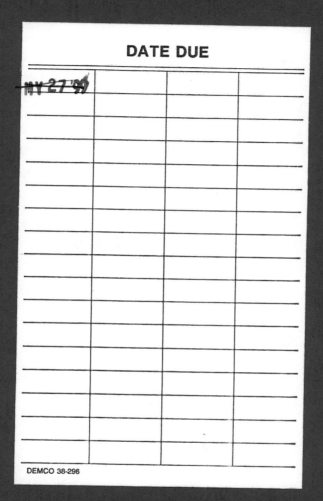

DATE DUE

MY 27 '99			

DEMCO 38-296

Dancing in Spite of Myself

DANCING

IN SPITE OF

MYSELF

ESSAYS ON POPULAR CULTURE

Lawrence Grossberg

DUKE UNIVERSITY PRESS   Durham & London 1997

© 1997 Duke University Press
All rights reserved
Printed in the United States of America on acid-free paper ∞
Typeset in Melior by Keystone Typesetting, Inc.
Library of Congress Cataloging-in-Publication Data appear
on the last printed page of this book.

If you prefer not to exaggerate,
you must remain silent,
you must paralyze your intellect
and find some way of becoming an idiot.
—Ortega y Gassett
The Revolt of the Masses

ontents

Acknowledgments

There are so many people to thank. Some of them allowed me to borrow their ideas—and sometimes even their words (but as Nick Lowe was purported to have once said, "I only steal from the best"). Some of them allowed me to bounce ideas and words off them, and were good enough friends to not always bounce them back to me. Some of them stood by me and others told me when to get off. Some have laughed and danced with me, others have mourned and prayed with me, and many have done both. Some have held my hand, and some have patted me on the back. Some have thanked me, and some have gone on without saying a word. Some have gotten high with me, and some have shared my lows. But all of them have taught me something, and I hope that I am a better teacher for having been able to touch so many wonderful people. I cannot thank everyone. Many are there in the notes to particular essays, and although I know it is not enough, I also know it will have to do.

My work and my life as a scholar and teacher have been shaped by three wonderful people, three of the best teachers/political intellectuals in the world: Stuart Hall, Jim Carey, and Meaghan Morris. I was fortunate enough to study with Stuart and Jim. And Meaghan has been what I used to call in graduate school a dialogic partner—every intellectual's dream. They have all been and remain more than friends and more than teachers. They have helped to shape my sense of myself as a political intellectual, and they serve as constant and powerful reminders of what an intellectual can and should be. They each continue to have an enormous impact on my work, even though I have moved in different directions, along different paths, over the past decade. They have influenced me more than I can ever say and I know that I will never find the words to express my gratitude to them. I also need to thank

Catherine, Becky and Jesse, Betty, and Andre: they were all generous enough to let me into their lives, and they have become an important part of my life.

I have been more than fortunate, over the years, to work with many wonderful graduate students. I have had colleagues and friends more supportive than I could possibly deserve: Chuck Whitney and Ellen Wartella (my other dialogic partner), Daniel and Barbara O'Keefe, Steve and Laurie Weidemier, Eleanor Blum, and James Hay. I left them all to move with my family to warmer (and more hospitable) places, and found colleagues and friends who made us feel at home: Della Pollock and Alan Shapiro, Bill Balthrop and Nancy Keeshan, Beverly Long (and Bill Long—we will miss him), Ken Wissoker and Cathy Davidson, Judith Farquhar and Jim Hevia, and more. I would also like to thank those people who supported my early efforts to think and write about popular music, including Richard Hoggart, Simon Frith, Dick Hebdige, Iain Chambers, Angela McRobbie, Andrew Goodwin, Will Straw, Jody Berland, Marcus Breen, Van Cagle, Jon Crane, The Quaker, and others whom I met through the International Association for the Study of Popular Music, and my undergraduate rock class. There are other friends, around the country and the world, that I want to thank, for many things: Tony Bennett, Henry Giroux, John Clarke, Paul Gilroy, Jennifer Slack, Marty Allor, Jan Radway, and all the rest of you (I hope you will forgive me for not trying to list everyone). Finally, I want to thank John MacGregor Wise for providing me with the title of this collection, and John Moran, for helping to dress me so well.

I would not be who or what I am were it not for my parents and family, and I am eternally grateful to them (at least at those moments when I like myself).

But in the end my life and whatever energy I have, whatever faith I have in myself and in the possibilities of a better world, rest with my wife, Barbara Anne Claypole White. Because she thinks I am better than I am, I am constantly trying to be what I can. (Thank you for loving me, and for putting up with me.) And there is my son, Zachariah Nigel Claypole White, born on Christmas Day 1994, named after the prophet who called for the rebuilding of the temple. He cannot yet read the words gathered here; he may never care enough to even bother. But he makes the future so much a part of my present, and he enriches my present so much every day. He has brought new meaning to my fears and rekindled my dreams. More than anything, I hope he will want to thank us for the world he inherits.

I dedicate this book to Zachariah Nigel, and to Barbara, and to my mother, Miriam Grossberg, who has always stood by me.

The essays in this volume originally were published as follows: "Another Boring Day in Paradise: Rock and Roll and the Empowerment of Everyday Life" in *Popular Music* 4: 255–58 (with permission of Cambridge University Press); " 'I'd Rather Feel Bad than Not Feel Anything at All': Rock and Roll, Pleasure and Power" in *Enclitic,* no. 8: 94–111; "Rock, Territorialization, and Power" in *Cultural Studies* 6: 358–67 (with permission of Routledge); "Is Anybody Listening? Does Anybody Care? On 'The State of Rock' " in Tricia Rose and Andrew Ross, eds., *Microphone Fiends: Youth Music and Youth Culture* (New York: Routledge, 1994: 41–58); "The Indifference of Television, or, Mapping TV's Popular (Affective) Economy" in *Screen,* no. 28: 28–45 (with permission of Oxford University Press); "Postmodernity and Affect: All Dressed Up with No Place to Go" in *Communications* 10: 271–93 (with permission of Gordon and Breach Publishers); " 'It's a Sin': Politics, Postmodernity, and the Popular" in Lawrence Grossberg with Tony Fry, Ann Curthoys, and Paul Patton, *"It's a Sin": Essays on Postmodernism* (Sydney: Power Publications, 1988: 6–71); "From Media to Popular Culture to Everyday Life" in *Metro,* no. 86: 20–26. I am grateful for permission to publish these essays here, but I am especially grateful for the opportunity, however long ago, to publish them in the first place.

Dancing in Spite of Myself

Introduction: Re-placing the Popular

Too often the rise of cultural studies is automatically linked to the rapid growth of interest in the study of popular culture, as if cultural studies were somehow defined by popular culture. In fact, the two discourses are not the same nor even necessarily connected, although they have been articulated together in at least some discourses and networks. What remains unspecified is the precise nature of those articulations, the choices strategically made in specific contexts and enacted in specific critical practices. I want to use this question as an opportunity to reflect on my own work, since my project, begun over twenty years ago,[1] can be situated here: between an interest in the social effects and logics of popular culture, especially rock music and youth culture, and a commitment to the possibilities of cultural studies as a form of progressive intellectual work.[2] On first glance, my work has followed four trajectories: a concern with the specific practice of cultural studies; a philosophical interest in cultural and communication theory; an exploration of the popularity and effectivity of rock music; and an investigation into the apparent success of the new conservative hegemony.[3] In retrospect, these appear less as separable projects than as interconnected components of a larger and more pressing attempt to find a critical practice adequate to the challenges of understanding "the politics of the popular" in the contemporary United States, all the while recognizing that national contexts can no longer be so confidently isolated from the global circulations of people, power, capital, and culture. By the "politics of the popular," I do not mean merely the political inflections of particular texts nor the relations of such texts to ideological positions, subjectivities, or pleasures. Rather I mean to point to the intersections of popular culture, popular politics (or political identity), and systematic structures and forces of political and economic inequality and domination. It describes what Meaghan Morris (1988c) calls the links between the politics of culture and the politics of politics.

Cultural studies has always argued that popular culture cannot be defined by appealing to either an objective aesthetic standard (as if it were inherently different from art) nor an objective social standard (as if it were inherently determined by who makes it or for whom it is made). Rather it has to be seen as a sphere in which people struggle over reality and their place in it, a sphere in which people are continuously working with and within already existing relations of power, to make sense of and improve their lives. Cultural studies has questioned the authority of any specific line that can be drawn between popular culture and its other (whether elite or mass culture). But this does not go far enough, for it potentially leaves in place two problematic assumptions.

Recognizing that the line between popular and legitimate culture is a political struggle, too much work in cultural studies satisfies itself with merely struggling over the line rather than rejecting the very practice by which the line is constituted. While I agree with Hall that "The changing balance and relations of social forces throughout . . . history reveal themselves, time and time again, in struggles over the forms of the culture, traditions and ways of life of the popular classes" (1981, 227), I am not willing to accept the assumption of a constituted category of popular culture that somehow necessarily corresponds to or even is made to correspond to the ways of life of the popular classes. If there is "a continuous and necessarily uneven and unequal struggle, by the dominant culture, constantly to disorganize and reorganize popular culture" (233), then it is the very process that must be contested. And that means abandoning the category of popular culture as part of a sociological or normative economy. This it seems to me is at least one reading of Hall's warning that to unravel a history of popular culture, "one could not begin without talking about many things which usually don't figure in the discussion of 'culture' at all. They have to do with the reconstruction of capitalism and the rise of collectivisms and the formation of a new kind of educative state as much as with recreation, dance and popular song. As an area of serious historical work, the study of popular culture is like the study of labour history and its institutions" (230). But too much of cultural studies has continued to locate popular culture within two binary normative economies: on the one hand, the popular (as poaching, fragmented, contradictory, bodily, carnivalesque, pleasurable) versus the legitimate (as reified, hierarchical, intellectual, etc.), and on the other hand, the popular (as stylized, artificial, disruptive, marginal, resisting) versus the mainstream (as naturalized, commonsensical, incorporated, etc.). Even Hall's often repeated warning to approach popular culture as "the double movement of containment and resistance" (228) has not stopped critics from distributing texts, audiences, and reading practices into these dichotomous judgments. Critics divide up popular culture, identifying specific forms as resistance and relegating all others to a cultural mainstream in which they are "contained" by the existing structures of power. At best, the "dialectic" is given a temporal sense (what was resistant is then contained, perhaps later to escape and become resistant again), or a spatial sense (while the practice resists over here, it is contained over there), or it is traced onto different aspects of the form (this element is resistant, that is contained). The real dialectic—the articulation—of the relationship between the two movements (which might say that, because of its specific resistance, it is also contained, or vice versa) is rarely examined. And at the same time, the tensions between dominant and legitimate culture are often ignored as well.

Moving beyond this normative and still static model, my own work has presupposed a more dynamic model of the circulation of popular practices. Instead of constructing some homogeneous mainstream, I see it as a social pastiche, a structured distribution of practices, codes, and effects, constantly rearticulating itself by incorporating pieces of the margins and excorporating pieces of itself into the margins. The distinction between mainstream and margin is then a question, quite literally, of social space, a distinction that does not carry with it any guarantees about either textuality or effects. The mainstream is not a unity but is marked by differences: it is a collection of overlapping cultural styles, defined by sets of productive and consumptive practices. It is differentiated both through the various local alliances that articulate it to concrete places and audiences and through diverse fractions that compete for public attention, whether in fact they define the economic mainstream. Thus, for example in my own work on music, I have always focused on one "face" of the mainstream: when talking about the '60s, I have been concerned primarily with the counterculture, and when talking about the '70s, with disco and punk, although these were never the center of success, as it were. Rather they were the leading edge of the mainstream, dominant fractions that were most visible, most influential, that most indelibly marked their social and cultural contexts at that moment.

And the margins are not inherently marginal; they only come to be expelled in this way in the context of the ongoing fluid articulations of the mainstream. Thus my work has always involved a defense of the mainstream of popular culture, or at least an unwillingness to begin by subdividing popular culture into intrinsically politically resonant categories. I want to defend popular culture not only against those who are hostile to any of its forms (by measuring it against "legitimated" culture), but more importantly, against those who are hostile to the largest part of popular culture because they champion those marginal trends or appropriations, as in subcultural theories. I am not a great fan of marginality for its own sake or for the sake of the critic's own cherished assumptions. In fact, I rather think that marginality functions as something of a residual force in the 1990s. I do not see popular culture in opposition to legitimate culture (it is even possible that "high" culture is someone's popular culture). Nor do I see a "co-opted" mainstream against a resistant margin. Instead I see a complex range of possibilities for the differentially articulated effects of cultural practices. In other words, being "in the mainstream" is never defined in purely textual terms, nor is it solely a matter of audiences; rather it is a description of a relationship between cultural practices and their contexts, that is, a question of the balance of forces in the field.

But if cultural studies should demand that we refuse to begin with such normative judgments, that we refuse to organize the diversity into predefined opposed unities, the fact is that such judgments are an integral part of the behavior of those who produce and consume popular culture. And since we too are implicated as participants/consumers of popular culture (in fact, often as fans of what we write about), we face a particular challenge when trying to write as reflective critics: the challenge to postpone judgment until the last instance. Writing as a cultural critic, at least on this model of cultural studies, is not about justifying one's own tastes or the ways they are inserted into one's life. That doesn't mean we don't use those tastes or write about them. Rather we have to distance ourselves from our tastes (or anyone's, for that matter) in order to write about taste itself, to write about what it means to be a fan of different popular cultural practices and organizations, in different contexts. In the end, the question is not whether or how one defends popular culture, but what such practices are doing and what is being done with them. As John Frow puts it, "our attention must be turned away from that mythical popular subject immediate to observation, and focused instead on the relation between two different kinds of practice: a 'first-order' practice of everyday culture, and the 'second-order' practice of analysis of it conducted by a reader [sic] endowed with significant cultural capital" (1995, 87). It is not a question of judging people so much as it is of trying to describe how their everyday lives are articulated by and with popular culture, how they are empowered and disempowered by the particular structures and forces that organize, always in contradictory ways, their lives, and how their everyday lives are themselves articulated to and by the trajectories of economic and political power. Otherwise we risk conflating our own academic project with that of the various cultural formations (e.g., youth culture) we are studying.

The second assumption that I find problematic in much of the cultural studies work on popular culture is that popular discourses can be neatly divided and distributed into domains—the social, the cultural, the political, and so forth—with their own specific modes of practices and planes of effects. Popular culture, then, is simply a subset of the larger category of cultural practices. Obviously this not only throws popular discourses into the problem of normative differentiation, of discrimination and value, it also locates any attempt to make sense of popular discourses within the logic of the modern concept of culture. According to this logic, culture is the necessary excess filling in for the lack of an adequate instinctual apparatus in human beings. Culture is that which mediates between people and reality, turning chaos into order. Therefore all cultural practices necessarily involve the production of meanings and representations, of subjectivities and identities (making it into little more than the form of ideology or the content of common sense). This notion of culture as a plane of cognitive meanings turns critical analysis into a question of individuated (often defined through social identities) and psychological interpretations and tastes. Additionally culture is all too easily assumed to be equivalent to communication, and all cultural practices are treated as instances of the communicational relationship between text and audience.

I have challenged, on both theoretical and strategic grounds, the dominance of such communicational models of culture. I have argued against any analysis that finds meaning in texts or in an audience's experiences of texts. Perhaps my theoretical antagonism to this model derives in part from my position within the discipline of communication itself. But it seems to me that the so-called linguistic or interpretive turn in contemporary theory is actually built upon an assumed centrality of communication in human life and a very limited set of taken-for-granted but rarely elaborated assumptions about the nature of human communication. Within this "turn," power and struggles against domination increasingly are displaced into and imagined within a reified realm of culture and communication.[4]

Alternatively I have attempted to hold onto a contextual notion of discursive practices and effects, arguing that both texts and audiences are themselves located within and articulated by broader contexts that determine the identity and effects of any cultural practice. And while I have never wanted to deny that cultural practices enable us to "make sense" of the world and our experiences, I do want to contest the reduction of sense-making to cognitive meaning and interpretation, and the model of culture as somehow standing apart from another plane that it interprets. I have argued that cultural practices always operate on multiple planes, producing multiple effects that cannot be entirely analyzed in the terms of any theory of ideology, consciousness, or semiotic. Thus the problem may be more general, involving not merely the equation of culture and communication, but the very logic of culture itself. Perhaps the problem is the very subsumption of popular discourses into the category of culture.[5]

Consequently I have never been particularly interested in either cultural texts or audiences, nor have I conceived of the object of analysis as simply the relationship between them. I suppose one could say that I have been investigating the question of taste, but I refuse to see it in individual or psychological terms, or to explain it as an excess of determination. Rather I began with the question of popularity: What does it mean that something is popular? But I quickly translated the question from an attribution made to a text to a question of the nature of the relationship of fandom. A "fan" is a particular sort of relationship that can be distinguished from a number of other possibilities. First, fandom is a positive relationship, as compared, for example, with an opponent or antagonist. Second, fandom is immediate and, to a certain extent, unreflective, as compared, for example, with a critic. Third, fandom is different from consumption or simple enjoyment (although it may incorporate it), because it involves a certain kind of identification or investment; one can like something (enjoy it, find pleasure in it) without being a fan per se. Finally, fandom is different from what I have called fanaticism, by which I mean an (ideological) identification that involves the production of identity. In fanaticism, the investment in particular cultural practices becomes the dominant structure of one's self-imagination (such as in subcultural identities). It seems reasonable to assume that taste describes the quality and quantity of one's relationship to particular practices, that it is a matter of the investment people make in particular things, of the ways they matter. Fandom then describes a particular slice of the range of possibilities for such investments, located largely (but probably not entirely) in what is generally called "the mainstream." But fandom is not reducible to a relationship between a text and an audience member, for it involves a more complex set of relations and investments between practices.

But if culture is not simply a matter of meaning and communication, then the struggle over "culture" is a struggle over the behavior of the population, especially the different and differently subordinated fractions (which in the contemporary world includes the vast majority of the population), and the role of discursive practices in constructing the machinery by which such behavior is controlled. Is it about constructing the line between legitimate and popular culture? Perhaps that is one of the (increasingly minor?) mechanisms of power. Is it about distributing the population into the dominant and the subordinate, about constituting the subject of "popular culture" as the popular classes (as opposed to the power bloc)? Again, that may be one of the ways in which particular discursive practices of the popular may be deployed, but it is not the primary site of the subordination of people or practices, nor of the construction of their identity as subordinated. We fail if we forget what has always been for me the primary lesson of Stuart Hall's classic article: not that popular culture is inherently subordinated or resisting, but rather that it is a force in political struggles: "Popular culture is one of the sites where this struggle for and against a culture of the powerful is engaged: it is also the stake to be won or lost in that struggle. It is the arena of consent and resistance. It is partly where hegemony arises and where it is secured. It is not a sphere where socialism, a socialist culture—already fully formed—might be simply expressed. But it is one of the places where socialism might be constituted. That is why popular culture matters. Otherwise, to tell you the truth, I don't give a damn about it" (1981, 239). I am not as concerned with Hall's apparent faith in the revolutionary potential of popular culture as I am with the political drive in his work. The point is that popular discourse is not about culture but about the struggles to articulate the relations between social and economic power, political forms of agency, and modes of discursive practices. Ironically, the New Right seems very much aware of this and, as I have repeatedly argued (e.g., Grossberg 1992), it uses popular culture and popular strategies all the time, in a variety of ways, in the service of its larger political struggle. To put it another way, as Shiach (1989) suggests, the rhetorical power of the discourse of popular culture is much greater than its descriptive specificity or, I would add, its political utility. Instead we might do better by foregrounding the notion of "the popular" in order to explore the relationships between popular practices, everyday lives,[6] and machineries of power. If we want to begin to understand popular culture, we may need to stop talking about it.

I have tried to understand the increasing power of a popular conservatism in the United States. In many ways, the challenge of this new conservatism merely recreates the question that has troubled political analysts for so long: Why do people agree to their own subordination? or, perhaps less judgmentally, What is it people are doing when they appear to be acceding to specific structures of inequality and power? How is popular culture deployed not only in contemporary political struggles but also in the very construction of the crisis that now drives those struggles forward? How is popular culture implicated in the changing and emerging forms of leadership and authority? How can we describe the complex ways in which a new structure of power is being organized, built upon contradictory political, ideological, economic, and cultural commitments? How is political power being restructured in such a way that ideological and economic subordination are articulated to certain forms of cultural empowerment? How is culture made into the site of the struggle as well as its weapon? Where do contemporary forms of cultural practice engage with the struggle for hegemonic leadership?

In attempting to answer some of these questions, or at least to provide the terms within which such an answer might be given, I have come to the conclusion that it is impossible to understand the project of the new conservatism, as well as the form and strategy of its success, apart from its relationship to the popular. It operates largely in the realms of the popular and everyday life (although the sites of power from and into which it is reaching are both political and economic). Moreover its successes depend to a large extent upon its ability to appropriate some of the very "operational logics" that made postwar popular culture different and that gave it its central and often threatening place in everyday life, and to make them, simultaneously, into positive and negative allegories for a new kind of political struggle.

In other words, I am interested in the changing relations between the popular and a specific hegemonic struggle in the contemporary national (and global) context, and in the ways these planes are being rearticulated to reshape the balance of forces in the social formation of the United States. I have a particular reading of hegemony in mind, which starts from Stuart Hall's notion (1988) of the struggle of a power bloc to win the position of leadership over and against the "people." Hegemony is a matter of consent and not consensus, and it is a specific, historically recent (since it depends on the emergence of "the masses" as a political and cultural subject) form of the struggle for power. But I want to go a step further and argue that there are significantly different hegemonic struggles, depending upon the way in which leadership is constituted and won. While Hall's analysis of Thatcherism depends on a struggle over common sense, I believe that, in the United States, the struggle is around a certain "national popular," which is not the same as, nor reducible to, common sense.

The development and increasing urgency of these concerns have always driven my efforts to understand some of the tendencies of postwar American popular culture. If nothing else, this defines for me the difference between doing cultural studies of and with rock, and studying rock as another genre or medium. I have always been opposed to carving up the field of popular culture into a series of new disciplines: film studies, television studies, popular music studies. To my mind none of these makes sense (in terms of the ways popular practices are inserted into everyday life), and all of them lose sight of the political practice of cultural studies. (I do not mean to suggest, however, that every moment of work in cultural studies has to be saturated, as it were, with political intentionality. Rather the issue is the way one articulates any analysis of popular culture to political projects and possibilities.) My project is to understand how the popular defines at least one set of the conditions of possibilities for the increasing appeal of a new conservatism. But certainly one cannot stop there: one has to transform the understanding of the context as a set of conditions to a more politically productive understanding of the context as a set of possibilities or effectivities. Just as cultural practices are no longer to be taken as merely representational but rather as productive, so the analysis itself must be seen as not merely reconstructing the context but as actively producing or fabricating it, as empowering the practice within the context of its own analysis. Or perhaps we can think of this in Gramscian terms: Analysis is always an attempt to "prise open already existing contradictions . . . thereby renovating and making critical an already existing activity."

Transforming the context in this way requires a detour through theory, and it requires as well a theory that is adequate not only to our object, but to the question and the context as well. That is, theory cannot be taken for granted, put in place, as it were, before the work of describing the context and transforming that description has begun. Of course, it is never that simple or easy; one always begins within a theoretical discourse that has to be measured by its ability to actually enable the project. But at the same time, such an "empirico-political" judgment cannot be entirely separated from an ongoing and simultaneous theoretical investigation, an investigation that takes the form of a critical engagement with other theoretical trajectories and critical practices. Thus, despite my rhetorical excesses, I have not attempted to offer a universal theory of culture, or of anything, for that matter.

I have been seeking a theoretical and analytic vocabulary that is capable of transforming itself as it engages with the contingencies of politically defined contexts. I have attempted to bring together two different theoretical perspectives, two different practices of cultural studies: a modernist theory of articulation and hegemony (Gramsci, as read through Stuart Hall) and a radically nonmodernist theory of effectivity, spatiality, and "machinics" (Michel Foucault, Gilles Deleuze and Felix Guattari, often as read through Meaghan Morris).[7] The result has been a set of emphases and commitments that I have described elsewhere as a "spatial materialism" which sees power operating in the production of a material context that is itself the space of the production of effects.

I also believe that political strategy, as well as assumptions about the nature and sites of struggle, have to be deferred until the empirical and theoretical work is actually under way, if not completed. To begin already knowing what and where the real and possible struggles are is to give up what I take to be the responsibility of the political intellectual. This has led me to seek a political position that acknowledges differences without organizing social space according to a logic of identity.

Not surprisingly, I have never been particularly sympathetic to any of the dominant modes of critical practice available for studying popular culture. It seems to me that all of these practices miss the very heart of Hall's description of the importance of the popular because they fail to address the actual context of relations, the articulations, between popular culture and systemic politics (or, in my own terms, a context constituted at the intersection of popular discourses, everyday life, and the machineries of power). Rather than treating "the ordinary" as a text, then, I have always attempted to treat the text as ordinary, and in so doing to find knowledge on the complex and multidimensional (dare I say fractal) surfaces of social life.

But accepting the consequences of articulation, of a radically contextualist model, threatens to make all analysis futile: Imagine you are confronted with a box containing the pieces of an undisclosed number of jigsaw puzzles. All of the original boxes are lost so you don't know what the puzzles are supposed to look like. It is also possible that the same piece will fit in several different puzzles. Thus the identity of each piece is only the set of its possible places in the as yet undefinable contexts. It *is* its possible functions. Thus you cannot name a piece or describe its contribution before the puzzle itself is assembled, but of course you cannot know ahead of time what is being assembled. No piece can be taken for granted, and in the end the significance of any piece—its possibilities for serving a range of functions—might never be exhausted. Yet while there is no necessary correspondence between the surface of a piece and its place, the surface is never blank or innocent and its functions are determined in part by its shape and appearance. It is scarred by traces of its history, a history of functions and effects that mark its emergence and survival and articulation. Read as a signifying practice, any piece can be related to any other piece and interpretation is undecidable or reduced to the "impossible science of the individual." Read alternatively as a function that allows and is allowed by particular connections, analysis is a process of mapping the vectors of effects that traverse and encircle any piece as a possible practice. The metaphor of a jigsaw puzzle, however, too easily suggests a static representation (as recuperation) of a real situation and needs to be replaced with a more active and multidimensional one: a functioning or machinic apparatus (imagine a *Lego* creation that could actually move, and in so doing transformed itself). My own cultural practice attempts to map out the lines that distribute, place, and connect cultural practices. This for me is the import of "everyday life" as a description of the distribution of practices across social space in such a way as to define the differential access that social groups have to specific forms of enactment.

Rather than asking how texts communicate, or how discourses construct subjective identities and experiences, or how people use culture, I want to explore the ways in which everyday life is articulated by and with the specific forms and formations, the material deployment and effects, of popular discursive practices. At the same time, I want to identify the different ways in which volition and "will" (i.e., forms of agency) can be enacted contextually to construct people's lives and history. This analytic model allows me to try to describe the various ways in which both discursive practices and human actors are effective. Moreover it now follows that the relations between individuals, culture, and reality cannot simply be defined as the necessary mediation of ideological effects. The site of this intersection must also be opened up, and I have used Bourdieu's notion of sensibilities (1984) to describe the specific planes on which forms of cultural effects and agency are produced. Sensibilities empower cultural practices to work in certain ways, and they empower individuals to enact them in certain places. Sensibilities define the dialectical production of active audiences, everyday practices, and productive contexts.

This has important consequences for the study of the popular as a sphere in which people struggle over reality and their place in it. I see popular sensibilities delimiting the effects of discursive practices. I have argued that "popular culture" is characterized by the production of affective logics and relations, that is, relations of volitional power, mood, investment, and energization. In fact, the need to radically distinguish affect from the more common notions of desire and pleasure became a dominant theme in my work over the course of the decade that these essays map. Obviously this understanding has been shaped in part by my concern with popularity and fandom on the one hand, and by the fact that the object of my analysis, the rock formation, places musical practices at its center. Talking about the rock formation requires a way of understanding the ability of such sounds both to become the points at which a wide range of practices and commitments can be articulated and to travel across and into different contexts and configurations. Thus I disagree with the new (Derridean-derived) common wisdom that the Western (logocentric) tradition has always privileged the presence of the aural (speech) over visual (writing). In fact, Derrida's vision of aurality makes it into little more than writing (meaning) with an excess of immediacy. But that immediacy is never explored—it is simply assumed as presence (more like breath than sound). I want to make the more limited claim that within North Atlantic modernity, the visual (and the legible) has usually been privileged as the model of perception, knowledge, and sense-making, and hence of our relationship to the world. It seems to me that most work in popular culture, by starting with the visible and the legible, ends up foregrounding the distinction between popular and "high" culture. At the same time, North Atlantic modernity has recognized that there is something to human existence beyond the epistemological, but it has quickly assigned this excess to the domain of the irrational, the unstructured, the unmappable (e.g., as desire or creativity). Interestingly, much of contemporary cultural theory and criticism seems to assume a binary opposition between affect/the body/ materiality and the concrete on the one side, and ideology, subjectivity, consciousness, and theory on the other. Drawing upon Freud, I began to think about affect as the plane of cathexis (including more than just libidinal modes); drawing upon Nietzsche, I began to think about affect as the plane of effectivity (the ability to effect and be effected). My dilemma has always been the relationship between these two understandings of affect.

So, using Deleuze and Guattari (1977, 1987), I began to think of affect as a structured plane of effects (investment) that is the very possibility of agency (of acting willfully). That is, affect for me is the plane on which any individual (persons and practices are the two most obvious forms of individuation) is empowered to act in particular ways at particular places. "Affect" is the term I use to describe the observable differences in how practices matter to, or are taken up by, different configurations of popular discourses and practices— different alliances (which are not simply audiences). But perhaps this makes affect sound too mental, for affect is both psychic and material; it demands that we speak of the body and of discursive practices in their materiality. This foregrounding of affect is also probably connected with my reading of Pierre Bourdieu's often overlooked insight that "The resistance of the popular occurs on terrains altogether different from that of culture in the strict sense of the word . . . and it takes the most unexpected forms, to the point of remaining more or less invisible to the cultivated eye" (1990, 155). I am interested in the various ways popular discourses can empower and disempower specific groups and practices, in the ways different cultural alliances operate in and produce different "mattering maps."

In that sense, I think popular culture cannot be limited to those practices that we might normally locate within the circumscribed (modernist) region of culture. For many generations and for many people, religion itself was within the popular. It served not as an exact body of knowledge but as an affective structure, one that helped make sense of the world by producing the feeling that the world was a totality, that life must have a meaning. The nature of that meaning may have been less important than the confidence that the world, despite its contradictions, still made sense. The popular, in the narrower sense of popular culture, can still serve this function, but it rarely can do so by producing a stable and enduring affective horizon.

The question of empowerment is a crucial one. On the one hand, for me empowerment has never been intrinsically political. (Actually, as a careful reading of this essay demonstrates, this is probably not true. It may be fairer to say that I have always felt uncomfortable with models that locate power in an economy of domination and resistance and that see cultural practices as immediately resistant. The necessity of inserting a space between empowerment and resistance became clearer as my work developed.) But I have always conceptualized empowerment as involvement and investment, as a matter of vectors of energy connecting positions in space. And as such it is a necessary condition for the possibility of agency, of any form of action or commitment, and hence of any form of resistance or opposition. However, to leave it at that—at what some writers have called the level of micropolitics (but this is not the Foucauldian sense) or what others describe as everyday life (again, not my sense)—is to render it impotent and irrelevant. For the question is always how structures of empowerment are themselves articulated to and by other forms of practices and effects. It cannot be thought of simply as the articulations between micro and macro levels of politics, but rather of the articulations between different practices and effects which, taken together, make inseparable the politics of everyday life and the politics of "politics" (both of which exist at both the micro and macro levels).

The popular articulates everyday life as a structured mobility by constructing the spaces and places of everyday life, the spaces within which and the places in which people live their everyday lives. In other words, popular culture is constantly enacting and enabling specific forms and trajectories of movement (change) and stability (agency). It defines certain formations of practices as the possible sites of individual investments, sites at which subjects and identities are constructed. It defines the vectors by which people and practices can or cannot move between, and connect, such investments. And it defines particular practices as billboards or guideposts along these vectors. In this way, popular discourses empower and enable specific forms of agency and action in everyday life, and they become crucial sites of both the appeal to authenticity and the construction of authority. Admittedly then, my conclusion—that the new conservatism is an affective struggle to change the maps of what matters through the operating logics of specific popular formations,[8] that it is producing a particular structured mobility (what I have called a disciplined mobilization [Grossberg 1992]) that is articulated in significant ways to and by the struggles of contemporary capitalism—is as much a result of the choices I have made as it is a "description" of an empirical reality. Yet the question is not, Is this an accurate representation? but rather, Does this open up new political strategic possibilities? Yet I would also now stand back from this conclusion a bit, for I believe that my own interdisciplinary efforts in economics (Grossberg 1992) were premature and guided as much by my own theoretical assumptions as by my work in economics. I jumped into the "regulation school" and postfordism as the obvious way to bring economics back into cultural studies, rather than starting at ground level, as it were. Were I to do it over again, I would focus less on abstract notions of economic change and more on the actual sites of economic agency, for example, changes in the tax codes.

It is in the context of this larger project that I would position my own researches on rock music: the attempt to analyze the new conservatism's articulation with the popular requires not only that we find a way of understanding the functioning of popular discourses in terms of their operating logics, but also that we describe the specific operating logics that are being deployed in this hegemonic struggle. It is these questions that have defined my interest in rock (although my faith that rock is at the center of the relevant formations is probably more the result of my own position as a fan, and my particular generational identity as a baby boomer, heavily invested, in different ways at different times and places, in rock). Consequently, I have never been particularly interested in talking about what is good or bad music, or about my own taste. I have preferred to assume (and enjoy) the fact that there is always lots of good music. Instead my interests were always in music's relationships to—as part of—a larger context. In asking what music does for its fans and vice versa, I was asking about music's effects in that broader context. Because its effects, however, are shaped in part by how one understands what it can or is supposed to do, my work often starts by describing something like the assumed ideology of rock; but it is more material, for it is lived in the body and the soul. As a fan and a scholar, I have always been intrigued by the imagination of music's transformative possibilities.

Thus my research questions about rock have always been about its political possibilities rather than about any judgment of its aesthetic quality or cultural authenticity; about its effects on everyday life (and its potential deployments into larger hegemonic struggles) rather than about any judgment of its immediate impact as containment within or resistance to some abstract structure of ideological power. I was always interested in the ability of rock to interpellate so many people in particular ways, ways that can only be described by saying that rock mattered: people gave it a real power in and over their lives—without becoming the dominant characteristic in their identity. Being a rock fan has always had significant consequences, but it would be a mistake to assume that interpreting the music or its fans' experience offers an adequate description or account of what drives its fans. Rock seemed to operate somehow as an affective articulatory agent; my questions were how this was accomplished, why, and with what effects.

Answering these questions, using a wide variety of research methods (although, I must admit, almost always too informally and without the proper care, but then cultural studies has always had an uncomfortable relationship with questions of methodological rigor), I have studied rock culture as a configuration of cultural practices and effects that have been organized around rock music, the ways its fans have empowered it and been empowered by it. But I have never thought of myself as studying rock music/culture as an isolatable cultural phenomenon—as a set of texts and audiences and communicative relations. My notion of rock as an object of study has always operated at a particularly high level of abstraction, a level that I have called "the rock formation." This phrase is meant to signal a specific material, spatial, and temporal identity. Thus I assumed that rock's identity (whether as a musical genre or a specific text/practice within the genre) and effects depend on more than its specific textuality or sound. To describe rock culture as a formation is to constitute it as a material—discursive and nondiscursive—context, a complex and always specific organization of cultural and noncultural practices that produces particular effects: specific forms and organizations of boredom and fun, of pleasure and pain, of meaning and nonsense. The rock formation cuts across any attempt to divide up the field of popular discourses and practices, bringing together genres, media, styles, and so forth. To speak of a formation is also to constitute rock culture spatially, as a particular dispersion of practices across time and space. I was never interested in the empirically describable details of various specific organizations of fans and practices (what I have called apparatuses, scenes, and alliances) per se, but in the more abstract questions of how such assemblages and their effects might be understood. I have never been interested in the concrete as a local, empirical phenomenon (that I leave to better critics and analysts than myself) but in the formation of rock culture at the broadest level—that is, as a particular organization of *American* popular culture; my disinterest in any concrete instance (geographically and temporally) of rock culture has been defined (and to my mind justified) by my interest in the concrete context of American political hegemony. I have never championed the local; rather I have always argued that political projects define the appropriate definition of contexts and objects of analysis. For, given my project, the particular articulations and manifestations of the rock formation were less important than its existence across practices, time, and space.

At the same time, the rock formation has a temporal extension and boundary: it is a historical event and production that emerged at a particular moment, made possible by and in response to specific conditions of possibility, conditions that enabled rock culture but also constrained it, that defined it but also opened up its trajectories of transformation, that empowered it but also set limits on its shapes and effects. But if the rock formation is an event, it must also have the possibility of an end, which explains my obsession with the notion that rock is dead, again not as a judgment I want to make about particular musical practices or variants of rock culture but as a discursive haunting within the rock formation and, of course, as a possible eventual reality. That is, I simply assumed that if the rock formation emerged as a response to particular conditions, eventually, when those conditions changed and the effects of the discourses within the formation changed (not necessarily in some simple corresponding way), then whatever music sounded like (perhaps even exactly like some of the music in the rock formation), the set of relations and effects articulated around it would not be the same. In fact they would be so different as to no longer be usefully described as another variant of the rock formation. The discontinuities would be more significant than the continuities.

Understanding this formation involves trying to map the conditions and effects of its emergence, understanding why this particular popular formation appeared rather than another. What sort of forces and dimensions constituted the context of the emergence of the rock formation? How have these conditions—and the relations among them—been transformed over the course of recent American history? Obviously it is impossible to know in advance what conditions are the most pertinent, which have the greatest purchase and the greatest reach. But I believe one can put together a sense of the context of the rock formation by describing at least the following aspects: the economic and political terrain; the structural position of youth and generations; the state of play of the various axes that articulate power and identity; the dominant structures of feeling; the media economy (the availability and popularity of various media with different audiences); the state and structure of the music technology and industry; the availability (to youth audiences) of images and discourses of alienation and rebellion; and finally, the emergent structures of feeling (including that of youth in its various articulations).

But the real work begins when one tries to describe the effects of this context and the ways in which particular cultural practices and formations emerge and function as responses to and transformations of that context. Even to put it this way is to risk the danger of falling back into a model of culture representing an external social and political reality. Instead what I am attempting to do is to redescribe the context, to fabricate an other map that enables us to better see the contradictions, fault lines, and struggles that are already at work in the context, either as actualities or as possibilities. If people make the world but in conditions not of their own making, then we must move from a description of the social context as a structure of social relationships and experiences to another description of the context as a field of forces. My own critical investment in the popular leads me to understand such a field in terms of—and as constituted by—a struggle over the production and distribution of operating logics: modes of articulation by which particular organizations of practices are able to produce particular organizations of effects. That is to say, if we assume that contexts (everyday life) are not static structures but active configurations of possibilities, of mobilities and stabilities, of the spaces and places at which forms of agency become available, then popular formations define possible ways of producing and navigating one's way within and across the spatial field of everyday life, even as they constitute that field.

This theoretical apparatus developed as I attempted to describe the logics— what I have called the politics—of the rock formation and how they have changed over the past forty years (and eventually how they have played into the new conservative hegemony). This involves laying out the affective geography of the rock formation as it has moved across the various configurations of everyday life (i.e., the first description of the context). This "geometry" describes a functioning apparatus that is transformed by its conditions even as it transforms itself. It is a matter of material effects and agencies that need not be consciously experienced or represented. It describes the possibilities—the forms and locations of empowerment and disempowerment—that the rock formation makes available to those placed within its logics.

Given the lack of any available vocabulary for describing the forms, quantities, and organizations of affect, this geography or operational logic cannot be described directly, but the parameters and possibilities of its articulatory power can be laid out at least schematically. The only significant continuity I "discovered" in the process of mapping out the conditions of the emergence of the rock formation is a certain "postmodern vector" operating at the intersection of the rock formation and everyday life in postwar America. For me, the postmodern is a very specific and restricted (always local, partial, and temporary, although also mobile and increasingly powerful) rearticulation of everyday life (or experience, as long as experience is not reduced to the ideologically constructed realm of meaning, knowledge, and subjectivity). It involves the proliferation of sites in everyday life where the relations among ideology, desire, and affect are attenuated. Whether I describe it as indifference or authentic inauthenticity, then, the postmodern is not an experience of subjects or a representation of an external reality, but a form of practice that produces particular sorts of affective alliances.

And this vector is rearticulated into the popular logics of the rock formation—although its importance, pertinence, and power have varied significantly over time—where it defines the affectivity of the formation itself. The result is a new articulatory logic and a rapid movement, into the center of contemporary cultural life, of the various figures of this affective logic. I want to make clear that I do not think that this logic, or the vector that it rearticulated, constitutes a crisis in and of themselves. It is only when they are themselves deployed within and linked to specific hegemonic struggles that the postmodern becomes a crisis of sorts.

In this effort I have too often ignored important differences and contradictions within the broader rock formation, and I have given too little attention to the changing shape of the rock formation across space and over time. However, the inability to deal with change in rock in anything other than the most simple terms is not only my problem. I would like to think that my work has begun to develop some tools that might enable one to describe the different spatial and temporal articulations of the rock formation, according to the following dimensions:

—the *rock terrain* describes the internal differentiation of the alliances within the formation itself (e.g., mainstream, countercultural, undergrounds, alternatives)

—the *affective machine* describes the primary register of rock's productivity (e.g., fun, lifestyle, style/fantasy, attitude)

—the *ideologies* of the formation describes its more or less explicit politics (e.g., liberalism, anarchic utopianism, self-conscious commodification)

—the articulation of rock as a *differentiating machine* describes its investment in its own sense of difference (whether differences in taste do matter; whether they are articulated to generational, social, and political differences and to identities)

—the *politics of fun* describes both the antagonism around which the formation is structured (fun versus boredom, insanity, reality, or despair) and the primary sites of investment (youth, movement, pleasure, experimentation, body, pain, style, reflexivity, entertainment, etc.)

—the *politics of everyday life* describes different projects in relation to the conditions of possibility of everyday life (relative deterritorialization, the fantasy of absolute deterritorialization, reterritorialization, polemological struggle)

—the *geometry of affect* describes where rock locates itself in the formation of everyday life (e.g., as topical it has a place of its own; as pantopical it is everywhere; as heterotopical it is only in other's places; and as atopical it is a space without a place, which is to say, at the border)

—*affective differences* describes the nature of its borders within the dominant culture (independent, alternative, oppositional)

—*affective alliances* describes the nature of its self-positioning (experiential, utopian, critical)

Together these dimensions might enable us to describe rock's politics of empowerment, its operational logic as different ways of allowing people to navigate through and even to respond to their lived context. I have always thought of rock as a practice that helps us make it through the day. These dimensions, taken together, can be used, I think, to chart the trajectory of the rock formation and to mark the point of its possible disappearance.

If I am right that the rock formation is coming to an end or at least being replaced by something different enough that it must be recognized as such, if I am right that the rock formation is no longer as powerful a site of agency and articulation as it has been for the past forty years, then both the terms for analysis and the political stake in such studies will have to be rethought. I think this partly explains the increasing professionalization and discipliniza- tion of popular music studies, a development with which, I must admit, I have limited sympathy and in which I have no interest. Ironically these de- velopments have done little to advance the potentialities of such writing. In fact, I would suggest that writing on popular music—whether journalistic or academic—is rather unique (compared to writing on other popular cultural forms) in that it has not moved very far in the past forty years.

But perhaps it would be more accurate to offer a slightly different descrip- tion of this disappearance (and in so doing to revise my conclusion in the essay "Is Anybody Listening? Does Anybody Care?"). The formation that I have described throughout the body of my work emerged in the 1950s to become the dominant cultural formation of youth (if not of the United States) from the 1960s until the mid-1980s. But by the end of the 1980s, I believe, it is more appropriately described as a residual formation, still active and impor- tant around the edges, as it were, it occasionally moves into and is expelled from the center. But this formation, increasingly organized around generic commitments and differences, is no longer dominant and sometimes has the effect of marginalizing other forms of cultural practice and social relation- ships. What has replaced it? I now think that my essay "Is Anybody Listen- ing?" conflated the new dominant cultural formation with an emergent for- mation. I would describe the new dominant as a mainstream committed to (and invested in) eclecticism and hybridity. It is a formation that operates without the mediations of the ideology of authenticity; hence it willingly and simultaneously embraces the global megastar and the local rebel. As I de- scribed it, it gives up rock's differentiating function even as it tries to hold onto its territorializing power. But it is not, in the last instance, a musical formation insofar as its center is defined as much by visual practices and commitments as by musical ones. On the other hand, I now believe that there is also an emergent formation that can only be described as a network of scenes (including dance, rap, and rock). These scenes are geographically identifiable and define a system of differentiation that is not binary but ter- ritorializing. It is this formation I described as having a polemological (ex- plicitly antagonistic) politics, as operating on the borders of everyday life by imagining an identification between the country's poor white trash, black youth, and white middle-class youth. Somewhere between these new forma- tions I would like to begin to imagine new possibilities for a popular politics.

If particular cultural formations and historical events come to an end, then some old political possibilities may no longer be available. We may lament such closures, but we would be better advised to ask what new political possibilities have become imaginable. That is, my interest in the death of rock is actually an interest in the possibility of rock's becoming something else, in an attempt to ask what a new popular politics might look like and how it might be discursively constructed. In fact it seems to me that the disappearance of any progressive political movement (not as an institutional organization but as an organization of spaces and places) has been actively constructed, for particular fractions of the populace, at three sites, all being actively constructed through rearticulations of postmodernity and the operating logic of the rock formation: first, the impossibility of investing in the political (i.e., whether in the government or "the people" as agents of change or in some utopian field of political and ethical values); second, the active discouragement of any investment in the possibility of political community (i.e., of rethinking the relation of the individual to the group and of identity to struggle); and third, the impossibility of articulating a theory and practice of agency (of reconsidering how people make history but not in conditions of their own making). These are, in the first instance, problems of everyday life, constructed in struggles in and over the popular. They are also problems at the intersection of everyday life and the tendential forces struggling to determine it. But they are also challenges for the intellectual, and we will have failed if we cannot find ways to address them outside the limits of our own theoretical and political positions, if we cannot speak, as intellectuals, through the popular, in order to connect everyday life with the very real struggles and sufferings of economic and political injustice.

I have tried to suggest throughout this essay something about my project—about its contextual and strategic approach—but equally important, I have tried to imply that it is as much a collective project as it is my own. After all, cultural studies is itself an intellectual practice that not only claims to belong somewhere but also claims to belong within a collective intellectual enterprise. It challenges not only the boundaries between the disciplines but, more importantly, the boundary between the academy and the world outside. Much like rock, it has always been for me empowering and enabling, and like rock, it is always fun. But also like rock, it offers a challenge I have always taken seriously: In a struggle in which the dominant mattering maps are being restructured—when the individual and the concrete matter so much more than the general and the abstract; when the freedom of the market matters so much more than caring for the people—the political intellectual has no choice but to enter into the terrain of the popular. When the very possibility of political struggle is being erased—not because the scene of politics (or the public sphere) has disappeared in some postmodern apocalypse, but because there is an active attempt to use popular discourses to restructure the possibilities of everyday life—the political intellectual has no choice but to enter into the struggle over affect in order to articulate new ways of caring.

JUST WHEN YOU THOUGHT YOU WERE THROUGH . . .

Introductions are almost too tempting; they provide a magical opportunity to rewrite if not one's own history, then at least the history of one's own labor. By substituting the geography of placement for the history of production, an introduction becomes the natural point of departure (home?) from which the reader can embark on his or her journey, retracing the steps of the mysterious author in search of whatever knowledge or insight he or she may have discovered (destination?). But the reader knows it is a fabrication (and the author knows the reader knows . . .), for this starting point has been constructed along the way and the author has never reached his or her destination.

So perhaps it is necessary, in the last instance, to acknowledge briefly some of the choices that have been made and the weaknesses that they attempt to hide. Publishing a collection of essays written over the course of a decade poses some immediate problems. First, there is the threat of redundancy. While I have attempted to limit the amount of redundancy (largely through my choice of essays), I have by no means erased all of it. Redundancy after all is a fact of intellectual life, but more importantly, it can be productive. It may involve elaborations or subtle shifts in emphasis and direction; it may inscribe different takes on the same theme, attempts to try new vocabularies and new frames, or to find better articulations of a problematic and a position. These essays are, after all, only provisional takes, attempts to move without ever knowing where I am trying to get to.

Second, there is the choice of how to present the essays: thematically or chronologically. I am drawn to the latter because it provides material evidence of the actual labor of intellectual investigation, with all of its fragility, instability, and repetitiveness. I have chosen the former, however, because it more clearly demonstrates the ways in which the different foci of my work

intersect and rearticulate each other. I also believe it highlights certain continuities: a commitment to contextuality and materiality; a concern with productivity rather than interpretation; a focus on the hegemonic organization of
affect; a desire for a politics that is not based on notions of identity; and a
rhetoric of spatiality and geography.

Third, one is forced to confront the questions and criticisms that colleagues—both sympathetic and not so sympathetic—have raised over the
years. Some of the things they have pointed to I would change if I could, other
things I would not change, and still others I know I cannot change. My work is
admittedly abstract and speculative. Some have argued that for me theory has
become a constant detour deferring the concrete; others have suggested that
my arguments lack the mediations that link the abstractions of theory to the
materiality of the ways hegemonic struggles are played out in everyday life.
There is, no doubt, some truth to both of these. And yet I choose to remain
abstract and speculative. Like Deleuze, I believe that philosophy seeks to
make concepts that can touch and affect the real. Moreover, I want to find a
way to interrupt the comfortable rhythms of narrative coherence. While I
want to leap metonymically, back and forth and across the concrete and the
abstract, I want to avoid the pitfalls of postmodern synecdoche, which lets
the particular stand in for the general. This no doubt contributes to the fact
that my writing is, too often, too difficult. I take this criticism seriously if only
because I would like to think that some people might find my work useful and
that it may offer some new directions for both intellectual and political en-
deavors. I have no doubt that many of these essays could be rewritten more
effectively, but I fear that those who found them inaccessible would still find
them inaccessible even if better written. I apologize to those who put in the
effort to read these essays and, in the end, do not find the effort worthwhile,
but I hope that there are some out there who do find their efforts rewarded. At
the same time, I do not believe that accessibility is a criterion of potentially
useful knowledge, at least not in the first instance. I do not know of any
correlation between accessibility and significance, which is not to claim that
inaccessibility is a measure of significance. I would like to think that at least
part of the difficulty of my work is the result of my project: to find a radically
contextual theoretical vocabulary that can describe the ongoing production
of the real as an organization of inequality through an analysis of cultural
events. Moreover, such a vocabulary would have to offer a viable notion of
agency without falling back on models that privilege either human subjec-

tivity or processes of epistemological mediation. I am interested in a theory of how reality is made, but I am not willing to assume that human beings are consciously in control of the mechanisms or practices of that making.

Finally, I want to comment on the fact, often observed, that I have too often avoided raising issues of gender and race in my researches on the politics of the popular. I do not want to deny that such cultural identities have become crucial sites of political investment in the contemporary world, nor that there are important questions about the relations between the popular and structures of race, gender, and sexual identity. In fact I think there are many critics exploring these questions, while issues about everyday life and hegemonic struggles remain largely ignored. In an ideal world, these two political vectors would be connected in all their complexity, but politics does not often afford us the luxury of ideal interventions. In truth, I do have theoretical reservations about theories of identity and difference and strategic concerns about the efficacy of a politics organized around investments in cultural identities. Nevertheless, the mere absence of a topic from a discussion, however important, does not, in my opinion, necessarily constitute a serious weakness; the real question is whether that absence could be addressed in some terms or whether it is a necessary consequence of the position itself.

In the contemporary political climate, where self-reflexivity is too often reduced to a litany of cultural identities—I am middle-aged, middle-class, Jewish, heterosexual, male, married, with one infant son, of Eastern European descent, and so on—pronouns have become as significant as the identities they are assumed to represent. The problem of how one may speak of and for others has become almost insurmountable. The political intellectual is caught in an impossible dilemma: either constructing or negating the other. Consequently, "we" has become one of the more dangerous words to use: Let the speaker beware! But I choose to use it and I will continue to do so, although I am constantly challenged by its exclusionary operation. After all, it is claimed, the very presumption of inclusion that "we" carries with it also entails the exclusion of significant fractions of the population. But I do not accept the assertion that "we" necessarily reinscribes the particular economy of space and identity on which so much of contemporary politics seems to be based. Apart from the fact that I am increasingly opposed to political strategies that privilege identity (and that conflate subjectivity, cultural identity, and political agency), I am also convinced that this view of the deployment of "we" depends entirely upon an unacceptable—referential—theory of language. My use of "we" is neither referential nor singular. It is intended to be slippery and multifunctional. It is, I hope, invocatory, productive, even seductive. It is an invitation to belong within the space opened up by my discourse, although I hope it does not limit the ways one might belong. It is an invitation to care.

DANCING . . .

(POPULAR MUSIC)

Another Boring Day in Paradise:

Rock and Roll and the Empowerment

of Everyday Life

About five years ago, I began to teach courses on the cultural history of rock and roll. My approach was simple: I would try to describe the texts, interpreting the significance produced by the unique synthesis of musical texture and lyrical content. Then I would suggest correspondences to the situation of its audiences which were mediated through the institutional practices of production and consumption. The music obliquely represented and responded to the structure of experience of at least certain portions of its youth audience. As I sought more adequate readings, the correspondences became increasingly refracted; the music had to be located in an overdetermined context: class, race, subcultures, gender, as well as age exerted unequal pressures on and were represented in rock and roll. Nevertheless, my students—as well as the rock and roll fan in me—were noticeably dissatisfied. While they often assented to my readings, it was clear that my readings failed to capture something important, something that was intimately connected to rock and roll's power as well as to its cultural politics.

As I tried to respond to their discomfort, I found myself confronting two features of rock and roll: its heterogeneity and its affectivity. Rock and roll is not only characterized by musical and stylistic heterogeneity; its fans differ radically among themselves although they may listen to the same music. Different fans seem to use the music for very different purposes and in very different ways; they have different boundaries defining not only what they listen to but what is included within the category of rock and roll. Thus they objected to my attempt to define one experience or use of rock and roll as the only one. Sometimes, for example, the meaning of particular lyrics was significant; other times and more commonly, the experience was a purely affective one.

Thus if I wanted to understand the cultural significance of rock and roll (assuming that it has some unity despite its heterogeneity), that is, if I wanted to examine the specific social effects of postwar youth music, I had to recognize that the affective power of rock and roll goes beyond that of leisure itself. Of course, the observation that music has powerful emotional effects is hardly controversial. On the contrary, it is the assumption that musical texts, even with lyrics, function by representing something—meanings, ideas, or cultural experience—that is problematic. When applied to rock and roll, the assumption does not seem false, merely incomplete: particular instances of rock and roll may represent different things for different audiences and in different contexts. Much of the recent writing on rock and roll is similarly incomplete. For example, Frith argues (1981) that rock and roll is a form of leisure activity that represents various fantasies about the possibilities of a life constituted entirely as leisure. The matrix of these fantasies is the dialectic of working-class—urban—street culture and middle-class—suburban—creative culture. Hebdige, coming out of the tradition of British subcultural studies, locates (1979) rock and roll within the larger category of subcultural styles which represents and provides an imaginary solution to the experienced contradictions of British working-class life. Both Frith and Hebdige treat rock and roll as a "representation" located within a context of class relationships. And while they each capture important aspects of the place and effects of rock and roll in contemporary culture, neither one is able to account for the reality and the generality of the affective power of the music: "The most disturbing thing . . . is how little the establishment as such acknowledges what is a kind of continuous guerilla warfare . . . Rock . . . is the only medium that makes any sense of life—aesthetically or politically—at all" (Frith, cited in Marcus 1981b, 124).

Each of these writers proposes, adjacent to his interpretation of rock and roll, an alternative strategy. Frith proposes that we study the ways in which the audiences use the music, while Hebdige suggests that the effects of rock and roll depend upon its existence as a range of signifying practices. Still, though, neither approach is able to respond to two significant questions that I wish to raise: How does one describe the specific effects (and popularity) of particular forms of rock and roll? How does one describe the consistency that constitutes rock and roll as a determinate cultural form? Nevertheless, my own approach takes something from each of these writers. Like Frith, I propose to examine rock and roll functionally. But rather than assuming its audience in advance and asking how individuals, either consciously or unconsciously, use the music, I will focus on the ways rock and roll produces the material context within which its fans find themselves, a context defined by affective investments rather than by semantic representations. Thus the rock and roll fan is a part of the effects of the functioning of rock and roll itself. My concern is with the possibilities opened up between, by, and for the music and its audiences within the everyday life of postwar America.

Like Hebdige, I propose to treat rock and roll as a set of practices, but practices of strategic empowerment rather than of signification. Rock and roll structures the space within which desire is invested and pleasures produced. It is thus immediately implicated in relations of power and a politics of pleasure. I am concerned with the ways in which rock and roll provides strategies of survival and pleasure for its fans, with the ways in which rock and roll is empowered by and empowers particular audiences in particular contexts. Rock and roll becomes visible only when it is placed within the context of the production of a network of empowerment. Such a network may be described as an "affective alliance": an organization of concrete material practices and events, cultural forms, and social experience that both opens up and structures the space of our affective investments in the world. My aim then is to describe the parameters of rock and roll's empowering effects in terms of the production of affective alliances. (For the basis of this position, see Grossberg 1982.)

I will propose five general hypotheses to describe rock and roll, framed within the problematic of power as the organization of desire. The first suggests that the dominant affective context of rock and roll is a temporal rather than a sociological one. While class, race, gender, nationality, subculture, and even age may be partly determinate of specific effects, the emergence of rock and roll is enabled within the context of growing up (in the United States, for my purposes) after the Second World War. This context defines the practice of rock and roll's continued self-production. The second hypothesis argues that the power of rock and roll cannot be sufficiently described in ideological terms, either as the constitution of an identity or the production of a critical utopia. Rather rock and roll inscribes and cathects a boundary within social reality marked only by its otherness, its existence outside of the affective possibilities of the ruling culture (the hegemony).[1] In more traditional terms, rock and roll inscribes the particular mark of postwar alienation upon the surface of other social structures of difference. The third hypothesis describes

the strategic functioning of rock and roll: it brings together disparate fragments of the material context of the everyday life of its audiences within
different rock and roll apparatuses. It is the rock and roll apparatus that maps
out particular lines of affective investment and organization. It therefore both
locates and produces the sites at which pleasure is possible and important for
its audiences; it provides the strategies through which the audience is empowered by and empowers the musical apparatus. The fourth hypothesis
describes the diverse possibilities of rock and roll by using the concepts of
"encapsulation" and "affective alliances." The final hypothesis discusses the
notion of "co-optation" as a significant strategy by which rock and roll produces its own history and reproduces its affective power. My conclusion will
argue that rock and roll is a historically locatable event and that changes in
the contemporary context of everyday life raise the question of the impending
"disappearance" of rock and roll.

HYPOTHESIS 1. ROCK AND ROLL
IN THE POSTWAR CONTEXT

Any reading of rock and roll must begin by identifying the context within
which it is to be located and its relations identified. Despite the increasingly
prevalent gesture toward overdetermination, the dominant features are almost always identified as sociological variables, that is, the sociological characteristics of the music's producers and consumers. Such variables, while
often locally significant, must constantly confront their own exceptions. The
response that this is no longer rock and roll or that it has lost its real cultural
significance (and politics) seems merely to evade the issue. Further, such
sociological descriptions do not provide convincing accounts of the emergence and continued power of rock and roll. Is there, then, some feature that
remains common to all contexts of rock and roll? If we start with the simple
assumption that rock and roll is related in some way to youth's experiences of
alienation, powerlessness, and boredom, can we locate the context within
which these experiences emerge and function as specific responses of a
"youth culture"?

   The adolescence of the rock and roll audience, especially in the fifties but
continuing through today, is obviously an important determinant of the music itself as well as of its cultural politics. The frustrations, desires, fears, and
resentments of puberty provide much of the energy and many of the concerns
of rock and roll. However, even this apparently simple determination is me-

diated by other emotions, experiences, and events. While the first audience of rock and roll was in fact teenagers, the statement certainly no longer holds. And similarly, while the class experience represented in rock and roll may function significantly in one context, it may not function similarly in different contexts, and in some it may be generally absent. Attempts to generalize Hebdige's reading of punk as working-class music must confront not only Frith's argument that it emerged out of a largely art school and "bohemian" context, but also those situations in which punk functions in a largely middle-class context without any romanticization of the working class. The fact that particular forms of rock and roll, and even perhaps rock and roll in general, have specific class roots does not necessarily say anything about its reception and social effects in particular contexts. This of course does not deny that the fact of (class) origin may have specific mediated effects, particularly through local iconographies.

Consider by contrast the obvious fact that rock and roll emerged in a particular temporal context, variously characterized as late capitalism, postmodernity, and so forth. The dominant moments of this postwar context have been widely described: the effects of the war and the Holocaust on the generations of parents; economic prosperity and optimism; the threat of instant and total annihilation (the atomic bomb); the cold war and McCarthyism, with the resulting political apathy and repression; the rise of suburbia with its inherent valorization of repetition; the development of late capitalism (consumption society), with its increasingly sophisticated technology for the rationalization and control of everyday life; the proliferation of mass media and advertising techniques and the emergence of an aesthetic of images; the attempt and ultimate inability to deal with the fact of the baby boom; the continuation of an ideology of individuality, progress, and communication (the American Dream); and, to echo Sontag, an increasingly receding threshold of the shocking. The result was a generation of children that was not only bored (the American Dream turned out to be boring) and afraid, but lonely and isolated from each other and the adult world as well. The more the adult world emphasized their children's uniqueness and promised them paradise, the angrier, more frustrated, and more insecure they grew.

These cultural effects were themselves located within an even broader apparatus whose significance is only now being recognized: they operated in a world characterized by a steadily rising rate of change. What is unique, however (since this process had been going on for some time), is that change increasingly appears to be all that there is; it does not allow any appeal to a stable and predictable teleology. There is in fact no sense of progress that can provide meaning or depth and a sense of inheritance. Both the future and the past appear increasingly irrelevant; history has collapsed into the present. The ramifications of this fact are only now becoming visible as we confront a generation that no longer believes that their lives will be better than that of their parents, even though the "rhetoric of progress" is still present. Suddenly, "we are obliged to remake from scratch the foundation of our taste, as of our politics and our very lives. Old ways of judging linger [only as] unexamined habits, comforting defenses against the recognition of our common lostness" (Schjeldjahl 1981, 67). As history loses its sense, it can no longer be a source for the values by which one chooses and validates one's actions. As John Berger writes,

> Today what surrounds the individual life can change more quickly than the brief sequence of that life itself. The timeless has been abolished and history has become ephemerality. History no longer pays its respect to the dead: the dead are simply what has passed through . . . This means that the common experience of moments which defy time is apparently denied by everything which surrounds them. Such moments have ceased to be windows looking across history toward the timeless. The experience which instigates the phrase *for ever* has now to be assumed alone and privately. And so its role is changed: instead of transcending, it isolates. (Berger 1980, 89)

As history becomes mere change—discontinuous, directionless, and meaningless—it is replaced by a sense of fragmentation and rupture, of oppressive materiality, of powerlessness and relativism.

This new sociohistorical context further reinforced youth's conviction of its own uniqueness; indeed it determined their dominant generational needs and perceptions in the fifties and since. If adolescence is a time when one seeks not only pleasure but also a viable adult identity, then the collapse of the deep structure of history undermined the traditional models. The significance of Holden Caulfield, James Dean, Marlon Brando, and the Beats as cultural heroes lies in their struggle to achieve some identity consistent with this new set of experiences, and the Beats' turn to the model of the black hipster pointed the way for the rock and roll/youth culture.

Rock and roll emerges from and functions within the lives of those generations that have grown up in this postwar, postmodern context. It does not simply represent and respond to the experiences of teenagers, nor to those of a particular class. It is not merely music of the generation gap. It draws a line through that context by marking one particular historical appearance of the generation gap as a permanent one. Similarly, class divisions are reinscribed and realigned as they are traversed by the boundary of postmodernity, of the desires of those generations who have known no other historical moment. Postmodernity is, I shall suggest, not merely an experience nor a representation of experience; it is above all a form of practice by which affective alliances are produced, by which other practices and events are invested with affect.

While many commentators have described rock and roll as watered-down rhythm and blues (or more accurately, a synthesis of blues and white hillbilly music), I would argue that the fact of its production and reception by white youth involved a real transformation of its musical roots. It located them within a different, emergent historical formation, whose contours I have described in terms clearly meant to echo the aesthetic of postmodern practice: a denial of totality and a subsequent emphasis on discontinuity, fragmentation, and rupture; a denial of depth and a subsequent emphasis on the materiality of surfaces; a denial of any teleology and a subsequent emphasis on change and chance so that history becomes both irrelevant and the very substance of our existence; a denial of freedom and innocent self-consciousness and a subsequent emphasis on context, determination, and the intertextuality of discursive codes.

The question is whether the postmodernist rejection of meaning in favor of the production of fragments is merely the logical conclusion of the capitalist commodity fetish. In what sense is the postmodernist fragment, even when it accepts the inevitability of its existence as a commodity, something other than a commodity? The commodity in late capitalism exists at the site of the contradiction between modernist and postmodernist cultural practices. The commodity as such is still determined by a representation of totality; it signifies a fragmentation only in the context of a totalizing impulse that gives meaning, not only to the particular object (e.g., as status, fashion, or exchange value) but also to the general process of commodification. Postmodern practice denies any such totalizing impulse. We might say that the object in late capitalism functions in the context of an ideological aesthetic on the one hand and a structural aesthetic on the other. The former describes the way the object is represented; postmodern fragments are appropriated into the context of the commodity by defining them in purely economic or aesthetic (avant-garde) terms. This is made easier by postmodernism's propensity to use capitalist commodities within its discourse. A structural aesthetic describes postmodern practice as a demystification of the commodity, its aesthetic reduction to a fragment sans context or significance, a signifier without a signified. Postmodernism is the aesthetic practice of deconstruction.

The object within late capitalism then exists in the space of the contradiction between these two practices: an ideological mystification that turns it into a commodity and a structural demystification that returns it to the material context. By their very nature, postmodern objects cannot be merely consumed unless they have been recuperated by being re-presented as commodities. Thus the postmodern aesthetic of rock and roll does not determine the music's existence as a commodity but rather as a constant struggle between commodification and fragmentation.

I can now try to specify the particular form of postmodern practice that characterizes rock and roll as an appropriation of hegemonic practices into its own discourses. If the response of the hegemony to resistance is through practices of incorporation (see Williams 1981), then the power of rock and roll lies in its practice of "excorporation," operating at and reproducing the boundary between youth culture and the dominant culture. Rock and roll reverses the hegemonic practices of incorporation, by which practices claiming a certain externality are relocated within the context of hegemonic relations. Rock and roll removes signs, objects, sounds, styles, and so forth from their apparently meaningful existence within the dominant culture and relocates them within an affective alliance of differentiation and resistance. The resultant shock—of both recognition and an undermining of meaning—produces a temporarily impassable boundary within the dominant culture, an encapsulation of the affective possibilities of the rock and roll culture. Rock and roll is a particular form of bricolage, a uniquely capitalist and postmodern practice. It functions in a constant play of incorporation and excorporation (both always occurring simultaneously), a contradictory cultural practice. The most obvious result of this is the particular form of irony in rock and roll (which connects it with the tradition of symbolism—dada—surrealism). As Piccarella has noted, "What has always separated rock and roll from its roots in blues and country music, the essence of its youthfulness, is ironic distance from direct personal expression. In its outlandish styles and exaggerated mannerisms, rock showmanship tends toward the defensive self-alienation of adolescence" (1982, 83). Rock and roll practice is a form of resistance for generations with no faith in revolution. Rock and roll's resistance—its politics—is neither a direct rejection of the dominant culture nor a utopian negation (fantasy) of the structures of power. It plays with the very practice that the dominant culture uses to resist its resistance: incorporation and excorporation in a continuous dialectic that reproduces the very boundary of existence. Because its resistance remains, however, within the political and economic space of the dominant culture, its revolution is only a "simulacrum." Its politics emerge only at that moment when political consciousness is no longer possible. Its practice is surrealism without the dream/nightmare, dada without the representation of a political option.

Unable to reject, control, or even conceptualize this postmodern reality, it becomes both the source of oppression and the object/context of celebration and fun. Repelled and angered by the boredom (repetitiveness), meaninglessness, and dehumanization of the contemporary world, youth celebrates these very conditions in its leisure (technology, noise, commodity fetish, repetition, fragmentation, and superficiality). Despondency and pleasure become mutually constitutive. Rock and roll seeks its place within and against the very postmodernity that is its condition of possibility. Of course, at moments rock and roll has sought as well to flee that impossible denial of representation. For example, while the subculture of acid rock played with signs and objects as if they were merely the pieces in a bricoleur's game, that culture also denied its postmodern practice by appealing to a myth of natural reality. Although its texts were not transparent, they were located within a larger context in which resistance was harnessed in the interests of a utopian retreat into the "natural" life.

HYPOTHESIS 2. THE POWER OF ROCK
AND ROLL: AFFECTIVE DIFFERENCE

We might begin to understand how rock and roll works by affirming that it is, above all, fun—the production of pleasure (e.g., in the sheer energy of the music, the danceable beat, the sexual echoes, etc.). In fact, the most devastating rejection of a particular rock and roll text is to say that it is "boring." Thus rock and roll can never take itself too seriously. To be effective it must constantly deny its own significance; it must focus the attention of its audiences on its surfaces. Its power lies not in what it says or means but in what it does in the textures and contexts of its uses. For in fact different audiences interpret the same texts differently, and there seems to be little correlation between semantic readings and uses/pleasures. I do not mean to suggest a disjunction of lyrics and sounds (which may operate in a variety of relations to each other) but rather that rock and roll cannot be approached by some textual analysis of its message. Rock and roll, whether live or recorded, is a performance whose "significance" cannot be read off the "text." It is not that rock and roll does not produce and manipulate meaning but rather that meaning itself functions in rock and roll affectively, that is, to produce and organize desires and pleasures. When David Susskind asked record producer Phil Spector what the meaning of the song "Do Doo Ron Ron" was, Spector responded, "It's not what I say it means. It's what it makes you feel! Can't you hear the sound of that record, can't you hear that?" (Marcus 1969, 11–12). What both Spector and his fans knew was that the answer to his question was no.

But of course, on the other hand, rock and roll does take itself seriously. Not only is it extremely self-conscious, but it continuously reconstitutes and re-encapsulates itself (e.g., in its intertextuality, its self-references, its recreation of its history through the incorporation of "covers," etc.). In fact, it is an essential sign of the popularity of rock and roll that it constantly marks its difference from other musical cultures, whether popular or not. Rock and roll is, from its own side, not merely a subset of "pop," and there must always be music that is not rock and roll. Such "other" music is "co-opted," "sold out," "bubblegum," "family entertainment," and so on.

If the power of rock and roll, then, depends not upon meaning but upon affective investments, it is related not so much to what one feels as to the boundary drawn by the very existence of different organizations of desire and pleasure. Its oppositional power is not the result of its offering a particular desire that the dominant culture cannot accept, nor of the particular structure of pleasure, nor of its calling for the unlimited realization of desire. Rock and roll need not always offer an ideological critique of the dominant culture, although at some moments it certainly has, aimed at particular repressions as well as the very presence of repression itself. However, rock and roll does not project an antinomy of freedom and constraint, since rock and roll always produces its own constraints on itself and its fans. Its history is rather the deconstruction of that antinomy; it plays with the relation of desire and its regimentation by always circumscribing its own possibilities for the production of pleasure. Rock and roll's relation to desire and pleasure serves to mark a difference, to inscribe on the surface of social reality a boundary between "them" and "us"; it constantly rearticulates and recathects a permanent rupture at the point of the intersection of postmodernity, youth, and pleasure. It makes a particular historical moment—and the generations emerging within it—into an apparently permanent rupture. This rupture is accomplished through the production of "affective alliances" that disrupt the hegemonic control of desire and pleasure; in the ideological register, these effects are most visible within the so-called emotional life of its fans.

This mark of difference is not, however, a simple boundary between inside and outside, hegemony and revolution. Rock and roll locates its fans as different even while they exist within the hegemony. The boundary is inscribed within the dominant culture. Rock and roll is an insider's art that functions to position its fans as outsiders. This "encapsulation" may sometimes be produced through ideological representations that either explicitly attack the hegemony or define an alternative identity for those living within its affective alliances. But these local considerations too often cloud the general stratification of social space that rock and roll produces: it defines an exteriority for itself inside the dominant culture through particular practices that constitute affective alliances. To use a psychoanalytic metaphor, rock and roll "incorporates" itself into the "belly of the beast." It is "internalised but unintegrated," included within the dominant culture but "alien to it, inaccessible; . . . enclosed, entombed, encysted inside" (Nelson 1978, 57–58).

Finally, we must ask in what sense this boundary constitutes a political relationship between the rock and roll culture and the hegemony. The most common descriptions of rock and roll's power of affirmation locate it within the attempt to reconstitute community in the face of industrial mass society. Thus if rock and roll apparently begins with private desires, it creates common experiences out of them. For example, rock and roll in the fifties produced a community based upon the shared experiences of teenagers. But it is arguable that the production of this identity—one that always reasserts itself and rebels against older generations of rock and roll fans—is the dismantling rather than the source of rock and roll's political function. The politics of rock and roll is not the production of an identity but the constant struggle against such identities (which could be incorporated by the dominant culture) even as it creates and politicizes them. The source of this tension can be located in the confrontation with postmodernity. Rock and roll transforms the despair of its context into an embracing of its possibilities as pleasure. But it cannot dismiss the despair. For what rock and roll is inescapably drawn into is the attempt to find meaning and value in the historical moment and in its own existence. The attempt is, of course, the refusal of postmodernity, of its own postwar context. And so rock and roll seeks new forms of identity, new values and meaning, yet it must always place these back into the context of a world that undermines all meaning and value. For example, it is not simply that youth's sense of loneliness is met with romantic myths of love obviously condemned to failure; it is rather that rock and roll seeks such paths out of postmodernity. And the reality of their immanent failure, the frustration of knowing that they will fail despite our desires, is partly responsible for the real sense of desperation behind the concern for love in pop (e.g., the Beatles, the teenage death songs) and teenage (e.g., Meatloaf) rock and roll.

The politics of rock and roll must be understood within this tension, caught between the desire to celebrate the new and the desire to escape it, between despair and pleasure. The politics of rock and roll arises from its articulation of affective alliances as modes of survival within the postmodern world. It does not bemoan the death of older structures but seeks to find organizations of desire that do not contradict the reality in which it finds itself. Rock and roll at its best transforms old dreams into new realities. It rejects that which is outside of its self-encapsulation not on political grounds but because their organizations of affect are no longer appropriate in the postmodern world. It celebrates the life of the refugee, the immigrants with no roots except those they can construct for themselves at the moment, constructions that will inevitably collapse around them. Rock and roll celebrates play—even despairing play—as the only possibility for survival (e.g., Elvis's pink Cadillac, the Beatles' antics, punk's shock tactics, and postpunk's dissonance). It does not oppose its own ideological representations to those of the dominant culture: it locates itself within the gaps and cracks of the hegemony, the points at which meaning itself collapses into desire and affect.

HYPOTHESIS 3. THE WORK OF ROCK
AND ROLL: AFFECTIVE ALLIANCES

The question remains, however, of why rock and roll fans so confidently assumed that Susskind could not "hear" the music. Nor have we acknowledged the existence of boundaries and differences within rock and roll, and its cultures: What one audience takes to be rock and roll, another may dismiss as co-opted. I want to suggest that a particular music exists as "rock and roll" for an audience only when it is located in a larger assemblage that I will call "the rock and roll apparatus." Within such a context, the music is inflected in ways that empower its specific functioning. The rock and roll apparatus includes not only musical texts and practices but also economic determinations, technological possibilities, images (of performers and fans), social relations, aesthetic conventions, styles of language, movement, appearance and dance, media practices, ideological commitments, and media representations of the apparatus itself. The apparatus describes "cartographies of taste" that are both synchronic and diachronic and that encompass both musical and nonmusical registers of everyday life. For example, not only do particular apparatuses define differing boundaries of "acceptable music," they place different forms of rock and roll in different affective positions; they empower them in different ways. At any moment, rock and roll is constituted by a number of different forms, and while certain forms or conventions may remain common, their effects change in terms of their synchronic and diachronic relations as defined within the apparatus. Furthermore, these positions are always changing as new forms appear and disrupt the musical economy.

To treat rock and roll as a set of musical texts whose effects can be read off their surface or be located within the isolated relation between music and fan is already to assume an interpretation of its place within a particular rock and roll apparatus. Instead the music's effects and identity can only be described within the apparatus, which connects particular fragments of the heterogeneous domains of social, cultural, and material practices. It is, then, the rock and roll apparatus that encapsulates itself, that inscribes the difference between "them" and "us." And it is the apparatus that exists as a bricolage through the "excorporation" of hegemonic signs and events. By treating them as fragments, it reinvests them within a different "topography of desire."

It would be a mistake, however, to see the apparatus as a passive collection of discrete material events; it is the apparatus itself that is constantly producing ever-changing structures of desire and thus reproducing itself. The rock and roll apparatus organizes the seemingly random collection of cathected events and codes that interpenetrate the rock and roll culture. It is an array of strategies with which youth organizes its affective existence. Such "topographies of desire" might then be described as "affective formations" in order to affirm both their relation and irreducibility to ideological, political, and economic formations.

The power of the rock and roll apparatus, therefore, lies not mainly in its "theft" of partial objects from the various domains of social life, nor even in the mere fact that it draws lines connecting them. Rather its power lies in its foregrounding and production of particular organizations within and between these fragments. The apparatus is a machine that, in constantly reproducing itself, reshapes our affective life by mapping the vectors of its own economy of desire upon our material life. My claim is that the continuity of rock and roll is constituted by the continued inscription of a three-dimensional topography that describes its "affective formation." By operating at this level of abstraction, I am ignoring questions about the specific fragments upon which the apparatus works at a particular moment, as well as the particular inflections these axes of the apparatus may be given at such moments. Rather than looking at particular apparatuses and formations, I want to begin by describing the boundaries of the rock and roll apparatus: the moment of its emergence, the possibility of its cessation, the range of its variability, and so forth.

The rock and roll apparatus affectively organizes everyday life according to three intersecting axes: (1) youth as difference: the social difference of generations is inscribed upon the phenomenological field of social relations; (2) pleasure of the body: the celebration of pleasure is inscribed upon the site of the body; and (3) postmodernity: the structure of uncertainty (the fragment) is inscribed upon the circuit of history and meaning. I will comment briefly on each of these.

Most obviously, the rock and roll apparatus is constructed around the category of youth; and while it is certainly true that "youth" has a number of different ideological inflections, youth is also a material body that can be located socially and historically—a body that is traversed and inscribed both affectively and ideologically. In fact, the rock and roll apparatus has produced a "generational politics" that can be described structurally as a politics of difference and exclusion and substantively as a politics of boredom. As I have argued, rather than defining any necessary identity for its fans, the rock and roll apparatus functions as a boundary that encapsulates its fans and excludes the others. It is this difference that affectively invests the category of youth within the apparatus itself and defines the site of youth culture. The "other" that is excluded from the apparatus is not, however, defined chronologically but rather by a phenomenology of boredom. The rock and roll apparatus institutionalizes a politics defined only by its opposition to boredom as the experience of hegemonic reality. The politics of youth celebrates change: the work of the apparatus transforms the very structures of boredom into pleasure.

The second affective axis of the rock and roll apparatus involves its celebration of the body as the site of pleasure—in its transformation of identity into style, in the centrality of rhythm and dance, and in its courting of sexuality and sexual practices. The musical practice itself is inserted into the apparatus at the site of the body: it is a music of bodily desire. There is an immediate material relation to the music and its movements. This relation, while true of music in general, is foregrounded in rock and roll. At its simplest level, the body vibrates with the sounds and rhythms, and that vibration can be articulated with other practices and events to produce complex effects. The materiality of music gives it its affective power to translate individuals (an ideological construct) into bodies. This material relation is there, within the apparatus, available to its fans. The body becomes the site at which pleasure is restructured and desire potentially redirected. One might examine, for example, the complex and often contradictory relations between rock and roll and black music in the United States (the fact that it is both so compatible and so distanced at various moments) in terms of the changing investments of this axis. Furthermore, it is here that one might try to articulate the possibilities of an oppositional sexual politics within the rock and roll apparatus.

Of course, these suggestions are not meant to occlude the relations between the affective formation of the rock and roll apparatus and its position within the ideologically (as well as economically and politically) produced structures of racism and sexism within American society. Clearly, many of the institutional practices of production, marketing, and distribution, as well as patterns of gendered and racial consumption, reinforce and reproduce hegemonic structures of difference and oppression. For example, many of the feminist critiques of rock and roll are quite legitimate. Musical texts and cultures are often quite repressive. Often, such inflections produce their own "pleasure of the emotions" which, most commonly, involve experiences of romance and self-pity. Here the body is reinscribed as the site of selfhood. On the other hand, such critiques cannot justify global condemnations of the affective political possibilities of the rock and roll apparatus. The concrete "politics of pleasure" can only be identified and evaluated contextually. Further, at the level of the affective formation, desire is at least conceptually independent of ideology (in this case, of gender); it is at least difficult to maintain that the desires and rhythms of rock and roll are intrinsically gender coded (see the exchange between Catharine A. MacKinnon and Ellen Willis in Nelson and Grossberg 1988).

The third axis of the rock and roll apparatus foregrounds the postmodern context within which it emerged. Whether understood as the absence of a future by which we can organize our lives ("The future is a hoax created by high school counselors and insurance salesmen"; "Life is hard and then you die") or of meaning ("Even if there were a meaning to life, I probably wouldn't agree with it," as one of my students said), the rock and roll apparatus is materially structured by this absence of structure. The rock and roll apparatus functions to provide strategies for escaping, denying, celebrating, finding pleasure in—in other words, for surviving within—a postmodern world.

This third axis reflexively positions the rock and roll apparatus within its postmodern context and constitutes rock and roll's ambiguity toward its own importance and power. Unlike other forms of popular culture, the "postmodern politics" of rock and roll undermines its claim to produce a stable affective formation. Rather it participates in the production of temporary "affective alliances" that celebrate their own instability and superficiality. While such alliances may apparently make claims to totality within their own moment of empowerment, they are decisively marked by their fluidity and self-deprecation ("Nothing matters, and what if it did?" [John Cougar]), and by the ease with which the rock and roll apparatus slides from one alliance into another. In other words, the rock and roll apparatus incorporates and even celebrates the "disposability" of any affective alliance without thereby sacrificing its own claim to existence.

The existence of the rock and roll apparatus is, then, precisely in its production of itself as an affective alliance that locates the sites of empowerment between the music and its fans. That is, the rock and roll apparatus affectively organizes the everyday life of its fans by differentially cathecting the various fragments it "excorporates" along these three axes. The result is that it locates, for its fans, the possibilities of intervention and pleasure. It involves the investment of desire in the material world according to vectors (quantities having both magnitude and direction) that are removed from the hegemonic affective formation. It is not that the desires or pleasures themselves are oppositional but rather that the affective investments of the rock and roll apparatus empower its audiences with strategies that, taken topographically, define a level of potential opposition and, often, survival.

HYPOTHESIS 4. THE DIVERSITY OF
ROCK AND ROLL

The most commonly observed division within rock and roll (and its fans) is between the punk—violent, sexual, and emotional—and the poet—critical, sensuous, and intellectual. These correspond roughly with the images of working- and middle-class life. In the popular rock press, one finds descriptions and categorizations of the different musical styles in rock and roll (e.g., pop, rhythm and blues, art, folk, country, heavy metal, etc.). The concern is often with musical lines of influence. However, it is difficult to see how rock and roll can be circumscribed by any musical characteristics. And the fragmentation of the music has to be complemented by an appreciation of the heterogeneity of listening practices: styles, contexts, and functions. For example, the same music can be used by different groups (e.g., new wave); different styles can be used for similar functions (e.g., dance music, drug music); and different groups within a common style may yet have different audiences (e.g., Beatles, Ramones, REO Speedwagon, and dB's all use pop conventions; Heart, Styx, and AC/DC are all "heavy metal" bands). There is not "only one way to rock."

We can, alternatively, describe the diversity within and the difference of rock and roll on the basis of the considerations of the power and the work of rock and roll advanced above: first, by specifying the ways in which the rock and roll apparatus has cathected a boundary between "them" and "us" through its history; and second, by identifying the vectors that are foregrounded in particular affective alliances. In both cases, I shall have to abstract from the concrete history of the production of local affective alliances. I do not wish to claim, for either of these typologies, that they belong exclusively to rock and roll, or that they limit its future possibilities in predictable ways.

The Inscription of Difference. I propose to construct a two-dimensional schema: the horizontal axis specifies the various structures by which rock and roll differentiates its culture from the other; the vertical axis describes the different affective statuses that rock and roll has assigned to or invested in its own existence.

Rock and roll has produced three forms of boundaries: oppositional, alternative, and independent. An oppositional boundary inscribes the fact of difference explicitly; both "us" and "them" are affectively charged. Its effectiveness depends upon the presence of the other as an enemy. Thus oppositional rock and roll presents itself as a direct challenge or threat to the dominant culture, perhaps even confronting the power of the dominant culture with its own power. It might be expressed in the phrase "We want the world and we want it now." An alternative boundary is inscribed when the other is only implicitly present. The enemy is negatively charged only as that against which the rock and roll culture differentiates itself. Alternative rock and roll mounts an implicit attack on the dominant culture; the fact of its existence implies a potential substitution for the hegemonic organization of desire: "We want the world but on our terms." An independent boundary is inscribed when the other is effective only by its absence. Independent rock and roll does not present itself as a challenge, either explicitly or implicitly, to the dominant culture, although it may function as such. It apparently exists outside of its relation to the dominant culture; it does not want the world. It seeks to escape, to define a space that neither impinges upon nor is impinged upon by the hegemony: "We want our world." We can represent these three structures of difference, in terms of Us and Them (U and T), as follows: U/T, U/(T), U/( ). Without recognizing these different structures of difference, whatever affirmations rock and roll may produce are likely to be described independently of the particular historical context. While it is possible that some music may consistently produce the same positive affects across different contexts, the effects of the affirmations are bound to change as their particular relations to the dominant culture are differentially cathected.

What then is the nature of the affirmative affect of rock and roll? I have argued against seeing it as the representation of identities; the subject-positions articulated by rock and roll are often multiple and contradictory. Rather it defines particular affective statuses for its own culture. By describing itself as a particular structuration of affect, rock and roll locates *social* subjects in a *nonrepresentational* space. One can identify three such self-cathexes: visionary, experiential, and critical. These are, essentially, self-attributions; they describe different forms of affective alliances, modes of affectively relating to and surviving within the world. Again, it is not the content of the particular affirmation that is effective (although ideological representation may play an important role) but the status that it assigns to the existence of its own desires.

Visionary rock and roll projects itself as a utopian practice. Its power derives from its claim to be a stable structure of desire. The particular rock and roll culture lives out—in its music—the possibility of a moment of stability in the face of change and regimentation. Whether the real audience succeeds in actualizing its utopian possibility and the particular content of the vision are only secondary. The affective and political power of the music depends upon its constituting itself as something more than just a mode of survival, as a vision of a potentially permanent affective alliance. Experiential rock and roll is more modest; it projects itself not as a necessary mode of survival but only as a viable possibility in the present context. It valorizes its own affirmation of change and movement. The alliances that it organizes are at best temporary respites. It celebrates the behaviors and images of its own youth cultures (e.g., driving, dancing, sexuality, rhythm), which deny both regimentation and the possibility of stability. Its affirmation is only in the very pleasure of the music, in engulfing oneself within the musical context, in participating within the practices of youth culture. Such an affirmation tends to be neither as optimistic and pretentious as the visionary, nor as pessimistic and self-destructive as the critical. A critical affirmation refuses even the claim that it can produce temporary spaces within which the audience might control and make sense of its life. By rejecting any possibility of stability and value—including that implied by the valorization of change itself—it undermines its own status as a viable mode of survival. It affirms and valorizes only its own negativity. Its status as pleasurable depends upon its status as the only response to the reality of postmodernity. All that can be affirmed is the practice of critique, the deconstruction of all affective alliances, including that produced by its own inscription of the difference between them and us. The affirmation of critical rock and roll is a self-reflexive affirmation of difference, a decathexis of any affirmation.

The matrix of "stances" that these two dimensions generate (see Fig. 1) describes the possibilities of an affective politics offered by rock and roll. It is not a description of musical styles nor of a group's intentions. Further, no group or style can be stably located within a category; groups can play with a number of stances simultaneously (e.g., the Clash). The affective stance of particular music is, as I have emphasized, locally produced. It may depend on a wide range of determinants, including the image of the band and different degrees of knowledge of the lyrics (rock and roll fans often "float" in and out of the lyrics). Fans of different musics (e.g., punk and heavy metal) often place a great weight on what appear as minute musical differences to outsiders. The ways in which one listens to music, as well as the music one

NEGATION

		Oppositional	Alternative	Independent
AFFIRMATION	Utopian	Jimi Hendrix (late sixties) / Tom Robinson Band (late seventies)	Grateful Dead (late sixties) / U2 (seventies)	David Bowie (early seventies) Electric Light Orchestra disco (mid-seventies)
	Experiential	Doors (late sixties) / Bruce Springsteen (mid-seventies)	Chuck Berry (mid-fifties) / Ramones (late seventies)	Beatles (early sixties) Blondie REO Speedwagon (late seventies)
	Critical	Clash Tonio K (late seventies)	Sex Pistols (mid-seventies) Gang of Four (late seventies) New Order Aztec Camera (eighties)	Joy Division (late seventies) Culture Club Orange Juice (eighties)

Figure 1

listens to, is a product of already differing and often antagonistic affective alliances. Thus while the emergence of folk rock (e.g., the Beatles' *Rubber Soul*) redefined the listening habits of particular audience fractions (one had to listen to the lyrics in new ways), it is doubtful that younger kids listening to the music on AM radio found it making the same demands on them.

Two consequences of this approach to rock and roll are worth noting. First, it points to the existence of a real ambiguity within many critical evaluations between judgments of musical quality and affective politics. This has always been a dilemma for the rock and roll culture itself, for the two are often in conflict. The music of the Beach Boys, the recent series of revivals (e.g., ska, rockabilly, glitter, pop, and psychedelic rock) are potentially good music with questionable political effects. On the other hand, punk was about the possibility, indeed the necessity, of politically "good" rock and roll whose musical quality was, by any traditional standards, dubious. Finally, the neofascist tendencies of some new wave music (e.g., oi) pose the question of the content-free nature of these affective stances and the possibility that rock and roll may succeed in inscribing a powerful affective boundary by representing a regimentation of desire even more oppressive than that of the hegemony.

Second, this approach opens the possibility of using a reading of rock and roll as a way of understanding and interpreting the more general social context at a particular moment. What this matrix makes obvious is that, at different times, different stances are available as resources and that some of them may dominate or define the struggles both within the music and between the youth culture and the hegemony. The power of this approach, however, must obviously be judged on the basis of what it allows one to say about particular examples. In Figure 1, I have included within each category examples of groups whose music might be generally associated with that particular affective function. I have further specified a time frame and, were I to be more precise; I would have to include some definition of a particular fraction of the youth culture.

The Structures of Affective Alliances. There are at least two problems, however, with this schema. First, it leaves unaddressed the differences that may exist between musics located within the same position. For example, while the Sex Pistols and the Gang of Four may both be located as "critical-alternative," this says nothing about the differences between the rock and roll apparatuses within which they are effective. Second, rock and roll fans, as well as many critics, act as if the same music has the same function for its entire audience. We forget that there is no stable and homogeneous rock and roll audience except as it is constructed through the marketing practices of the dominant economic institutions. Our analysis must allow that the same music can be located within different apparatuses, and that different apparatuses may coexist within the same position of difference (as given in Fig. 1). The particular "politics of pleasure" and structures of empowerment effected by a particular music will, therefore, depend upon the range of apparatuses within which the music exists.

Consequently the music itself cannot be assigned a social power apart from the different affective alliances within which it is implicated. But such apparatuses/alliances are only partly described by their structural position vis-à-vis the hegemony. We have already alluded to the terms with which particular apparatuses can be identified, but I want to propose a strategy that will allow us to schematize the positive differences between major forms. If the rock and roll apparatus is defined by the particular arrangement and inflections of the three axes (youth, the body, postmodernity), different apparatuses can be described as foregrounding particular ones. That is, I propose to locate a significant positive difference among affective alliances according to the relative investment made in each of the three axes. It is tempting, and perhaps historically accurate, to identify the three axes with the three affirmative affective positions (youth, the body, and postmodernity with the utopian, the experiential, and the critical, respectively). However, the equation is not a necessary one and would have the effect of occluding new possibilities (e.g., a postmodern utopianism). It seems best, therefore, to treat the two schemas as conceptually independent and concretely interactive.

The most common cathexis within the rock and roll apparatus foregrounds both the axis of youth (difference) and that of the body (pleasure): Chuck Berry, Elvis Presley, and others. A second possibility is that one of these two becomes, to various degrees, relatively less important. While soul music foregrounds the axis of the body and pleasure, clearly it need not direct its audience to invest its desire or locate its pleasure in its "youth." On the other hand, as many critics have noted, there is a relative decathexis of the body in much of the music directed to and effective for a general "teenage" audience. I would also suggest that much of the "acid rock" of the counterculture, and the singer-songwriter tradition that followed it, were defined in part by a continuing decathexis of the pleasure of the body (by deflecting it toward an ideologically defined concept of "love" and "relationship"). It is not surprising, then, that both glitter rock and heavy metal, which emerged as rejections of the counterculture's affective alliances, recathect the axis of the body (and in fact define the axis of youth and difference by reference to it).

Finally, the apparatuses constructed around punk and postpunk musics apparently foreground the axis of postmodernity. I would like to develop this particular example, beginning with punk. Hebdige has argued (1979, 62–70) that punk emerged from the working-class experiences of historically changing racial relations and of economic pessimism (no work, no future, no meaning) in England. Frith has rejected this view of its origins: "The pioneering punk-rockers themselves were a self-conscious, artful lot with a good understanding of both rock tradition and populist cliché; their music no more reflected directly back on conditions in the dole queue than it emerged spontaneously from them" (1981, 158). He could also have pointed to the emergence of American punk bands in the mid-seventies (Television, Patti Smith,

Ramones, Residents, etc.) as further evidence for his view of the origins. Frith proposes to read punk instead in the context of its representation of a "new sort of street culture . . . punk's cultural significance was derived not from its articulation of unemployment but from its exploration of the aesthetics of proletarian play" (267). However, Frith goes beyond this to locate punk within the history of rock and roll conventions:

> The original punk texts had a shock effect. They challenged pop and rock conventions of romance, beauty, and ease. Punks focused their lyrics on social and political subjects, mocked conventional rock 'n' roll declarations of young virility and power, disrupted their own flow of words with their images and sounds. It soon became apparent though, as the shock wore off, that punk was constricted by its realist claims, by its use of melodic structures and a rhythmic base that were taken to tell-it-like-it-was just *because* they followed rock 'n' roll rules—the 4:4 beat, shouted vocals, rough guitar/bass/drums lineup. (160)

Greil Marcus has similarly argued that the Sex Pistols "used rock and roll as a weapon against itself" (1980a, 452; see also Marcus 1980b, 1981a). Punk recathected the boundary between rock and roll and the outside world precisely by rejecting what rock and roll had become not merely economically and aesthetically, but affectively as well. It rejected the affective possibilities that had defined and constrained rock and roll, structures I have described as "utopian" and "experiential." It affirmed only its own negativity, constituting a set of "critical" apparatuses, while leaving open the possibilities of its structural relation to the hegemony. It did this, in part, in much the same way disco operated, by an explosion of its own practice of "excorporation"; anything could be incorporated into punk (or disco) culture. But, unlike disco, punk made the excorporative practice of rock and roll the only possible response to the context of everyday life. As Hebdige has argued, punk "deconstructed" all signs, all value and significance. Punk acted out its negative deconstruction of the world and of rock and roll itself. By foregrounding the artificiality of all taste, the risk of all affective investments, it attempted to decathect anything below its own surfaces, including rock and roll itself. There is a sense in which, after punk, one can no longer reasonably believe in the "magic that can set you free."

Regardless of its origin (in the reality of working-class experience or the image of proletarian play), the punk apparatus was constituted by its foregrounding of the axis of postmodernity: it made rock and roll into its own postmodern practice. Further, punk (unlike disco) often decathected the axis of the body as the site of pleasure, rejecting not only love but sexuality—the musical crescendo (orgasm?) is replaced by pulse, drones, and continuous noise. On the other hand, the punk apparatus often continued to invest its power in the axis of youth and made the body itself into the site for the inscription of difference (through clothing, style, etc.). But the cathexis of difference forced it back into the context of an implicit faith in youth and, consequently, in rock and roll itself. As Marcus has observed, "Perhaps the only true irony in the whole story was that, in the end, it all came down to rock and roll—nothing less, but nothing more" (1980a, 455).

But punk was part of a larger set of possibilities emerging in the rock and roll culture, and it often functioned within them.[2] Thus it could have its impact in the United States despite the fact that it was neither particularly visible nor popular.

Punk called into question the affective power of rock and roll; it attempted to incorporate its own possibility of incorporation, and its only strategy for survival was constantly to proliferate its own excorporative practice. It tried to celebrate rock and roll even as it acknowledged its conceit. The effect of the punk apparatus within the rock and roll culture has enabled a number of different alliances to emerge. First, apparatuses constructed around both "oi" and "hardcore" continue the "shock techniques" of punk and often recathect the axes of youth and the body, while apparently decathecting that of post-modernity. Second, what I will call "new wave" apparently accepts the inev-itability of incorporation and attempts to reclaim the affective power of rock and roll by reviving older rock and roll apparatuses (e.g., rockabilly, acid, garage bands, pop, and soul). Third, "postpunk" uses punk's technique of deconstructing rock and roll in order to excavate and extend the limits of rock and roll. Its deconstruction is always followed by at least a partial reconstruc-tion of rock and roll conventions. And finally, "new music" refuses the lim-itations of rock conventions entirely and seeks intentionally to alienate itself, not only from those outside of the rock and roll culture, but from that culture as well.[3]

A number of relations exist between these different apparatuses. Both the continuations of punk and new wave often recathect the axis of youth. New wave and postpunk often recathect the body as the site of pleasure (albeit according to very different inflections of that axis), and both postpunk and new music foreground, above all, the axis of postmodernity. On the other hand, new wave always balances this investment by recathecting at least one of the others, while hardcore/oi appears to invest itself in decathecting the axis of postmodernity.

That postmodernity has been described by John Piccarella: "A vision underlies the elegance and outrageousness—the artists are horrified by the seduction of the flesh turned to image and identity determined by fetish even as they celebrate it" (1980, 70). What unites new wave and postpunk is that both continue to go back to their own traditions as rock and roll. But such traditions become hollow fragments whose repetition reproduces them as both the same and different. Such apparatuses are constructed upon the postmodern realization that context is determining and, therefore, that reproduction in a new context must produce new effects. In new wave, the result has been a proliferation of revivals, genre exercises, and attempts to revitalize the stylistic conventions of rock and roll. But it is marked by a reflexivity that acknowledges its own superficiality and commodification. As Tom Carson has suggested:

When any hybrid can become an instant form, all categories look suspicious; instead of panicking because the music's in transition, musicians are taking the fact of transition as their starting point and building one disposable monument to ambivalence after another. Of course, it isn't just music this is happening to: it's people's lives. For all the militant anti-emotionalism of the smart DOR [dance-oriented rock, e.g., B-52s] fodder now in vogue, at its heart is a bewilderment that's all the more obvious because even the occasional authentic emotion has to be hedged into a pose. It's bad enough to live by surfaces, but it's worse when you find out the damned things are every bit as slippery, ambiguous and intractable as depths. Everything—manners, art, identity—is up for grabs; you don't have to commit yourself to any of it, and if you do, you still wonder. (1980, 59)

While this statement is also true of postpunk (and perhaps even new music), these latter two apparatuses attempt to explode rock and roll history by deconstructing its limits and conventions. Postpunk explicitly decodes and disrupts the surface of rock and roll, but it also recodes it, unlike new music. The result is a self-conscious peripheralization of the music. Such postmodern music denies anything apart from the concrete reality of everyday life and its own surfaces and recognizes that even pleasure is a struggle and an acquired possibility. Its emphasis on the materiality of surfaces, on fragmentation, and on reflexivity has produced a music that constantly proliferates its investments: a formally minimalist music whose apparent content is an almost random collection of discrete facts. Rather than being cryptic and intellectual, it is explicitly surreal and materialist. Rather than communicating an emotional response to outer phenomena, it describes the phenomena and leaves the interpretation unsaid, because interpretation itself cannot be trusted. The result is a music that is oddly detached and yet furiously energetic and affective. While postpunk and new music deny or distrust emotion, their very attempt to produce an apparatus that does not depend upon such affective codes has powerful affective consequences (e.g., Talking Heads, Joy Division, Glenn Branca, etc.). There are, however, significant differences between these two postmodern musics and their apparatuses: while postpunk is often characterized by a particular inflection of the axis of postmodernity that foregrounds its own sense of despair, futility, anger, and paranoia in the face of reality, new music apparently uses its cathexis of the postmodern axis to obliterate reality in favor of its own surfaces. Second, new music is content to deconstruct rock and roll, isolating and negating its various conventions and clichés and producing itself as confrontational, often inaccessible (especially to the rock and roll audience), and alienating. It includes two major strategies: (1) to appropriate non–rock and roll conventions (e.g., avant-garde classical and jazz practices, electronic and performance music); and (2) to produce intentionally dissonant and arrhythmic sounds (e.g., DNA, Pere Ubu). On the other hand, postpunk reconstructs its place within rock and roll by reintegrating various conventional codes (and recathecting axes of youth and the body), creating a music that is alienated but more consonant and accessible and less confrontational (e.g., Talking Heads, Joy Division, Gang of Four, XTC). We might summarize this by saying that punk responds to postmodernity with anger, postpunk with paranoia and, along with new wave, with a celebration of superficiality, while new music retreats into postmodernity. We can, further, locate these various apparatuses within the different possibilities of relating to the hegemony within a "critical" stance. Although it is an oversimplification, we might say that oi and hardcore punk move between an oppositional and an independent position; new wave functions as an independent (and sometimes an alternative: e.g., Elvis Costello) apparatus; postpunk exists largely as an alternative possibility; and new music positions itself as a radically independent apparatus.

Of course, these descriptions treat these different musical apparatuses as if they were distinct, when in actual practice they have interacted with each other in a variety of ways to produce a range of concrete affective alliances. Further, I want to emphasize that although there is a relation between the musics commonly referred to by these terms and the apparatuses I have described, the relation is by no means necessary. The particular inflections of a musical text will depend precisely on the range of apparatus within which it is located.

I will offer an additional, albeit briefer, example of the possibilities for analysis made available by my descriptions of the dimensions of diversity within rock and roll: the importance of Bruce Springsteen in American rock and roll culture. My argument is, simply, that Springsteen's music has evolved in such a way as to make the two registers of rock and roll's diversity (its negative difference from the hegemony and its positive cathexis of specific axes within the apparatus) parallel. And for a particular audience, this has made his music a powerful affective center of their rock and roll apparatus. Springsteen has had, since the early seventies, a steadily growing audience of fanatical fans. Apparently, that audience was largely middle-class youth in college after the counterculture. In his earliest records (*Greetings from Asbury Park* [1973] and *The Wild, the Innocent, and the E Street Shuffle* [1974]), Springsteen not only locates youth as the dominant site for the investment of pleasure, but details an almost utopian existence around a particular image of youth culture. The music was, then, largely both utopian and oppositional. It is only in the mid-seventies, however, with the release of *Born to Run* and *Darkness on the Edge of Town,* that the power of his position becomes explicitly visible. And concomitantly, I think, the music is located within a different apparatus, perhaps one more widely accessible or more powerfully present. Rather than youth and difference, it is increasingly the axis of the body, sexuality, and movement that is invested in. He no longer paints pictures of utopian cultures, but rather valorizes a sense of movement and energy embodied not only in his images (especially to do with driving) but also in the sound, which, often carried by the saxophone, drives one forward as if in flight. Thus Springsteen's cathexis of the axis of the body is matched by a move into an experiential—and still oppositional—position.

The most interesting moment in Springsteen's career, however, came with the release of *The River.* With this album, his audience expanded rapidly, and he achieved the status of a superstar: his album topped the charts, he had his first hit single, and so on. There was, at the same time, some antagonism between the fractions of his audience. Both the sudden popularity and the relations between his audiences can be understood if one sees that, at that moment, his music functioned within two radically different apparatuses and produced radically different affective alliances. The album can be heard, in fact, in many ways, as transitional. Many critics have observed that the album is quite schizophrenic. On the one hand, it was incorporated into an experiential and independent apparatus. The music was taken, primarily by new and younger fans, as an affirmation of fun and excess, as a form of escape. The music itself provided a space within which they are apparently in temporary control of their lives. On the other hand, for others, the album continued to be located as oppositional, but it appeared increasingly pessimistic and critical. It seemed to celebrate only its own recognition of our common hopelessness.

With the release of *Nebraska,* Springsteen has not only reinforced his position within a critical-oppositional apparatus, he has increasingly foregrounded the axis of postmodernity as the only means of survival. The album was self-produced at home, with comparatively primitive technology. It is a solo, acoustic, almost "folk" album, a self-conscious attempt to remove himself from precisely those rock and roll conventions that gained him his "superstardom." In fact, the production quality and the sound embody a kind of retreat into an almost confessional, novelistic texture (much like his earlier albums). *Nebraska* seems, above all, to problematize *The River*'s place within Springsteen's career and its ambiguity. Images of love and hope, which appeared in *The River* in the contradictory contexts of fun/innocence and sadness/anger, have disappeared. Extremes dominate the iconography: images of criminals and cops, acts of despair and acts of rigid social norms offer us no alternative, no way out, and no end to the journey. A rather uncomfortable religious imagery evokes not salvation but the impossibility of hope, of ever washing the blood from our hands. Whether it be the hero of "Atlantic City," shrugging off the likelihood that he has chosen his own death by intoning "maybe everything that dies someday comes back," or the narrator of the closing song, invoking scenarios that point to the only reality, "At the end of every hard earned day, people find some reason to believe," we are left with the inescapable reality of "Nebraska": "I guess there's just a meanness in this world." No way out except the lonely cry "Hey somebody out there, listen to my last prayer/Hi ho silver-o deliver me from nowhere." And yet, two songs later, the prayer is readdressed; no longer imploring an anonymous other, it is to "Mr. Deejay" and to "rock 'n' roll" that *Nebraska* turns. Thus the album tries to reconcile the contradictory moments of *The River* by alienating itself from the latter's valorization of youth and the body and foregrounding instead its own "postmodern" perception.

Springsteen has, as a result, charted in his music the evolution of the rock and roll apparatus for at least a part of the larger rock and roll audience. He has remained at the center of the apparatus, and at the center of rock and roll itself for his audience, only by mapping the affective history of that audience.

HYPOTHESIS 5. THE HISTORY OF ROCK
AND ROLL: CO-OPTATION

Discussions of "co-optation" usually focus on the techniques by which rock and roll, youth culture, and the more general context of postwar experience have been exploited and transformed by the economic system and the various "ideological state apparatuses," especially the mass media. By the end of the fifties, the youth market was recognized as an enormous source of consumer expenditure, one considered easily manipulatable. Further, the sheer numbers of the baby boom generation made them a potential economic and political threat that had to be incorporated into the dominant culture. Clearly this exploitation and incorporation have often been quite successful through a wide variety of strategies that have remained largely unexamined. According to most histories of rock and roll, this process has been going on since the late fifties, and at each stage rock and roll loses its power and becomes a commodity that can be produced, marketed, and consumed. But it is also apparently true that each time it has happened, rock and roll breaks out of that co-opted stance and reaffirms its affective power, creating new sounds and new political stances. The result is that the history of rock and roll is read as a cycle of co-optaton and renaissance in which rock and roll constantly protests against its own co-optation.

This reading is reinforced by the view that the co-optation of new sounds, styles, and stances seems to take place at an increasingly rapid rate. We seem today to be caught in a situation in which the vast majority of the rock and roll audience is incapable of making the distinction between co-opted and non-co-opted any more:

> Sitting around with friends one night, I remember saying that instead of being the triumph of our lives, rock and roll might be the great tragedy. It had given us a sense of possibility so rich and radical that nothing could ever feel as intense—and then the world went back to business as usual, leaving us stranded . . . As mass-media folk culture, rock and roll was always an anomaly. Since the direction of mass culture is toward more control and less spontaneity, the record industry has worked ceaselessly to suborn rock back into the status quo of entertainment, and succeeded. Nearly every band that still thinks rock and roll was meant to change your life now labors under the contradiction of creating popular culture that isn't popular anymore. Yet they can't give up the dream of making as big a difference as Elvis or the Beatles, because their music doesn't make sense any other way. If such grand ambitions are now meaningless to the mass audience, the attempt is tragic for them; in so far as we give credence to their ambitions, it's tragic for us. (Carson 1981, 49)

Even worse, one must face the argument that this process is inevitable, since co-optation is simultaneous with commercial success.

This rather pessimistic reading of the history of rock and roll assumes that it is a form of mass art. Others argue that rock and roll is either folk art or the product of individual creativity, but these do not escape the cycle of co-optation and the ultimately pessimistic reading of rock and roll's history. In order to challenge such views, we need to recognize that there are two meanings of rock and roll as product (or commodity): music and records. Although good rock and roll is often produced locally, even out of a local community with a set of shared experiences, and is as well often the product of individual talent,[4] its audience is always more inclusive: some subset of youth who have grown up in an increasingly urbanized, electronic-technological society—and the music uses the sounds, rhythms, and textures of that common environment. The notion of community (and hence of "folk art") is problematic when applied to youth culture, for the so-called community of rock and roll cannot be defined geographically. But the notion of community is a spatial one: everyday face-to-face interaction has been assumed to be the dominant determinant of shared experience and the criterion for community. But if temporality has replaced spatiality in defining the rock and roll audience, then the music requires widespread dissemination to be shared among the members of its appropriate audience. The musical product must be reproduced as an object (e.g., a record) precisely if it is to be available to those whom it addresses, to those existing within its boundaries. The music must voluntarily enter into various systems of economic practices and hence accept its existence as apparently mass art.

This suggests a very different understanding of co-optation and a different reading of the history of rock and roll. The problem with both the "folk" and the "mass" art views of co-optation (and this is true of Frith's approach as well) is that they define it in purely economic terms, as if it were simply the result of strategies imposed on rock and roll from without. They assume that rock and roll is co-opted when the demands of the economic systems of production and distribution are allowed to define the production of the music as well as of the object. Thus the attempt is to make rock and roll into a commodity, to make it salable to an audience without any acknowledgment of differences within the youth culture. While such views are partially correct, they ignore a number of characteristics of "co-optation" in rock and roll. First, they ignore the tension within rock and roll—for mass distribution is a real part of its functioning. The appropriate audience for any particular music cannot always be defined ahead of time (consider the new listening alliance made up of "high school kids, housewives and assorted adult-contemporary types" [Considine 1981, 5]). Second, they ignore the fact that the question of co-optation is raised and answered at specific moments within the rock and roll culture.

In fact, the notion of co-optation allows us to see clearly the existence of rock and roll at the intersection of youth culture and the hegemony. Rather than assuming a homogeneity of either external strategies or internal formations, a study of co-optation would have to begin with an analysis of the concrete forms it has taken at various points in the history of rock and roll.[5]

Thus co-optation no longer appears only as an external action perpetrated upon rock and roll—a hegemonic strategy that is at best reflected in the judgments of rock and roll fans. To see it in these terms is to set rock and roll against the capitalist mode of production, distribution, and consumption. But in fact, as Frith argues, rock and roll is always a form of capitalist commodity. To describe certain rock and roll as co-opted is to acknowledge and contribute to its normalization. Co-optation is a decathexis of the boundary, a de-encapsulation of the music and its culture and an incorporation of its affective alliance into the hegemonic organizations of desire. Co-optation indicates an affective realliance of the music rather than an alteration of the aesthetic or ideological constitution of the text. Co-optation is the result of a recontextualization of affect, a restructuring of the affective alliances penetrating and surrounding the music. What may serve in one context as a powerful cathexis of difference may, under a variety of circumstances, lose or be deprived of that affective function.

Co-optation is one form of rock and roll's production of its own history. Rock and roll constantly marks differences within itself just as it marks the difference of its audience. Co-opted rock and roll is music that no longer potently inscribes its difference and the difference of its fans. And this is measured from within the culture of rock and roll. Co-optation is the mode by which rock and roll produces itself anew, rejecting moments of its past and present in order to all the more potently inscribe its own boundary. "Co-optation" is a particular affective charge made from one stance within rock and roll against others; it produces new affective alliances within the corpus and cultures of rock and roll. This entails a very different reading of the history of rock and roll. Rather than a cycle of authentic and co-opted music, rock and roll exists as a fractured unity within which differences of authenticity and co-optation are defined in the construction of affective alliances and networks of affiliation. These alliances are always multiple and contradictory. Thus the "co-optedness" of a particular form of rock and roll is a historically unstable judgment; it may change in response to developments within the changing musical and political possibilities of rock and roll. It certainly changes as one moves between particular fractions of the rock and roll audience.

CONCLUSION. "ROCK AND ROLL IS DEAD AND WE DON'T CARE" (THE RUBINOOS)

The *New York Times Magazine* a few years ago published a cover story claiming that rock and roll is all that remains of the generation gap and is slowly losing its appeal to America's youth (Zion 1981). Ira Robbins, editor of *Trouser Press,* has mourned the death of rock critic Lester Bangs: "There won't be any more like you, but then maybe your era died before you did" (1982, 46). Bangs, perhaps more than any other critic, celebrated the affective politics of rock and roll, and his death occurred at a moment when the very possibility of rock and roll has been called into question. In the same issue of *Trouser Press,* Mick Farren wrote that "Rock music faces its biggest threat . . . We are witnessing the arrival of a generation who neither desire, nor require rock music. The obvious question is what is going to happen to rock?" (1982, 52). The rhetoric of the possible death of rock and roll has become increasingly common, entering the pages of such prestigious rock journals as *New York Rocker* and *New Musical Express;* it has become a common topic of conversation among rock and roll fans as well.

This is not the first time that such rhetoric has appeared. It was common in the early sixties, only to be put aside with the arrival of The Beatles, and in the mid-seventies, again to be put aside with the arrival of punk. Yet there is something unique about the present moment and the challenge it poses to the affective power of rock and roll. It is not merely an economic crisis that reflects the effects of a recession on leisure expenditures. The potential rejection of rock and roll arises simultaneously from two interpenetrating vectors: the arrival of a new generation of youth, traditionally a source of revitalization for rock and roll, and the dilemmas that punk brought to the surface of the rock and roll culture.

I have argued that the affective politics of rock and roll depend upon its particular temporal context. Rock and roll describes "how a life lived in continual motion might ideally sound to someone half in love with and half oppressed by this state of affairs" (Hunter 1981, 71). It appears that the context within which rock and roll works for the new generations of youth is changing: the promise of a booming economy has been replaced by the threat of continuous recession; the dominance of the baby boom's images of youth and change has been replaced by images of the baby boom's attempt to deal with responsibility and "middle age"; rock and roll as a symbol of rebellion has been replaced with its status as nostalgia. Youth today confronts a generation of parents who were themselves weaned on rock and roll; it is no longer a stigma, a point of antagonism. "Nice" kids can make rock and roll and their parents will come to see them, even support their efforts. Further, the centrality of music in the affective life of youth seems to be giving way to new media and new sounds: video-computer technologies. While they continue to listen to rock and roll, it has receded into the background of their emotional lives and leisure.

There are two accounts that can be given of this development. First, rock and roll is no longer able to constitute a powerful affective boundary between its fans and those who remain outside of its culture. While it is still vigorously attacked in some quarters, it has become an accepted and even appreciated feature of the modern world. It is interesting to note the vehemence with which video games, for example, are being attacked and the rhetorical similarities between these attacks and those that greeted rock and roll. The second account is that youth no longer desires a strongly cathected boundary, being satisfied instead with a return to a more temporary and fluid experience of the generation gap. Perhaps history has taught them that one cannot live in celebration of postmodernity; they seek instead to celebrate moments of possible stability. Survival for this new youth seems to demand adaptation to and escape from the hegemony rather than a response to the historical context within which they find themselves.

The question, however, must remain unanswered, for it raises a much more problematic issue: the status of youth in postmodern daily life. That is, the very historical emergence and transformation of youth is part of a larger apparatus of power that takes the body of the population as its object of control. While it is true in one sense that the category of "youth" emerges after the war, it is equally true that rock and roll exists at a particular cusp between the rise of youth and its problematization/disappearance (see Hebdige 1982).

There is also a vector of the contemporary crisis that is internal to rock and roll, a vector that can be traced back to the emergence of punk and which I have discussed above. Rock and roll in the eighties is not merely fragmented; it is constituted by three vectors fighting against each other. First, commercial (MOR) music merely reproduces the surface structures of existing styles despite the fact that they have lost their affective power. Second, new wave rock seeks to reaffirm pleasure as resistance but cannot escape its own desire for commercial and popular success and thus its own complicity with the dominant culture. Third, postpunk and new music seek to articulate a pleasure and cathect a boundary that no longer coincides with the rock and roll culture. While MOR seeks stability behind its surface and new wave seeks the stability of rock and roll, postpunk and new music appear increasingly to reject anything not consistent with their postmodern practice. These three directions in rock and roll have created a situation in which the affective alliances surrounding each, and thus their audiences, have little in common. There is no center around which they can exist as fringes or at which they can intersect. They are on opposing trajectories, moving at increasing velocities, despite commercial attempts at incorporation and the fact that some music remains shared within all three contexts.

The result of these developments both within and outside of the music is that, apparently, rock and roll no longer generally serves the affective functions I have described. For the younger generations, as well as for many of the baby boomers, it has become background music that, even as leisure, can provide no challenge to the dominant organizations of desire. For those who seek to reaffirm its affective power, the boundary has been relocated. The result is that new alliances are being formed, and the cultural and political ramifications of this moment in the history of rock and roll may be as powerful and interesting as those that emerged with the "birth" of rock and roll in the fifties. Whether it is the "death" of rock and roll remains to be seen.

I'd Rather Feel Bad than Not Feel Anything at All":

Rock and Roll, Pleasure and Power

I want to begin with a paradox: Although we are inundated with words about rock and roll, we understand very little about its place in the lives of its fans and its relation to the structures of power in our society. Of course, this is only one instance of a more general lacuna in contemporary critical discourses: the mass media and popular culture. Armand Mattelart has identified some of these pervasive gaps, but he too notes the appalling state of popular music analysis:

> A lack of relations between semiological research and the genuine latent demand for discourse analysis on the part of journalists looking for a redefinition of their practices: a gap which contrasts with the fluid exchange between semiology and the advertising industry.
>
> A lack of any detailed understanding of the modes of re-appropriating media discourse on the part of the various social categories that constitute the "grand public."
>
> A lack of any analysis of the strategies of evasion and deviation directed by multiple social agents against the apparatuses of power.
>
> A lack of any study on the articulation, in a dialectical model of analysis, of the so-called experiments in social intervention (cinema, video, radio) and the functioning of the central apparatuses . . .
>
> [A] lack of any dialectical analysis of exchange, or absence of exchange between university research on cultural production and the field of criticism . . . In many apparently unrelated fields, it is the references and accomplishments of academic research which, one way or another, fix the limits of tolerance for any discourse. Vulgar discourse, or at least one version of it, is no longer acceptable in the analysis of film, while it is still

looked on at the dominant mode of analyzing popular music. *The nota-ble absence of research in this field* (there are only one or two serious French studies of the musical culture industry and even they are in-spired by an anthropological vision of the phenomenon of popular mu-sic) *means that credence is given there to the most idealizing and mys-tificatory discourses to be found in the whole range of media reporting.* (1988, 598; emphasis added)

One of the reasons that so much contemporary writing on mass culture is inadequate to the task may be that it fails to consider what Stuart Hall has called "the sensibility of mass culture," the ways in which various audiences select, appropriate, and make use of a limited set of the available media messages. This seems, almost inevitably, to lead us into questions of taste and pleasure. As Michele Mattelart has argued,

What is disturbing is the exhiliration that these tales [soap operas] con-tinue to give spectators who are critically aware of how alienating they are and who have located the mechanisms through which their nefari-ous work is carried on. We simply cannot ignore the question of taste, of the pleasure . . . produced by these fictional products of the cultural industry. There is a problem here, and one hitherto scarcely tackled. (1982, 141)

There is a problem here, but we should not be too quick to define it. Both "taste" and "pleasure" draw us, perhaps unwillingly, into individualizing and psychologizing discourses. As Bourdieu (1980) has demonstrated, there is a political economy of taste that problematizes its status as a surplus of determination. And, on the other hand, despite current efforts to define a "politics of pleasure," the concept is both too vague (often substituting for desire or affect) and too narrow (often serving as the opposite or absence of pain). "Pleasure" draws us back into a phenomenology of emotions, but often discounts the complex role of ideology in such processes.

The first issue is, then, to locate and define the problem. One site that opens into these questions is the category of the "fan" and the unique relationship that it implies. It is this relationship that I wish to explore in the present essay, within the realm of youth culture and rock and roll. What distinguishes the fan from the consumer? After all, both may enjoy the music, and both may use it as a significant part of "leisure" activities. What is it about this relationship that makes rock and roll so important both to individual fans and within the larger culture of contemporary youth? What is it about this relationship that enables rock and roll fans to invest themselves within it, using it at times not only as leisure but as a form of struggle and resistance? Of course, rock and roll does not always or necessarily function as resistance, no more than it necessarily and always functions as a form of hegemonic incorporation. The question is precisely how to identify the terms of the fans' relationship to the music that enables rock and roll to function in different ways, for different audiences, at different times. This bond—the dialectical product of an active audience and productive (con-)texts—may shed some light on the range of functions and effects, both positive and negative, that rock and roll produces. And it may help us understand the broader question of the "sensibility of mass culture."

DISCOURSES ON ROCK AND ROLL

How is it that all the words that have been written about rock and roll leave these questions unanswered? It may be helpful to identify some of the ways rock and roll is currently framed and read in critical writing, and to point to the inadequacies of these discourses. I propose to isolate four such frameworks. The first two are decidedly unsympathetic; they measure rock and roll according to standards that have little or no place within the rock and roll culture itself. For example, the first discourse attacks rock and roll as merely another commodity consumed by (ignorant) youth. Its only significant functions are (1) to make a profit; (2) to distract youth from real social problems; and (3) to produce youth as capitalist, gendered, and racist subjects. The music manipulates youth, making them even more passive and noncritical than they apparently already are. Rock and roll fans are "cultural dopes" who can't even recognize that what they think of as their own culture is being used to dupe and exploit them. This discourse is more concerned with the interface between rock and roll and the dominant political and economic institutions than that between the music and its culture. The only time the music becomes worthy of cultural analysis is when it transcends the normal patterns of consumption to create a pop culture phenomenon (e.g., Elvis Presley, the Beatles, Michael Jackson). The history of rock and roll is written from the perspective of *Billboard;* the culture is defined by the music that sells (as these are reported in statistically questionable Top 100 charts). Music on the margins, or even "bubbling under," as well as the fans, are entirely ignored.

Also ignored are the contradictions between economic and political institutions within the social formation, the changing and often antagonistic relation between rock and roll and the various hegemonic institutions of power, and the differences within the rock and roll culture (differences of genre, uses, structures of musical and cultural alliances and antagonisms, etc.).

A second framework compares rock and roll to art, usually concluding (not surprisingly) that it has little or no intrinsic value or originality. When used sympathetically, such a view appeals either to the artist's expressive sincerity or artistic abilities. More typically, rock and roll is seen as little more than a rip-off of the music of other peoples (and with their music, rock and roll supposedly steals and dilutes their experience and pain), such as black rhythm and blues, or white southern working-class country and western music. Of course, the illusion of creativity is there, produced by filtering the music through a technology (and system of distribution) to which the white audience has privileged access. On this view, the only rock and roll worth talking about is that which talks to us, as the work of genius—as poetry or art. We are locked into reproducing the practice of canonization, the "great texts" syndrome: Talking Heads but not the Ramones, Bruce Springsteen but not AC/DC, Bob Dylan but not Phil Spector, the Beatles but not Fear. The problems with this framework are obvious: First, rock and roll does not function as art even though its fans may occasionally appeal to such criteria. Second, the popularity and function of particular texts cannot be read off the text itself; the reasons that particular music is important to particular fans vary widely and depend upon a number of other, contextual factors. Finally, while it is true that rock and roll steals from other musical sources, this is not sufficient to account for the particular musical structures that have emerged during its history. Further, the appropriation from other sources has important effects, not only upon the music but also for the ways the audiences use the music. In fact, the history of contemporary popular music demonstrates a complex, intercultural, and international exchange of musical conventions. There is a dialectical relation, one between white and black traditions: one need only listen to the music of Sly Stone, Jimi Hendrix, George Clinton, Prince, James Blood Ulmer, or King Sunny Ade to recognize the complexity of this process.

The remaining discourses build upon the audience's phenomenological relation to the music and present a more sympathetic reading. The third framework emphasizes the fans' use of the music to celebrate their youthfulness and to have fun. Rock and roll becomes entertainment for kids, a kind of condoned irresponsibility of youth, a form of play existing outside of the constraints of future (whether real or imagined) social roles. A more sophisticated variant suggests that rock and roll projects a fantasy about the possibilities of leisure and play. Within this framework, the history of rock and roll is often constructed on the basis of representations of the rock and roll culture that speak for it rather than on the music or the practices of the culture itself. After all, children cannot speak for themselves and practices that seek only enjoyment rarely bother to represent themselves accurately, if at all. Again, the weaknesses are obvious. Such readings of rock and roll cannot easily discuss those moments in which rock and roll explicitly offers a vision of opposition, struggle, or despair: it can describe the Doors but not the Velvet Underground, the Ramones but not the Voidoids, Michael Jackson but not Joy Division. This is not because such a discourse cannot confront the issue of the politics of fun or leisure, but rather because it fails to recognize the contradictions that may exist among the social functions and effects of particular musical texts. And it ignores the different relations that listeners may have to the music; it collapses the fan into a moment of leisure. In particular, it oversimplifies the relationship between rock and roll and youth. This becomes obvious as at least part of the rock and roll audience "grows up," without surrendering its claim to be fans of the music. Further, the category of youth is not only historically constructed but constructed within the apparatus itself.

The fourth discourse focuses on the text as a representation of social reality. It interprets rock and roll as folk music, representing the psychological, economic, and political experiences of particular groups of youth. Consequently the history of rock and roll is a cycle of "authentic" and "co-opted" moments. At authentic moments, rock and roll is not only produced and controlled by youth (i.e., by what it signifies: youth's real experience of the world), it may even present itself as a form of political opposition. But when the demands of capitalist production take over, the meaning of the music is "watered down," the sound is "professionalized," and the same thing is produced over and over again. Rock and roll is then unable to offer any resistance to the structures of hegemonic power. Capitalism reduces rock and roll to the lowest common denominator, that which will sell to the largest audience. The music itself becomes part of the hegemonic culture, incapable of resistance and condemned to reinforce stereotypical visions of reality and of the audience's place within it. On such a view, only the authentic moments are worth talking about, and these are all that distinguish this discourse from the first one described above: the golden age, the counterculture, punk. Other moments—teen idols, bubblegum, singer-songwriter, disco, heavy metal, white soul—are dismissed and relegated to the status of either commodity or bad art.

The variations within this discourse often depend upon which moment in the history of rock and roll is valorized and privileged, allowed to define the essential authenticity of rock and roll. The first variant sees the oppositional force of rock and roll rooted in class and race conflict; it privileges the working-class audience supposedly constituted in the "golden age," with an explicitly populist politics. A second variant privileges those moments that celebrate the idealism of youth and its explicit projection of political alternatives (e.g., the counterculture). And a third variant emphasizes the music's ability to present, on its surface, as it were, a protest against the alienation, fragmentation, and meaninglessness of contemporary life (e.g., the politics of punk and new wave).

The weaknesses of this discourse are less obvious than previous ones, partly because this framework is common among fans. Nevertheless, there are a number of problems. First, it reproduces an elitism that exists within the rock and roll culture (every rock and roll fan believes that he or she knows what rock and roll really is). It fails to locate the question of the effects of specific musics within the context of the fan's life. Thus it cannot account for how the same music may be politically oppositional for one audience but not for another. Second, it fails to acknowledge that, even at its best moments, rock and roll, in its practice and ideology, is often sexist and racist and certainly not anticapitalist. Rock and roll is, in ways that need to be described, part of the hegemony. Perhaps this is due to the already ideological nature of the experience that is represented. Still, it may be more important to recognize that the political function of the music cannot be totally explained by the representational content of the music itself. Finally, this framework oversimplifies the relationship between commercial success and popular music—as a contradiction and a site of struggle. Economic co-optation and political co-optation are not identical, nor can one be deduced from the other (e.g., the popularity and continued transgressive power of breakdancing and the larger "hip-hop" culture, despite their commercial appropriation and success).

ROCK AND ROLL AS RESISTANCE

There is yet one more framework that must be considered here. It differs from the others in two significant ways: First, its origins are academic, although it has found some journalistic homes. Second, it is not homogeneous but fractured, defined by the space between two competing discourses: subculture theory and postmodern (or deconstructive) theory. It approaches the question of the politics of leisure by investigating how the forms responsible for the production of pleasure can be and are used to articulate resistance. Rock and roll is seen neither as an expression of an inner life nor a representation of an outside world, but rather as an active moment that can be appropriated by youth as forms of resistance to, transgression of, or at least coping with, the contradictory demands of the hegemonic culture. Thus, like the third view above, it is concerned with how fans use the music and what they gain from it. And like the fourth view, it is concerned with the music's relationship— now viewed as an active one—to the context of its fans' lives. Of crucial importance, however, and unlike all of the frameworks discussed above, resistance theory starts with the recognition that the meaning of the music cannot be read off the text, divorced from its context and its use. To give just two examples of this context-specific appropriation, consider what happens when Ibis, an all-female band, playing at a women's music festival, covers Pat Benatar's heavy metal hit, "Love Is a Battlefield." And in the film *More American Graffiti,* the Supremes' "Baby Love" becomes a statement of both community and resistance. The differences within resistance theory result from competing views of the source of the resistance itself. While subculture theory emphasizes the activity of the fans in reappropriating the music, postmodern theory stresses the activity of the texts themselves.

Subculture theory (Hall and Jefferson 1976) dissolves rock and roll into subpopulations of youth—usually white, male, urban, working class. It argues that such groups appropriate particular musical genres into a larger "subcultural style" which provides them with "magical" or "imaginary" solutions to the contradictions they experience, contradictions determined by their social position. This style provides "forbidden identities" with which the members of the subculture can represent their difference from both the hegemonic culture and the culture of their parents, even as they continue to live within both. There are, however, a number of problems with this approach. First, as Angela McRobbie (1980) has argued, it structurally excludes women from the rock and roll audience. I would extend this to argue that it systematically limits the definition of "fan," confusing it with subcultural membership, and thus excludes the majority of rock and roll fans, especially in the United States. Second, although it assumes that the subculture is somehow able to "fit" the music into its "style," these two notions remain vague. Consequently, it is unclear what role the music plays in enabling this correspondence, and how the fans read the relationship (or homology) between the style and their experience (Coward 1977).

More recently, Stuart Hall (1983) has proposed a broader theory of "ideological articulation" in which the meaning of a text is the product of an active cultural struggle to "articulate" the text into a network of relations with other texts and social practices. By positioning a text, its meaning and its specific claim to represent reality are constituted within a web of connotations. Thus the relations between texts and experience, and the possibilities for using a text within a structure of resistance, are neither pregiven (as if inscribed within the origins of the text) nor impossible. They are the ongoing product of people's appropriation of them in their attempts to represent their own experiences, to speak in their own voices rather than in the hegemonic codes. We can project the implications of this revision for the understanding of popular music. There is no reason that this theory need be limited to subcultures, for it suggests that rock and roll is used by its fans to construct identities that provide alternative representations of their real social experiences. There is nothing magical about such solutions—they are the very real matrix of culture and ideology. Further, one need no longer assume the existence of a preconstituted style embodying a series of homologies between different levels of texts and experiences. Instead, style is the active field in which such correspondences are themselves constructed by fans in the act of appropriating musical texts. The "fit" need not be measured by some correspondence to experience; rather it is the very nature of the struggle over and within representation itself. Still, there is little room in this theory for describing the limits on, or possibilities of, such struggles: How is it that texts are already received with possibilities, if not meanings, inscribed upon their surfaces? If one wants to avoid appealing to encoded meanings (after all, in the field of popular music, whose meanings are encoded?) and origins, where is one to locate the productivity of the music itself? While Hall emphasizes the active struggles of populations within culture, the cultural field itself remains the passive product of the fans' manipulations.

On the other side of "resistance theory," postmodern theory argues that texts, including musical ones, do not produce meanings and so cannot be understood in terms of their claims to represent experience or reality. It rejects interpretation as an act that seeks out and expands upon the meaning of the text, even a contextually constituted one. Postmodern theory makes meaning irrelevant and communication impossible. The text is not a system of signifiers, each of which is struggling to find a place within a structure of signification, waiting to be articulated into a network of connotation and representation. Rather the text is understood as a collection of fragments, signifiers constantly sliding across and under one another, transgressing the boundaries of any claim to unity, stability, and coherence. The text can only be read as deconstructing its own appearance, decomposing itself and undermining its own self-privileging moments. It is the gaps that fracture and undermine the text and its meaningfulness that provide the sites of its productivity. Thus postmodern theory returns to a kind of formalism that makes the text itself—not as a definable entity but as an ongoing process of self-appropriation—rather than the audience the source of active resistance.

One can identify two variants within postmodern readings of rock and roll. The first offers itself as an alternative to marxist theories of ideology as representation, locating the ideological power of the text in the way in which it positions the audience within its own spaces. The text does not produce social identities as representations of experiences; rather, the text produces those experiences by inserting or interpellating the audience into particular positions from which their perspective on reality is already constituted. Thus, for example, Graham (1983) argues that while traditionally rock and roll produces its fans in predefined hegemonic, gendered subject-positions, certain "postpunk" rock and roll texts fragment and disrupt such identifications, producing subjects necessarily resisting such hegemonic relations of power.

The second variant of postmodern theory replaces ideological interrogation with a concern for the politics of pleasure. Again, it is the text itself that produces the pleasure audiences find within its spaces. Not only is the pleasure inscribed within the gaps of the text as deconstruction, but the transgressive nature of the pleasure—its resistance to hegemonic structures—is also written into the process by which the text interpellates its audiences into its spaces. In what is almost a mirror image of Hall, then, postmodern theory locates resistance in the pleasure of the text, and that pleasure within the text's own resistance to hegemonic demands that it speak, that is, that it communicate or represent. Of course such a reading is likely to make the effects of music merely a mechanistic response, both between the music and the audience and between the music and its context. This paradox—that postmodern theory often leads one back into theories of reflection and simple determination—can be seen in *New Musical Express*'s appropriation of its discourse. For example, Penman writes that "We need all the hypnotic, insouciant, insensible dance music we can get, to insure that we are never tempted to join the ranks of virtuous monsters and scarecrows everywhere . . . everywhere spewing dogma and cataclysm" (1982), as if the pleasure were sufficient to guarantee the politics. Similarly, Morley celebrates "those objects of desire that can introduce into people's lives not only colour and glamour but also a stimulation . . . The boredom is like a sensation of emptiness that we've all got to fill" (cited in Harley and Botsman 1982, 259). Again, the music bears an almost mechanical relationship to the world, even in its active resistance.

In one of the most interesting postmodern readings of popular music, Pfeil argues that "the experience of this newly constituted mass audience for postmodernist work is most fundamentally this very unstable play between a primal delight and a primal fear—or, if you will, between two simultaneous versions of the primary aggressive impulse, that which seeks to incorporate the world into itself, and that which struggles to prevent its own engulfment" (1985, 386). Postmodern aesthetic practice reflects the "recent transformation of advanced capitalist society" in which bureaucratization, advertising and changing structures of family life have contributed to the "de-oedipalization" of the audience. It is, ultimately, this de-oedipalization that is reflected in the aesthetic experience itself. But does this homology not guarantee the political consequences of the pleasure of this experience? Can it remain neither necessarily liberatory nor repressive: "Is it possible that these audiences seek and take pleasure in the 'de-origination of the utterance,' presumably in order to either liberate ourselves from the spell of its codes, or to realize ourselves as the shifting, uneven product of their proliferation? To ask the question is, I think, to answer it" (Pfeil 1988, 387). The preoedipal space necessarily opened up by the postmodern texts—both a reflection of the structures of late capitalism and the transformation of these structures into the audience's pleasure—is politically ambivalent, depending upon the way in which it is recoded within ideology. Thus postmodern theory finds pleasure produced in the gaps opened up by and within the text itself, a deconstruction that mirrors the fragmentation of contemporary life. At its best, it interrogates the political effects inscribed upon that pleasure, the ways in which pleasure itself may be articulated as a form of resistance.

The problematic of resistance theory can be located in the contradiction between postmodern theory (with a productive textuality at the level of a politics of pleasure) and marxist cultural theory (with an active audience struggling to articulate the ideological claim to representation of particular texts). And it is in this space that I wish to locate my own reading of rock and roll. With the latter, I will assume that people are not cultural dopes. They are often quite aware of their own implication in structures of power and domination, and of the ways in which cultural messages manipulate them. And with the former, I will assume that the reading of rock and roll must be discursive rather than symbolic, describing the different relations between audience fractions and musical texts. Neither mass culture nor the mass audience (nor rock and roll and its audience) are homogeneous. This entails more than recognizing the variety of musics and audiences included within the culture. For if there is no necessary correspondence between a text and its meaning, or even between a text and its effects, it is the relationship itself that must become the starting point for analysis.

At the same time, I want to argue against both the formalism of postmodern theory, which renders the audience inactive in the face of a hyper-(active) textuality, and the culturalist's inability to theorize the determining role of the text, operating at a level other than that of messages and their interpretations. I will begin by proposing a number of modifications of both positions to avoid the weaknesses already described, as well as to the postmodernist's trap of describing both cultural practices and social reality in the same terms. This trap places both domains under a common sign and condemns resistance theory to a reflection model, social pessimism, and political terrorism. I will argue for both an active textuality and an active audience, describing a theory of articulation that owes as much to Foucault as to Hall, and that attempts to incorporate the insights of postmodern theory into what Hall has described as a "marxism without guarantees."

ROCK AND ROLL AS DISCOURSE: THE AFFECTIVE ECONOMY OF AN APPARATUS

First, rock and roll texts do play a significant role in determining their effects, but their "textuality" is not merely musical/linguistic nor deconstructive. The effects of rock and roll depend upon the fact that particular musical and verbal practices (often taken from other traditions) are always received as already having been inserted into (1) a range of apparatuses and (2) a particular social and historical site. An apparatus brings together musical texts and practices; economic relations; images (of performers and fans); social relations; aesthetic conventions; styles of language, movement, appearance, and dance; media practices; ideological commitments; and sometimes media representations of the apparatus itself. It is not merely a set of codes or resources that a particular audience brings to the text, as if the audience could be described through sociological sampling procedures. Rather the audience is defined by its place within the apparatus. Further, there is never one rock and roll apparatus. It is the complex array of overlapping, and sometimes antagonistic, apparatuses that constitutes rock and roll and defines the limits of its effects. The same musical text will often be located in different apparatuses, each of which articulates it differently. It will then, for all practical purposes, function as a different song, with different possible effects and meanings, for the different groups of fans. Consequently the issue of "encoding," of how particular texts are already weighted in ways that limit the audience's ability to appropriate them, is a question of the interpellation of both music and fans within various rock and roll apparatuses.

But even recognizing that the texts of rock and roll are constituted by the discourse of the rock and roll apparatuses is not sufficient, for the effects of an apparatus—the relations into which it is articulated—are always characterized by gaps and contradictions, by noncorrespondences as well as correspondences. The actual effects of particular rock and roll texts depend upon the fact that the discourse of its apparatuses functions at different levels of social life and power.[1] Not only is it involved in the distribution of capital and the constitution of economic relations (e.g., leisure, the star system), it is also implicated in an economy of ideological struggles. But the enormous general popularity of rock and roll and its specific power for its fans seem to point to something other than its imbrication in either of these domains. Postmodern theory describes this other level in terms of the production of pleasure, compelling itself to take the position that pleasure is transgressive or resistant. I propose, alternatively, to describe the site of the relationship of the fan and the source of the "sensibility of mass culture" as a level of affective existence.[2] The distinction between affect and pleasure is an important one. The affective economy of rock and roll is neither identical to nor limited to the production of pleasure. The same affective economy can produce multiple, different pleasures. Furthermore, pleasure itself is a phenomenological category already implicated within the space of ideology, if not hegemony, even as its supplement. Instead I will argue that the rock and roll apparatus functions, in part, by transforming the affective geography of the everyday lives of its fans. This transformation, which both builds upon and produces particular forms of pleasure, empowers the fans within the apparatus itself.

We might say that the rock and roll apparatus inserts, into the cracks and contradictions of its own hegemonic existence, sites of affective empowerment that can provide strategies of resistance, evasion, and even countercontrol. For example, the disposability of the commodity also places it at the disposal of the consumer. I know a woman who has simply erased from her records (literally scratched beyond recognition) those songs she finds objectionable. Similarly, many fans are creating their own texts, using tapes to select and even remix the songs that work for them. A more controversial example demonstrates the way in which the affective economy of rock and roll exists within the larger economy of its discourse. Affective empowerment is always engaged by ideological, economic, and political practices, often in contradictory ways. And although I am not immediately concerned with the ideological economy of rock and roll, it is important to acknowledge that affective empowerment is always articulated with—sometimes through and sometimes into—ideology. Rock and roll is often condemned for reproducing hegemonic definitions of gender and sexuality in both its ideology and the gendered patterns of its consumption. Yet particular apparatuses may also provide opportunities for resisting hegemonic constraints on desire and the construction of gender. They may restructure the body as the site of pleasure and power in the ways in which they make a space for and insert the female body and voice into its physical and social environment. Consider the case of rockabilly, which is often interpreted as (and was certainly marketed as) a male-produced and male-consumed genre. But women bought it, sang along with it, danced to it, and participated in its styles. Unless one is prepared to judge all such fans to be cultural dopes, one must account for their ability to use this apparatus. Further women even sang rockabilly, although these recordings were rarely released. But to hear Georgia Gibbs sing "Great Balls of Fire," even today, is to hear that song (not to mention that line) in a new way. Does it take on new meanings? Certainly, but only because something else—its affective investment—has been changed by the insertion of the female voice into that particular apparatus. This affective investment, while asignifying, is not a pristine origin (as the concept of libido might suggest) that precedes the ideological entanglements of the articulation of gender dif-

ferences. It is a plane of effects, a circuit of empowerment. Thus the ideological inflection of the affective economy of rock and roll as male testifies to an
important and powerful appropriation. But on the other hand, if the "pleasure" of rock and roll is already coded as male, there is the possibility of a
doubled pleasure in its reappropriation as female.[3]

The fact that we are dealing here with a musical apparatus makes it clearer
that this affective economy exists at a level of materiality that need not be
consciously experienced nor represented as such. Music's sensuous materiality transforms passive reception into active production. Music surrounds
and invades the body of its listeners, incorporating them into its spaces and
making them a part of the musical event itself. The listener becomes a producer in real and complex ways. Many of the musical practices of rock and
roll clearly function to guarantee if not exaggerate this effect. This transformative power is at the root of Guattari's observation that "the abstract machines of music [are] perhaps the most non-signifying and de-territorializing
of all" (1984, 107). This transformation is not merely the product of creative
consumption, nor of a new relation to objects that have no use value (Baudrillard 1983b). In fact most writing about rock and roll has failed to define
the production of the apparatus, which includes not only the production of
recorded music but also of concerts, of music that is never recorded (the
existence of live local bands is absolutely necessary), of art and dance, of
writing and fashion styles, and so on. Thus while Guattari argues that the
"collectivity of musical production is so organized as to hamper and delay
the force of de-territorialization inherent in music as such," I would argue
that the collective production of the rock and roll apparatus enhances and
prolongs the possibilities for investing in an affective economy that empowers its fans and opens new spaces for resistance and struggle.

Of course, that affective economy is not inherently oppositional or disruptive. Affective empowerment does not guarantee struggle, or even survival.
But it does provide the "energy" that is necessary for them. If, as Benjamin
suggested, the ideology of the commodity produces the "ever the same again,"
and what we might today call the hegemony of pessimism, the affective economy of rock and roll provides its fans with the possibility of organizing and
transforming that pessimism, of transcending the same by reproducing difference. It provides them with a new affective space and thus enables them to
articulate strategies for resisting, or at least surviving in the face of, the hegemony of pessimism. It is the affective position of the fan that the apparatus

empowers, providing the possibility of struggle, but only the possibility. At this level culture offers the resources that may or may not be mobilized into forms of hegemonic or oppositional popular movements. The organization of struggles around particular discourses depends upon their articulation within an affective economy, that is, upon the different investments by which they are empowered and within which people are empowered. While there is no guarantee that even the most highly charged moments will become active sites of resistance, without the affective economy of popular culture such struggles are likely to drown in the sea of ideological pessimism.

EMPOWERMENT: THE AFFECTIVE
PRACTICE OF THE APPARATUS

Empowerment, then, refers to a process of enablement or enervation. A description of the affective economy of rock and roll must go beyond the ways in which pleasure is both produced for and taken for granted by its fans. It must describe how that economy empowers its fans and how the fans are able to use that economy (and not merely the various pleasures of the apparatus) to make possible various affective relationships to the organization of their everyday lives, relationships of compromise and survival, or resistance, or opposition. How is the rock and roll apparatus able to empower its fans? One must be careful not to reduce this to the musical characteristics themselves, as if the volume, rhythms, grain of voice were sufficient in themselves. For the issue is precisely why the rock and roll apparatus articulates only some musical texts into a specific affective economy for a particular audience. I will describe the work of the rock and roll apparatus, its discursive conditions of possibility, as the practices of encapsulation, excorporation, and transference/reversal.

Despite the diversity of rock and roll styles, cultures, and apparatuses, these practices are always visible, on its surfaces. The first—encapsulation—is the most obvious, for rock and roll always constructs an identity and a history for itself from within the different apparatuses. That is, despite its synchronic and diachronic differences, differences embodied in musical, stylistic, and political parameters, the category itself is constantly reiterated, recreated, albeit never from scratch. In its self-nominations, as well as in its choice of historical precedents and covers, particular apparatuses always limit what is allowed into the culture. Further this circumscription of musical boundaries is also embodied in the structure of fans' judgments: there is not only bad rock and roll, there is always other music that is not rock and roll, that must be excluded from the category. Different fans are likely to disagree over where the line is to be drawn, and it is rarely an issue entirely defined by musical or economic criteria, although such appeals are common. Whether particular texts are located on one or the other side of the boundary is a matter of its affective power, that is, of whether it is locatable within the affective economy of the fan's apparatus. As a result, rock and roll is neither entirely outside of the dominant culture nor is it entirely incorporated. Rock and roll fans assume that it is perceived by those outside of the apparatus as alien and inaccessible; outsiders, including those within a radically different rock and roll apparatus, are assumed to be unable to "hear" the music, to feel its power and pleasure, to participate in its empowerment.

Thus the rock and roll apparatus inflects the music in such a way as to encapsulate it, and as a result it encapsulates its fans within its own spaces. It gives the fan a privileged possession of the music and a privileged access to its empowerment. The result is that the fans are interpellated into the apparatus, not necessarily through the production of a positive (visible, readable, or even representable) identity but as different from those on the other side of the boundary. In the rock and roll apparatus, you are not what you don't listen to (which is not necessarily the same as being what you do listen to). It is this boundary of encapsulation—always pluralized by the multiplicity of rock and roll apparatuses—that defines the space of an affective economy. But how and where is this economy produced? And what are its effects?

The second practice of the apparatus—excorporation—locates and produces this boundary. Rock and roll works by endlessly stealing from outside its already constituted boundaries. It relocates these cultural signs (texts, events, practices) within its own spaces and gives them new ideological and affective inflections. Not only does this undermine their ability to claim their own normality, as if they had stable meanings and functions, it makes this sliding across cultural formations have a particular shock effect, which in turn reinscribes the difference as a boundary. That shock effect depends upon making the normal into the other by reducing cultural signs to their material sensuousness. The rock and roll apparatus makes itself into another by reproducing the same as different. That is, it appropriates the signs of the excluded and marginal for the normal (e.g., the signs of black culture for white youth), and it expropriates the signs of the normal (mainstream hegemonic culture) for the already "other" (e.g., new wave's appropriation of Tin Pan

Alley styles, or the mods' use of "Italian modern" to dress up beyond their parents' expectations). The rock and roll apparatus deconstructs the opposition of normality and otherness by excorporating the signs of either into its own ambiguous spaces. Neither normal nor other, it guarantees its own difference and the boundary that encapsulates it.

It is, in a sense, on this boundary, on the surface of its difference, that the apparatus constructs its affective economy. Its style and attitude are a celebration of the artificiality of the same and the different. They valorize the "fake" and the ultimately unstable and temporary nature of their own difference. These strategies, in fact, define the site of rock and roll's affective economy, its geography of energy, pleasure, and power. For example, what made Elvis such a powerful figure was not that he realized the American Dream, but rather that he subtly reversed that dream, in front of everyone, on the surface of his life. Elvis was not the self-made man. The self-made man is boring, if nothing else. Elvis was the self-made king (Marcus 1981c; Marsh 1982). The surface, the place at which one lives out one's everyday life, defines a politics of style that is not merely a celebration of desire or pleasure as resistance. It is the ability to be empowered by the celebration of temporary pleasures. Style celebrates the pleasure and power of the temporary as empowering. In the pleasure of the artificial, rock and roll empowers artificial pleasure (e.g., as in love songs without an object).

The boundary of the rock and roll apparatus thus represents the site of an affective polarization. The reversal accomplished by excorporation transforms the affective investment of events and signs. Rock and roll apparently transforms the negative, the oppressive, the unpleasurable into the positive side of difference and pleasure, the site of empowerment. This is not to say that rock and roll transmutes unpleasure into pleasure. This would not only reduce affect to pleasure and pain, but it would also make rock and roll cathartic, a magical process by which unpleasant is defused. Rock and roll does not turn anger, boredom despair, and so on into pleasure. Rather it turns the material basis of such experiences (repetition, noise, anonymity, etc.) into the occasion for pleasure. It is this reversal that is the source of the empowerment, that enables one to find power in, for example, one's anonymity, or pleasure in the repetitiveness constitutive of rock and roll. This process echoes Freud's repetition compulsion: "the traumatic event is repeated not in spite of the unpleasure that is attached to it, but on account of this very unpleasure" (Safouan 1983, 74).

What appears as a reversal on the surface of the rock and roll apparatus (that rock and roll reverses the affective charge of the excorporated event) is, consequently, only the expression of the apparatus's functioning as a transference mechanism. The economy of the apparatus is constituted by the circuit it produces between the two poles of its own internal contradiction. For the apparatus to create its own "otherness," it must incorporate as well that against which its difference is defined. But by reproducing within itself the very structures of the everyday lives of its fans, it locates them within a different affective economy. Thus there is a relationship not only between the apparatus and the hegemonic reality within which it exists and to which it responds, but also within the apparatus. But in the latter relation, the apparatus is able to use the energy and pleasure of its own self-production (including the music, dance, sexuality, style, and the sense of difference) to reinvest the social lives of its fans as it is inscribed within its own spaces. It makes them into possible sites of pleasure. The productivity of the apparatus, located in this transference, enables the fan to find energy in the interstices of hegemonic lines of pleasure and unpleasure. The fan, interpellated into the very site of this transference, is empowered by the deconstruction of the dichotomy between reality and fantasy, power and pleasure. The fan finds pleasure within the very structures that, in a different economy, are oppressive. And thus the productivity of the apparatus not only provides pleasure in the response to particular forms of powerlessness and unpleasure. The very process of transference generates new energy and new forms of control with which fans can seek out strategies for living through and responding to the real problems and contradictions of their everyday lives (e.g., contradictions between economic, political, and ideological dreams and realities, between leisure and discipline, between freedom and responsibility, between power and powerlessness).

EMPOWERMENT: THE AFFECTIVE
SITE OF THE APPARATUS

I have said that the effects of rock and roll depend not only upon the functioning of the apparatus but also upon rock and roll's emergence from and insertion into a particular social and historical site. It is to this context that the rock and roll apparatus responds. But we cannot define that response as if the context existed outside of the apparatus. Rather the way in which the apparatus responds to its context must be understood through its transference mechanism. The apparatus incorporates its historical context and thus produces particular sites at which it empowers its fans. These sites are not merely reflections of reality, nor are they merely the transformation of points of oppression into the occasion for pleasure. Rather they are the spaces within which the rock and roll apparatus opens up the possibility for affective empowerment. I will briefly describe three interconnected axes that define the context of and within the rock and roll apparatus: style, youth, and the body. These are the conditions of possibility of the geography of rock and roll, the sites of its empowerment. They define the space within which its economy is active.

Style already defines a response to the historical conditions within which rock and roll emerged, the context into which youth and the body are inserted. For those who have grown up in the United States after the Second World War, existence has qualitatively changed as a result of many different events. For example, the new communications media redistributed social knowledge and gave youth access to their own media as well as their own education. The move to suburbia reorganized social space around principles of repetition and marginalization. The baby boom redefined social status and generational expectations. New forms of warfare (both cold and atomic) introduced new kinds of fear and insecurity into everyday life. New structures of technological, economic, and social practices contributed not only to a growing sense of alienation but also to a radical reorganization of daily life.

I have already described the effects of this material context as the hegemony of pessimism. We can dismantle this structure into changing structures of temporality and knowledge. We have been thrown into a maelstrom of constant change, apparently under no one's control and without direction. Both the past and the future have collapsed into the present, and our lives are organized without any appeal to the place of the present within a historical continuum. We have no sense of our indebtedness to the past nor of our obligation to the future. As a TV movie recently put it, "The future is a hoax created by high school counselors and insurance salesmen." Further the democratization of knowledge and the proliferation of mass communications have contributed to the emergence of new forms of uncertainty, relativism, and narcissism. The structures of meaning, purpose, and order that have been taken for granted have apparently collapsed. We no longer assume that there is a transcendent meaning that organizes our lives into coherent totalities and provides a justification and rationalization for our existence. As one student explained, "Even if there were a meaning to life, I probably wouldn't agree with it." This lack of meaning reduces the sign, the commodity, and identity to the same status—fragments whose only import is their existence on the surface of everyday life. As a popular T-shirt says, "Life is hard and then you die." Given this rapid rate of change, the increasing knowledge of risk and danger, the sense that the rules for survival no longer guarantee a good life, the commodification of all value, life is increasingly lived in a state of "controlled panic."

Of course, it is "epochocentric" to think that this is the first moment in which life appears fragmented and incoherent. Perhaps the *Annales* historians are right and it has always been this way. What has changed to produce the contemporary hegemony of pessimism? The answer lies in the changing practice of mediation and in the changing relationship between the material surface of reality and its unseen depth. For as that relationship itself is called into question, as it itself becomes the locus of techniques of power and control, then everything must be put on display. Where is one to find identities, or the sense that they are worth struggling over? If, as Benn says, "What is being policed is not the fact of [people's] existence, but the rules of their existence . . . it is imperative that they be controlled and managed, by slowing down and speeding up the tempo of paranoia—the self-policing method" (n.d., n.p.). What is displayed and controlled is not the totality of a lived reality or identity, nor even the fragments of such totalities but, as Baudrillard says, "the obscenity of the all-too-visible, of the more-visible-than-the-visible" (1983b, 131). How is one to struggle against a hegemony that only allows people to "project themselves into their objects, with their affects and their representations, their fantasies of possession, loss, mourning, jealousy" (127)? Since every object is a commodity and "ever the same" within late capitalism, the possibility for an empowering identity, for discovering something beneath or within the self-object relation, is constantly undermined even as it is declared necessary by the objects themselves. How is one to struggle against the hegemony of pessimism?

Style points to the transference of this economy of paranoia into the rock and roll apparatus and its transformation into both a strategy for reversing hegemonic surveillance (Hebdige 1982) and the site on which one celebrates the pleasure and the empowering possibilities of mobile, flexible, temporary identities. By fetishizing its own surfaces, and even the part and the movement of the surface, style undermines the relationship between the surface (the body as a screen onto which identities are projected) and identity. It challenges the look, both internal and external, which seeks to see beyond the images to the identity that is the real object of hegemonic control. But by embracing the absence of mediation, style gives density to the image. It creates its own "hyperreality" which is capable both of protecting identity and, at the same time, of denying it. It is into the space of this hyperreality that the body is inserted within the rock and roll apparatus.

Style does not refer to some other reality, hidden beneath or behind it. Style constantly displaces itself onto an other, but that other is merely another style, an attitude. Style makes the surface of life into the site of temporary investments and manipulations, without ever suggesting that there is a necessarily privileged agency behind them. It transforms the hegemony of pessimism—which is constantly and paranoically asserting that there is nothing below the surface—into a statement of protective transitions, an attitude of studied indifference, a celebration of fragmented narcissism. In the density of its ever-changing surfaces, youth find a space in which to empower their own transitional existence.

The close relationship between rock and roll and youth is obvious. But the place of youth in its discursive economy is less obvious. "Youth" is a semantically rich category, historically determined, full of contradictions and tangents. It is, before all else, a time of transition between childhood and adulthood, and it carries with it the changing reverberations of each of these categories as well; for example, childhood connotes on the one hand innocence and the need for protection and guidance and on the other hand a self-centered lack of ethical principles, which must be overcome. Youth is a time in which the resources of childhood are used to prepare for the responsibilities and constraints of adulthood, to acquire the necessary skills to fill adult roles. It is a time when one can take chances and risk oneself, a time to play with possibilities, and a time of fun. It is also the programmed moment of the transition from the "other" to the normal. For these very reasons, it is ambiguously valued by society: it is both envied and feared, both society's greatest hope and its greatest problem (e.g., delinquency) (Hebdige 1982).

Youth is also a material part of the body of the population; not merely a concept or a collection of individuals, it has its own density and integrity. It is constantly being worked upon and reshaped by various forces and influences, redistributed in time and space. Youth is a saturation point of hegemonic techniques of normalization, disciplinization, and the institutionalization of difference. It is located at the intersection of a number of institutions, including the family, school, leisure, medicine, psychology, and criminal justice. Thus, for example, in the fifties youth became an isolatable consumer market, with its own capital, its own desires, and its own commodities. But this was only one way in which the very existence of youth changed at the moment it entered into the rock and roll apparatus. My claim is that this relationship transformed a transitional culture into a culture of transitions. It created an impossible demand: that rock and roll deconstruct the very conditions of its possibility. Thus, modifying Rose's description of "children's literature," we might say that rock and roll "stands in our culture as a monument to the impossibility of its own claims—that it represents [youth], speaks to and for [youth], addresses them as a group which is knowable and exists for the [music], much as the [music] . . . exists for them" (1984, 1).

The construction of youth in rock and roll is a contradiction. It exists at the cusp of its isolation and self-identification on the one hand, and of its dispersion and self-negation on the other. Consider the opposition between the two most powerful sites of youth's production and productivity: the family and the peer group. It is interesting to note that the media, especially television, rarely portray both of these sites together. Rock and roll places its fans outside of the family, not only ideologically but physically and affectively as well. While Frith and McRobbie (1990) see this attack on the family—rock and roll's antidomesticity—as another example of its misogyny, a more accurate reading would see it as an attack on the institution itself, as a resistance to the very disciplinization that constructs its youth.

On the other hand, the places within which rock and roll locates itself and its peer culture—on the street, around the jukebox, at the hop—are the spaces between the various institutions within which youth is constructed and against which it rebels. The street is between the family and the school, between the private and the public. What is, in one economy, no place at all, merely a transition between places, becomes the privileged site of youth in the economy of rock and roll. The absolute distinctions between the privacy of one's room (into which one might escape to be surrounded by the music), the public surveillance of the school, and the "isolated anonymity" of the street are collapsed, conflating control and indifference. And as Brooks (n.d., n.p.) argues, it is in this new ambiguous space (e.g., the streets) that youths can enact their ever-changing identities, both reproducing and transgressing the constraints (including sexual and gendered) of hegemonic and consumer cultures.

How then do we describe the economy of youth within rock and roll? It is not merely, as Hebdige would have it, a politics of the sign and pleasure, nor of the conflation of fun and trouble. What these point to is the very real identification of youth with the rejection of the boredom of, the surveillance and control by, the straight world as their own imagined future. But even more importantly, youth displaces the question of identity and self-identity into the production of difference through a fragmented and narcissistic seduction. Instead of being different in the sense of having an identity, one has a difference through the possession of the music and of a style. Thus anonymity is transformed into difference. This transference evacuates the self-reflexive position of hegemonic subjects and empowers youth as the site of pleasure. Rock and roll youth is about the control one gains by taking the risk of losing control, the identity one has by refusing identities. It is about edges, flaws, changes, and incompleteness. Rather than seeking perfection, it celebrates the imperfections. Rather than seeking stability, it celebrates the instability. It reifies its own transitional status, locating itself as a permanent "between." It constitutes itself as a space of "magical transformations" in the face of its own necessary transformation into its own other, adulthood. Youth in rock and roll is a celebration of its own impossible existence.

Finally, the body plays a central role in the economy of the rock and roll apparatus, both as the space within which youth and style are enacted and as the site of pleasure. The pleasure of the rock and roll body is tied, most directly, to movement and dance. The music itself, in its volume and rhythms, in the particular tones, colors, and "grains" of voice to which it is always returning, not only foregrounds the motile body but deconstructs the identities of its fans and positions them as bodies. The body becomes the site at which pleasure is restructured and inserted into the gaps of hegemonic power and control. There is a "tactile appropriation" (Chambers 1985) of rock and roll that precedes any cognitive relation to the music. Rock and roll touches, fragments, multiplies, and propels the body of its fans. And this transitory and flexible rock and roll body in turn intersects the various emotional ideologies of hegemonic conceptions of youth (e.g., of romance and self-pity) that reinscribe identity as self-hood.

But the place of the body in particular apparatuses is not simply homologous to the music. The place of rhythmic motion—sexuality, but even more centrally, dancing—makes this obvious. Dancing not only inserts the music into the space of the body, it also inserts it into the body of space. The rock and roll body is not merely an ideological construct, nor is it a passive physical reality. It is not a stage on which fans "strike poses and pose threats." It is not an object but a space to be "constructed, deconstructed, and reconstructed" (Hebdige 1982). The rock and roll body produces itself in space by producing its own space. We can begin to understand rock and roll dancing by the transformation that it projects: from space as a vacuum within which the whole body (of the individual, couple, or group) moves so as to inscribe its unity and identity, to space as a material assemblage to be redistributed, reappropriated, and reassembled according to the temporary rules of a temporally constituted body. This body exists only as a dispersed collection of narcissistically cathected, and even fetishized, fragments and gaps. For the rock and roll body is only the way it organizes the space of the dance floor as it projects its own rearrangement. If, as Lefebvre (1984) argues, capitalism produces an abstract space in which its installations are a part of the flow of capital and in which time is reduced to the constraints of space, the rock and roll apparatus produces a space of fragments and difference that disrupts any tranquil flow of bodies. Space is reorganized by the constraints of time, by the demands of a rhythmic body.

This is not meant to deny the important role that dancing plays in gender relations and courtship behavior (Frith 1981). Dancing, like style, is a form of sexual display. This leads us back into the complex relations between affective and ideological economies. The centrality of the body does not mean that rock and roll is not concerned with representations. Encircling the rhythms of the body, in the spaces it produces, rock and roll often consciously represents its own representations. It cannot take any single narrative as definitive; rather it displays the images it finds, uses, discards, and reclaims. But if we are to understand the importance of dancing to rock and roll fans (for many fans, the need to dance is as powerful as the music itself, and someone who does not dance, or at least move with the music, is prima facie not a fan), and the real sense of power that it gives them (Pete Townshend of the Who is purported to have said once that while rock and roll won't get rid of your blues, it will let you dance all over them), we must find ways of describing its affective empowering relations to the fans.

In contemporary society, space has not only been reorganized but new spaces have been created—not only urban and suburban spaces, but the spaces of shopping malls, supermarkets, subways, and more. One can read different rock and roll dances as different projections through and of those spaces: different movements, relations, and fragmentations, but also different pleasures, risks, and empowerments. Rather than the self moving through a preconstituted space that has already defined its temporality, rock and roll offers the material vision of reifying transitional spaces, of the past rupturing and reconstituting space, of temporality empowering space. Like Benjamin's *flaneur* and Lyotard's drifting, the body draws new lines through old spaces, inserting the narcissistic body into its own positions of power within an otherwise hegemonically controlled space and time.

CONCLUSION

In *The Pleasure of the Text,* Barthes wrote: "Two edges are created: an obedient, conformist, plagiarizing edge . . . and *another edge,* mobile, blank (ready to assume any contours), which is never anything but the site of its effect . . . Neither culture nor its destruction is erotic; it is the seam between them, the fault, the flaw, which becomes so . . . Culture thus recurs as an edge" (1975, 6–7). I have suggested that the politics of the rock and roll apparatus cannot be located solely in its ideology but depends as well on the empowering effects of an affective economy. Unlike Barthes, I would neither make this a universal description of culture, nor would I locate it within a binarism of pleasure and bliss, which merely serves to reproduce the modernist tragedy. Perhaps we might say that rock and roll eroticizes the flaws, the transitions, the "edges" of its own ambiguous place within the hegemony. The point is not that such practices are always oppositional (while the ideology is always complicitous). Rather the empowerment that occurs at the intersection of the music and the economy of style-youth-body makes rock and roll more than either oppositional or complicitous for its fans, more than either leisure or rebellion. We will not understand the "sensibility of mass culture" unless we interrogate the necessity for empowerment in the everyday lives of fans in the contemporary world.

Rock, Territorialization, and Power

Most discussions of the politics of contemporary rock (using "rock" in its broadest possible sense) start by assuming that, in some sense, rock has lost its political edge. In its most sophisticated forms, such an argument is not intended merely to say that rock has become establishment culture or that it has been colonized by corporate interests (both of which may be true to some extent). Instead it points to the doubly paradoxical situation of contemporary popular music. First, there seems to be an enormous amount of political activity within rock culture (especially on the side of the musicians) and some very real efforts to explicitly reconnect rock to a sense of political activism. And yet these activities (whether in terms of lyrics, organizational identifications through such activities as concerts, or direct political involvement) seem to have almost no impact upon either rock audiences or the broader tendencies of rock culture.

Second, given that rock seems at the moment totally incapable of organizing any significant political oppositional force, it does seem odd that there is so much energy being directed against it. These attacks have taken a number of different, even contradictory forms: the effort to ban rock music entirely (e.g., the Christian fundamentalist rejection of all rock as the devil's work and Allan Bloom's attempt to blame rock culture for the failure of American values); the effort to regulate and discipline rock music by placing the authority to judge and discriminate between good and bad music in external—the state and family—authorities (e.g., the Parents' Music Resource Center and the various civil and criminal prosecutions of rock groups); and finally the effort to rearticulate the very meaning and possibilities of rock's social position (e.g., Lee Atwater as a rock star or Pat Boone's statement that he deserves to be in the Rock and Roll Hall of Fame for having made rock "nice").

In order to begin to make sense of these paradoxes, we need a better sense of where the politics of rock are located, of the possibilities of and constraints on its articulations. Rock has had a variety of political positions, powers, and effects since its emergence in the early to mid-1950s. Sometimes its politics have involved the organization of individual experience, the configurations of everyday life, the structure of social relationships and differences, even, on rare occasions, the explicit distribution of political and economic power. The history of rock can be seen to involve a series of interrupted struggles to articulate (or disarticulate) particular sounds, texts, genres, and styles, to specific meaning, social positions, and ideologies, and from there to specific political positions and effects or to the "necessary absence" of politics at a particular conjuncture. But unless we begin by acknowledging the constraints and limits operating on the articulation of rock to politics, we are likely to fall back into a naïvely romantic view that simply assumes that rock was and is supposed to be resistant and/or oppositional.

I want to suggest that, given the conditions of possibility that both called forth and enabled rock's existence as an articulation of musical, cultural, economic, and technological practices, it is simply mistaken to assume that rock was, in any significant way, outside of the political mainstream of American culture. Consider the political, social, and economic climate of the postwar United States (one set of the conditions of possibility for rock's emergence): an unstable and unequally distributed economic prosperity and optimism; the conversion of the productive apparatus to consumerist goals; a corporate compromise between labor and capital mediated by the state (committed to extending civil liberties in order to expand the consumer population); and most importantly a peculiar version of liberalism ("the end of ideology") built upon a precarious balance between a sense that difference mattered culturally and socially but not politically (i.e., it was no longer a disruptive or oppositional force).

The result was a powerful context of mobility and change, both in terms of images and experiences. But there was a particular image of the proper and possible form of mobility: ameliorism in both social and economic terms. This was a gradual process that had to be earned and that, when successfully completed, would reproduce the unity of the political consensus in the image of the social and cultural mainstream. America would create not only the first politically liberal society but also the first society that had created its own middle-class style as the consensual norm of everyday life. Of course, this mobility was counterbalanced by a very real quietism or conservatism, which pervaded every aspect of the nation's life. It was against the image of this social conservatism that the romantic vision of rock as an inherent statement of political resistance, or at least an expression of alienation, was formed. This then quickly became the necessary condition of "authenticity" in rock culture.

I want, instead, to emphasize the ways this context constrained the political possibilities of rock so that it was difficult, if not impossible, for rock to enter into any explicit ideological struggle or political resistance. Rock did not challenge the ideological consensus of American life, but it did attempt to escape the quietism of culture and everyday life. This has in fact always been the limits of rock's politics. Perhaps a part of the reason that the romantic version of rock's political agenda won out was the assumed identification of rock with a particular image: the rocker as the isolated and agonized rebel and delinquent, antisocial, antidomestic, and anticonsumerist. This is, of course, an inaccurate portrait, not only of the majority of rock fans but of the performers as well.

There is little evidence—even in the songs—that rock rejected the dominant liberal consensus of American society or its major ideological assumptions, including sexism, racism, and classism. It is not merely that most fans lived somewhere inside the vast center of U.S. society, it is also that they imagined themselves remaining within it (or even moving more toward the center insofar as it defined the middle-class image of success). This is not to claim that rock fans wanted to grow up living the same lives as their parents, but then what generation does? They assumed that the center would change, but their imagination of such changes was itself defined by the ameliorism of the dominant consensus. Nowhere in this was there any room for ideological questions. Rock's politics were firmly located within the commitment to mobility and consumerism, perhaps not as ends in themselves but as the necessary conditions for a life of fun. That is, rock culture never renounced the normative passion for comfort and success. Because rock fans were caught in the space between the discipline and boredom of the school and that of the family (the two dominant sites of youth's policing), they used rock to imagine their own space of enjoyment, pleasure, and fun, a space regulated only by the norms of the rock culture itself. But this space was not a replacement for school or family (although it may have suggested the possibility of less rigid organizations for these institutions). Being a rock fan certainly did not entail, and only rarely involved even imagining, the possibility of leaving school—it remained the necessary path to secure the consumerist lifestyle and its associated pleasures—or renouncing family and a domestic future.

Rock did not reject the domestic image of daily life, including the privileged position it gave to men in both gender and sexual relations. While rock as well as the image of the rocker were often positioned outside the family, the vast majority of songs and fans reproduced the desire for love and the stable relationships of the nuclear family. While rock did create a space in which women's sexuality and pleasure were publicly legitimated, it was often romanticized and almost always defined in relation to the male partner, viewer, or listener. This does not deny that the sexual power of rock music, performance, and dance was new to its fans, nor that it was seen, by its fans but even more by the mainstream population, as a rupture in, even a threat to, the quiet regulation of sensuality and sexuality.

Similarly the dominant class politics remained largely in place, reinflected only through romantic fantasies of different class experiences and of the possibilities these implied for the members of each class to escape the structures of control and discipline of their own class. So too regarding race relations, rock was firmly located within the ambiguity of the dominant consensus: both ameliorist and racist, rock's relations to black music, performers, and audiences has always been a highly selective one. The apparent absence of a gap between black and white music and musical taste in the 1950s—a gap that has been constantly reinscribed since then—says more about the organization of the economics of distribution (limited repertoires of available musics, limited number of venues for performance, etc.) than it does about the politics of the rock culture itself. Again, this does not deny that rock—performers, performances, and fans—positioned itself significantly further along the ameliorist ladder of improved race relations. But it did not challenge the taken-for-granted terms of the ideologically and institutionally constructed racism of the United States, and it most certainly did not offer any critique of the dominant ideology.

Yet once again, to the extent that this was seen—not by rock fans as much as by the mainstream adult culture—as having allowed the interracial mobility implicit in the rhetoric of the liberal consensus to be accomplished more quickly than the mainstream's racism desired, rock was seen as something of a political challenge. Thus it was precisely because rock so innocently accepted its place within the liberal consensus that it was so easily embroiled in and articulated to political struggles, but always by others. Thus I am not claiming that rock did not challenge, upset, distance itself from the dominant social systems of power and discipline. I am claiming that rock's challenge was rarely articulated by or from within the rock culture itself but always by those outside of and, to some extent, opposed to it. I am also claiming that, while rock sought to rock the cultural boat (quietism), it did so with little or no concern for the organization of political consensus and economic relations since it did not consider these connected to questions of culture and fun. Rock sought to open culture to the needs and experiences of its own audiences, not to deny or overturn the consensual and institutional structures that had made those experiences, and rock's existence, possible. Its politicization resulted primarily from the sustained attacks it elicited rather than from its own activities or intentions. Perhaps those who opposed rock recognized that it was not quiet aesthetically, culturally, or socially; perhaps they were afraid that its attempt to upset the consensual economy of cultural taste and pleasure would have wider social ramifications. In any case, the result was that the rock formation often found itself articulated outside of the very consensus in which it still located itself. We might say that rock was politicized "behind its back." In its effort to fight back against its own expulsion from the mainstream, rock did sometimes politicize itself further. And this was not always only the result of its attempts to protect itself. Nor was it merely because it occasionally realized that it wanted to fight for the very things for which it was being attacked; it was just as often because it was exciting, if not fun, to be placed—temporarily at least—in the position of troublemaker. It was, as Dick Hebdige might say, a way for youth to assert its own place. Ultimately, rock's distance from the mainstream, and its dissonant voice within it, was the result of the way rock mattered to its fans and of the things that it made matter as well.

Almost four decades later, everything has changed. The political, social, and economic climate is radically different. The economic boom is over; the optimism is gone; the corporate compromise is rapidly being whittled away. While mobility is still the dominant social norm, it has an entirely different face: it is defined in purely economic (monetary and consumerist) terms with no sense of a common social class being created; it is instantaneous and it does not require labor or merit. Finally, difference has returned with a vengeance; it is omnipresent, dangerous, and yet glamorous. Certainly there are those who would use this changing historical context to explain the two paradoxes referred to above: that it is increasingly difficult to see how rock can be articulated to political positions and struggles and, at the same time, that rock is under increasing attack.

But this response is, in the end, too easy, for it ignores two fundamental aspects of rock music and culture, aspects that may help us understand why it is so important to challenge rock's privileged status without rejecting it altogether. First, we need to remind ourselves that rock is a form of music—and while this is quite obvious, discussions of rock often miss the unique relation of music and power. Second, the specificity of rock as a form of popular culture depends upon its special relation to everyday life, a relation that makes it particularly important in the current political context.

In order to understand music's specific relation to power, we must come to terms with music's specific power. But in a society (and a history) driven to master the power of the word, and mastered by that power, it is difficult, to say the least, to describe the apparently immediate and almost mystical (because, to some extent, universal) relationship that music constitutes, both between itself and its audience and between its audience and their environment. By describing it as "almost mystical" I mean to register the necessary uncertainty that we must have about the social determination of music's power (remembering its use in ritual and religion), while at the same time acknowledging that the actual historical forms of music are always socially determined. Jacques Attali has described music as "a herald, for change is inscribed in noise faster than it transforms society" (1985, 5). Later he expands upon this: music "makes audible the new world that will gradually become visible, that will impose itself and regulate the order of things; it is not only the image of things, but the transcending of the everyday" (11). (I will return to the last phrase shortly.) For Attali, then, one can read changes in musical form, in the dominant and emergent codes organizing their production and consumption, as a "prophesy" of the political transformations looming in society's future. For Attali there is always a correspondence, somewhat displaced, between the technologies of musical production, the codes of music's regularity, and the political economy of the social formation. (In fact, he identifies four moments of such correspondence: sacrifice, representation, repetition, and composition.) But I am less concerned here with such structural relations than with Attali's recognition that "[l]istening to music is listening to all noise, realizing that its appropriation and control is a reflection of power, that it is essentially political . . . And since noise is the source of power, power has always listened to it with fascination" (6).

What does it mean to say that "noise" or, more to the point, music "is the source of power"? For if we can understand this relation, then we should have no trouble understanding why power would find it necessary to appropriate and control it. Attali is, I believe, too romantic when he writes: "Rumblings of revolution. Sounds of competing powers. Clashing noises, of which the musician is the mysterious, strange, and ambiguous forerunner—after having been long emprisoned, a captive of power . . . But a subversive strain of music has always managed to survive, subterranean and pursued, the inverse image of this political channelisation: Popular music, an instrument of the ecstatic cult, an outburst of uncensored violence" (1985, 12–13). I should perhaps add, at this point, that Attali does not see rock as popular music: "From Jazz to Rock. Continuations of the same effort, always resumed and renewed, to alienate a liberatory will in order to produce a market, that is, supply and demand at the same time" (103). Rather than follow Attali into this zero-sum game in which we must constantly seek to discriminate between the co-opted and the subversive text, I prefer to take my lead from a more direct, if somewhat more naïve, statement he makes: "Ambiguous and fragile, ostensibly secondary and of minor importance, [music] has invaded our world and daily life. Today, it is unavoidable, as if, in a world now devoid of meaning, a background noise were increasingly necessary to give people a sense of security" (3). We need only think of the image of the mother singing to her child!

But how does music give people a sense of security? To say that the answer has to do with music's enormous and, to a large extent, inexplicable ability to "move" or stir people is too vapid an understatement, for it treats music's power in purely figurative terms. Obviously it is true that music somehow calls people emotionally. But it is perhaps better to begin by acknowledging the insight in Carlos Mejia Godoy's explanation of why the contras would inevitably lose in Nicaragua: "They have no singers . . . We have singers." Would it not then be more accurate to say that music is the most powerful affective agency in human life; music seems, almost independently of our intentions, to produce and orchestrate our moods, both qualitatively and quantitatively. Here one need only think of the impact of background and sound-track musics, whether in media texts (e.g., the differences between the use of music in *Miami Vice* and *Twin Peaks*) or in the places of everyday activities (e.g., Muzak). Behind these diverse uses of music is the implicit recognition that, somehow, such musical environments strongly influence the rhythms, tempos, and intensities of our lives. They can in fact determine the sorts of investments we make and the activities we undertake in their musically constructed spaces. We might turn, for an image of this power, to Deleuze and Guattari's "refrain" of creation, made manifest in the construction of the musical refrain itself:

> A child in the dark, gripped with fear, comforts himself by singing under his breath. He walks and halts to his song. Lost, he takes shelter, or orients himself with his little song as best he can. The song is like a rough sketch of a calming and stabilizing, calm and stable, center in the heart of chaos . . . Now we are at home. But home does not preexist: it was necessary to draw a circle around that uncertain and fragile center, to organize a limited space. Many, very diverse, components have a part in this, landmarks and marks of all kinds . . . Sonorous or vocal components are very important: a wall of sound, or at least a wall with some sonic bricks in it. A child hums to summon the strength for the schoolwork she has to hand in. A housewife sings to herself, or listens to the radio, as she marshals the antichaos forces of her work. Radios and television sets are like sound walls around every household and mark territories (the neighbor complains when it gets too loud). For sublime deeds like the foundation of a city or the fabrication of a golem, one draws a circle, or better yet walks in a circle as in a children's dance, combining rhythmic vowels and consonants . . . A mistake in speed, rhythm, or harmony would be catastrophic because it would bring back the forces of chaos, destroying both creator and creation. (1987, 311)

Deleuze and Guattari are here attributing to music an enormous territorializing power. In my own terms, it is music that founds place. It is music that calls forth our investments and hence our affective anchors into reality. It is music that affectively locates us in the world by constructing the rhythms of our stopping and going. When we stop, when the music enables us to stop, we ourselves are positioned not by an already existing stable identity, but by the wall that our music (our affect) constructs around a bit of space. We are protected now to engage in whatever activities are necessary, and enabled to move on in ways that were not possible before, since the wall reconstructs the space outside just as surely as it constitutes a place inside. Everyday life is itself organized by the rhythms of places and spaces, and by the specific configurations of places. This is merely to say that music or, more specifically, rock culture organizes the mattering maps by which everyday life becomes navigable and hence, livable.

But there seems to be a contradiction here, for at another point in their work, Deleuze and Guattari refer to music as the most "deterritorializing" of all practices; they claim that music destroys the codes that guarantee the repeatability necessary to both power and everyday life. How are we to bring these two notions together? How are we to make sense of the claim that music is a primary agency of both territorializing and deterritorializing forces? But isn't that just what rhythm is about? Is that not the very function of rhythm: to regulate the relations of place and space, of territorializing and deterritorializing? Meaghan Morris (1992) has pointed to a different image of everyday life as travel. In this image, contrary to Western common sense (in which one leaves a home already established to travel to some other home), mobility precedes and is more basic than stability. Space then takes precedence over place.

We begin with a necessary contradiction: territorializing and deterritorializing. And yet somehow the story we tell always seems to put the former into the service of the latter: place in the service of space, stability in the service of mobility. Attali has described the same perplexing situation at a different level of abstraction, one to which I referred above and to which we shall have to return: "No organized society can exist without structuring differences at its core. No market economy can develop without erasing those differences in mass production" (1985, 5).

The image of everyday life that Deleuze and Guattari's myth of musical creation offers might be described as a disciplined mobilization. A disciplined mobilization is a particular dynamic structuring of places and spaces, a closed circuit of everyday life. Once you have entered into its spaces, there are no longer any frontiers or boundaries to cross, for any such line would mark the possibility of a place. Instead everyday life becomes a transit compulsion in which sites of investment are transformed into epidemics that appear everywhere (and hence nowhere, as in the war on drugs), and ultimately into pure mobilities. One can only continue to move along the frontier as along a Moebius strip. There is no longer an outside or an inside, only the constant movement within the frontier itself. A disciplined mobilization signals the triumph of an unconstrained mobility that is nothing but a principle of constraint.

Perhaps then it makes sense that the attacks on rock would appear at just the moment they did, when rock culture has been called back to its roots in rhythm and dance, when club rock so powerfully dominates the culture, and when, as Frith (1990) has described it, the most powerful pleasures in rock seem to be produced out of the contradictions between the central and powerful rhythms and the increasingly less memorable "soundtrack" melodies. In fact, we might consider that punk's self-referential attack on rock helped to undermine rock's ability to establish any place. In a sense, punk transformed rock into a disciplined mobilization of sorts (and in that sense, may have unintentionally played into the hands of the contemporary forces of conservatism and capitalism). The possibility of such a close relationship between rock and this particular cultural structure makes sense when we consider the way in which youth, the audience of rock, has been constructed in the postwar United States: shuttled around with no place of its own.

Perhaps this helps to make it clear why rock's regulation—its ownership and control—must become a priority in any struggle, such as that to put into place a new conservatism, explicitly directed to the structures of everyday life itself. Consequently the ambiguities, selectivities, and differences within the new conservatism's attacks on rock make perfect sense if the task at hand requires the appropriation rather than the disappearance of musical relations. Music is then precisely a force that needs to be harnessed to the project of the new conservatism. But even more directly, there may be a close relationship between the specific effectivity of contemporary rock and the specific project of the new conservative alliance, which is, I believe, precisely to construct everyday life on the model of a disciplined mobilization. For reconstructing everyday life itself on the order of a disciplined mobilization defines a specific form of depoliticization, one-dimensionality, and even narcotization. It is a socially constructed discipline of apathy built upon the very possibilities of postmodern cynicism and irony. In a disciplined mobilization, there can be no outside or, more accurately, there can be no way of connecting everyday life to the political and economic forces that are shaping it.

I want now to turn briefly to my second point: the specificity of rock culture as defined by its distinctive relationship to everyday life. This can provide further insight into the specific (different but coexistent) forms that the attacks on rock have taken and into their combined effectivity. Attali argues that music always transcends the everyday. I would change this statement, only partly to reflect my own use of everyday life as a historically produced plane of existence that is unequally distributed. That is, I am using "everyday life" here as a specific, historically produced form of daily life (following Lefebvre), built upon principles of repetition and redundancy (and ultimately boredom). Its unequal distribution makes it a privilege determined largely in economic terms. Consequently, unlike Attali, I would rather say that music produced by and for a population already living in everyday life is always about the possibility of transcending the specific configuration of everyday life within which it is active. Lefebvre in fact draws a close parallel between music and everyday life: "Music is movement, flow, time, and yet it is based on recurrence" (1984, 19). When he asks whether music "express[es] the secret nature of everyday life, or compensates, on the contrary, for its triviality and superficiality," our answer must be that it does both. In fact, it is precisely in attempting to transcend particular forms of recurrence (everyday life) that music is able to express its secret nature.

Returning to my earlier discussion of rock culture, I believe that the implication of its conditions of possibility in the 1950s was that rock culture could only seek to transcend the specific configuration of everyday life, the specific forms of repetition, mundanity, and triviality characterizing the everyday life in which it found itself imprisoned. That is, rock did not seek to transcend everyday life itself, to open itself out onto other planes of political, social, and economic existence. It operated with and within, it took for granted, the luxury and privilege of everyday life as the condition of possibility of its own struggle against the mundanity of its everyday life. At best, rock sought to change the possibilities—the rhythms—within everyday life itself. It did not construct for itself a space outside of everyday life. (Consider the music of the Pet Shop Boys.)

Instead it appropriated as its own the markers of places outside of everyday life that other musics, other voices had constructed. These voices and the places they marked became the signs of authenticity within the everyday life of rock culture, but they were the voices of peoples who had no everyday life, who existed outside the privileged spaces of the repetitiously mundane world of rock culture. Rock then attacked, or at least attempted to transcend, its own everyday life, its own conditions of possibility, by appropriating the images and sounds of an authenticity constituted outside of, and in part by the very absence of, everyday life.

Rock is not merely white boys singing the blues; it is the sound of those who are imprisoned within everyday life, who cannot imagine its negation (and only ambiguously desire it), trying to produce the sounds of those who have no everyday life. Consequently, rock could never address questions of politics, society, or economics directly; its politics are often determined by those moments when political realities impinge upon its everyday life (e.g., the draft rather than the fact of a genocidal war being waged against the Vietnamese) or when it can be reduced to a question of everyday life (e.g., it can protest the suffering of blacks under apartheid but it cannot acknowledge the international political economic system that sustains apartheid and a multitude of other repressive regimes). Its most powerfully resonant music comes when it acknowledges that it can only see the realities of such questions through the structures of its everyday life (e.g., the best countercultural music, and the most powerful punk music). Thus when Simon Frith writes that "American rock music now is a form of easy listening" (1990, 91), there is a sense in which it has always been true but only now is it becoming blatantly obvious.

Thus it is not surprising that rock in the United States has always had an ambiguous relationship to black music. At those moments (e.g., the various "soul" musics of the '60s, disco from the late 1970s into the 1990s) when, for a variety of reasons, black music seems to speak from within its own structures of everyday life, or can be articulated into more generic national structures of everyday life, rock and at least certain versions of R & B seem closely intertwined. At other moments, or when specific forms of black music operate explicitly and self-consciously outside of any possibility of an everyday life, the chasm between the two musical traditions seems unbridgeable. This may help illuminate the peculiarly ambiguous reception of rap within rock culture, and the extraordinary power of rap for many fractions of the black audience (but notably not the black middle class). Rap is about the lack of an everyday life, and hence it is constantly confronting the realities of politics and economics. If rock rejects sentimentality (pure affect) in favor of its affective rhythms, rap cannot afford the luxury of sentimentality. Rap is perhaps the only place in contemporary popular music where politics is and must be constantly marked. This necessity is formally reproduced since the words are both the source of the rhythm and the site of the politics of rap. It is not surprising then that rap is often subject to the most vehement attacks and active repressions.

At the other extreme of the popular music scene, heavy metal is the second form that is the object of unqualified attack and active suppression. But it is certainly not the case that heavy metal, like rap, is a site where that which is outside of everyday life—politics—can enter. Rather what distinguishes heavy metal affectively from other forms of rock is that, ultimately, heavy metal hates and rejects everyday life itself. In fact, the range of heavy metal music is approaching the point where it recreates the entire spectrum of rock, but it does so always from a very different position vis-à-vis everyday life. Consider the contradiction often noted within heavy metal: its two poles are defined by a desire to be entirely sedated so as to become literally dysfunctional, and a desire to literally destroy any suggestion of routinization and boredom. This contradiction helps to explain the importance of visual effects, solos, and distortion, the celebration of violence and "perverse sexuality," and the outrageous appearance of its performers, which so violently contradicts the actual tastes of its audiences. Heavy metal does not negate the possibility of politics nor does it allow politics back into everyday life; rather it champions its own antipolitics.

Neither of these musics—rap and heavy metal—can be articulated into the new conservative reconfiguration of everyday life. The former flaunts the absence of everyday life and, with it, the presence of that which remains outside of everyday life. The latter constantly and continuously, albeit futilely, attempts to escape everyday life, refusing to allow it to constitute itself as the boundaries of the lived. Rock, however, has a more ambiguous and ambivalent relation to everyday life and, given its power and popularity, can make a powerful ally if it can be "appropriated and controlled," inflected into a project other than its own, unknowingly articulated into a new vector of effectivity. It can become not only a site of struggle but an agent in somebody else's struggle. But this is a very unstable task and, at the very least, it must be constantly policed, and ways must be found to ensure that it will continue to move only within the lines of the disciplined mobilization of everyday life. The struggle over rock, then, is an ongoing but specific contestation within a larger field. But the questions remain, haunting any effort to understand the struggle: Whose struggle is it? What are the stakes? What can we do about it?

Is Anybody Listening? Does Anybody Care?

On "The State of Rock"

In this paper, I want to address some questions about the current state of the rock formation in the United States, and about the possibility not so much of the death of rock as of rock's becoming something else. Or in other words, in what sense is it meaningful—and in what sense could it be true—to talk about the death of rock? Let me begin by explaining my use of the phrase "the rock formation." In this context, "rock" refers to the entire range of postwar, "youth"-oriented, technologically and economically mediated musical practices and styles. By describing it as a formation, I want to emphasize the fact that the identity and effect of rock depend on more than its sonorial dimension. Speaking of rock as a formation demands that we always locate musical practices in the context of a complex (and always specific) set of relations with other cultural and social practices; hence I will describe it as a cultural rather than a musical formation. Finally, using the singular "the" signals my desire to operate at a certain level of abstraction, a level at which there is some unified sense to "rock." I don't mean to deny that this unity is always locally rearticulated, but the overemphasis on locality and specificity often leads us away from important generalities, as well as from the fact that such generalities are part of the reality of the local articulations (for instance, there is a history of this broad use of the term within the formation itself).

Rock as a cultural formation is a historical event, a historical production and organization of particular practices, activities, sounds, styles, and commitments, of particular kinds of pain and fun. It emerged at a particular moment, determined by specific conditions of possibility, conditions to which rock responded. These conditions not only enabled rock but also constrained it, setting limits on its shapes and effects. But if the rock formation had a beginning, it is also possible that it has an end, or at least a trajectory of disappearance. If it has a history of its own transformation (and it most certainly does), then presumably that history can be understood as its attempt to respond to changes in its conditions of possibility. But then we have to acknowledge at least the possibility that, as the conditions themselves become so radically transformed as to be in some sense unrecognizable, then the transformations of the rock formation may similarly become significant enough that we can no longer credibly speak about the resulting formation as rock, as if its continuities were more powerful than its discontinuities.

These reflections are motivated in part by my own personal political dilemma. In a book I published in 1992, I treated the rock formation as an allegory for a kind of politics which, I argued, has been increasingly appropriated to construct a new conservatism in the United States. In a sense, then, the reflections in this paper are the beginning of an attempt to ask what a new popular politics might look like, and how it might be culturally constructed. The paper's (unearned) optimism—trying to find that possibility in an emergent cultural formation—is a perhaps premature effort to balance the pessimism of my earlier argument.

I

Of course, talk about the end or death of rock is not a new theme. There is a long history of such discourses that goes back almost to the emergence of rock in the 1950s. Traditionally such arguments are about the power of rock to change its audience and the world, a power that, it is assumed, can be measured in the sounds themselves, in the audience's social marginality or in the imagined uses made of the music. This rhetoric assumes a binary, hierarchical, and cyclical map of the musical terrain. It is built upon a strategy of differentiation: always distinguishing between the authentic and the co-opted. This distinction, then, easily and often slides into a narrative war between authentic youth cultures and corrupting commercial interests. Rock is judged dead to the extent that the commercial interests, the co-opted music, seem to be in control, not only of the market, but of the music and the fans as well (leaving only a few die-hard fans on the margins, fanning the embers of authentic rock). In a sense, then, in this rhetoric rock is never dead, but it is constantly in the process of dying or of being killed. This rhetorical strategy still has a powerful presence among both fans and critics. For example, Simon Reynolds has recently described the present situation as one in which rock has become "a reflection of straight aspirations, a normative agent. The dreams of youth culture have been excluded from the center stage, outflanked and outmoded" (1991, 71).

In fact, this rhetoric dominates much of the discussion about the relationship between rock and rap, taking two different forms. Some locate rap within rock, positioning it as the new internal site of authenticity (reproducing the structure of rock versus pop). Others, claiming that rap is not part of the rock formation (usually by drawing a sharp distinction between white and black musical formations), nevertheless position rap as the heir to rock's vitality and potential as a nascent act of resistance. Rap replaces rock, even as it reproduces the logic of its effects. I would argue, alternatively, that it is necessary to avoid arguments about whether rap has merely replaced rock as the new authentic music, for this merely relocates rap in the logic of the rock formation. At the same time, we have to remember that the rock formation has, after all, encompassed various black sounds, apparatuses, and scenes. At times it has acknowledged them, at times it has appropriated them, and at times it has given them the space within which to develop. For example, we might point to the positive importance of rap's white audience to its commercial success, as well as to the perplexing fact that its popularity seems to increase as it becomes "more black," even as it becomes "more black" in response to that white popularity. Of course at other times and places, various rock alliances have "expelled" and even silenced those apparatuses and scenes they judged to be "too black" (for instance, funk, disco, and so on).

But I think that the contemporary rhetoric of the death of rock is different; something has changed, rhetorically at least:

> The question of the death of rock comes up again and again these days, and not just because of falling record sales, a collapse of the concert market, major labels consolidating to the point of monopoly, or desperately profligate, rear-guard superstar contracts . . . It isn't even that the music is empty . . . The question of the death of rock comes up because rock 'n' roll—as a cultural force rather than as a catchphrase—no longer seems to mean anything . . . *There is an overwhelming sense of separation, isolation: segregation.* (Marcus 1992, 68; emphasis added)

A number of other rhetorical strategies or organizing figures have gained an important and prominent place within the discourses of the death of rock. I will describe these as indifference, fragmentation, and Babel.[1] For the sake of space, I will give only one illustration of each, although it is easy enough to find many examples of them all. Indifference claims that the differences according to which judgments of taste, authenticity, and co-optation have been organized no longer work. The differences can no longer sustain the weight demanded of them for rock to continue functioning as rock. Consider the following example: "The pop versus rock debate that has organized . . . musical taste since *Sgt. Pepper's* is now played out. There is no longer any point in attacking pop silliness in the name of rock truth or denouncing rock stodginess in the name of pop flair" (Frith 1987, n.p.).

The second figure, fragmentation, speaks as if the entire musical field is now so fragmented that there can no longer be a center or an organizing principle that can bind the music and fans together into the unity of rock. For example: "Rock is slowly fading as tastes in music go off in many different directions . . . the age of rock as a prevailing cultural form is over. The music business as a whole is far bigger than it was when rock reigned supreme, but no unifying musical movement has taken rock's place . . . *We've never seen this kind of fragmentation before*" (Cox 1992, 1, 4; emphasis added).

The third figure constructs the contemporary rock culture as the latest appearance of Babel, without the necessary common language or experience. For example, Greil Marcus refers back to the diverse sounds of the 1950s and "the new spirit they seemed to share." He identifies this spirit as a certain "myth of wholeness . . . a myth less of unity or even rebellion, than of a *pop lingua franca*." And he continues: "There is no central figure to define the music or against whom the music could be defined" (1992, 68–69; emphasis added).

Perhaps paradoxically, I want to take these three figures, not as diagnoses of the death of rock (to be judged true or false), but rather as evidence for a significant transformation in the rock formation and of our inability to describe it. All of them seem to share a certain common assumption: namely that the fields of rock music and taste are structured in some predictable and stable way (as organized differences, as center/periphery, or as a unified whole). They all evince something like a common "terror" or mourning at the collapse of such structures. But what is it that these various assumed structures actually describe? And what is their status? I want to suggest the obvious: that they are abstractions—from the broad terrain of postwar popular musics and from the complex relations between musical practices, social relations, and the practices of daily life.

It is in fact necessary for the very practice of critical interpretation that one abstracts structures—unities-in-difference—from these dense and dispersed configurations. And these abstractions can and often do have a reality of their own, not only for the critic, but within the field that is being described (for instance, the appeal to an abstraction like "rock" has real power and effects in the lives of its fans and in the practices of the music industry). Moreover, the reality of such a structure ("rock" or my own "the rock formation") does not depend on any claim that the field of popular music is limited to a single formation, or that such a formation is homogeneous in any single or simple (for instance, musical) way. In fact, even what we may think of as "the particular" or "the concrete" is simply another—lower or more overdetermined—level of abstraction. Critical work always involves moving between different levels of abstraction, constructing the network of determinations that connect them. Consequently, analysts constantly need to "measure the distance" between different levels of abstraction, between "the abstract" and "the concrete."

Thus it is important to distinguish how such abstractions operate within the field of rock music, and how they operate within a critical-analytic discourse about that field, and the distance between them. In the following brief discussion, I want to describe three dimensions of this distance: empirical, structural, and conceptual. The empirical can be quite a problem if one is both a fan and a critic. Confusing the two contexts can often lead to serious misunderstandings in which critical and everyday categories slide into each other. For example, taste is never as neatly organized as critical abstractions suggest, especially when we are considering the overdetermined way people respond to particular texts. For, at one level, I can argue that people respond neither to individual songs nor to individual performers, but to sounds and images within larger contexts and logics. It is also true, at another level, that particular songs and performers can have a powerful impact, even outside one's apparent taste: "We were committed to rock and roll, but that doesn't mean that we turned out the opposition—what makes a hit a hit is that it penetrates your defenses. Nor did our pop tastes boil down to simple like and don't like. We responded to pop artists individually—for how they sounded, or who they seemed to be" (Christgau 1992, 87). Thus whatever our tastes may be "generically," we often cannot help but respond to other texts (for example, the popularity of romantic "make-out music" like Johnny Mathis's in the 1950s, or the ability of various AM "bubblegum" songs to insert themselves into our minds, our memories, and our tastes).

A second confusion that frequently results from conflating the different levels at which our abstractions (structure, unities-in-difference) operate is the reduction of the field of popular music to some predetermined set of texts: sometimes to best-selling records or the records we know and/or like (there are a lot of records out there no one ever talks about), and sometimes to particular "genres" (often ignoring not only particular genres within rock but also everything from country and western and jazz to Las Vegas pop to Broadway show tunes to film music).

A third consequence is that the field of popular music is often reduced to its commercial face, to recorded (professional) music. This ignores the density of musical practices in daily life. It ignores all the music made outside of the vector of commodity production (for example, local bands and parties). It ignores all the music consumed in contexts other than commodity purchases, concerts, radio, and music videos. And it ignores all of the activities associated with musical life.

These three problems might be described as "empirical," but there are also what might be called "structural" problems that arise from the ways we misuse various abstractions. These problems exist independently of the particular structures, but for the sake of simplicity I will take two reasonably similar examples: the models of center/periphery and mainstream/margin. Most attempts to describe the terrain of popular music in such terms, while useful in particular contexts (for instance, fans' self-representation), oversimplify the relations between the center and the periphery, the mainstream and the margin. They ignore the fact that there have always been multiple centers and mainstreams. This diversity, more than anything else, has its most powerful impact in the always fragmented and incoherent nature of the Top 40. These models also ignore the varied forms of "traffic" among the different centers and margins. The real question is less what or where a particular sound is, than how it travels.[2] What kinds of sounds travel? from where to where? What are the enabling and constraining conditions of such mobilities and stabilities? Let me give just two examples. Recently, some critics have observed that the success of one group does not seem to necessarily bring similar groups (or the entire subgenre) with it: consider R.E.M., Nirvana, Metallica, Guns N' Roses, or Garth Brooks. It seems increasingly difficult to describe a general movement into a center. Yet this situation may not be particularly unique to the present. On the other hand, what may be unique is the existence of a "hip mainstream," whether filled by grunge, house music, Lollapalooza, college rock, or simply, as one radio station put it, "Less music by dead White men."

There is, finally, a third—"conceptual"—set of problems with the ways critics use the abstractions they have constructed out of or taken from the dense configurations of musical practices in daily life. For such abstractions often move, without much self-reflection, between three different strata or fields of analysis. Within each of these strata, the configuration of popular music looks significantly different. And although "rock" appears in all three, one cannot assume any equivalence (or synonymity) between its three appearances. I want now to describe these strata, remembering that each is always internally complex and contradictory. I will describe these fields as (1) the logic of production and/or commercialization (apparatuses); (2) the logic of consumption (scenes); and (3) the logic of effects or the operational logic (a space of alliances).

The logic of production and/or commercialization, which produces "apparatuses" of music, describes the largely industrial attempt to market music by segmenting it, usually according to "generic" distinctions supposedly grounded in "objective" sonorial features. Two recent examples of logics operating in this strata are worth pointing to: first, the recent attempt to organize taste via the marketing of scenes; and second, the recent collapse of rock into guitar-based music as a new marketing strategy, which can be traced back at least to the "success" of the racist attacks on disco in the name of "rock." It is also important to point out that music criticism, as part of the economic logic of marketing, is often complicitous with the construction of apparatuses.

The logic of consumption describes the organization of taste-cultures according to particular configurations or scenes. Reinterpreting a recent argument by Will Straw (1991), a scene is characterized by a particular logic that may, in a sense, transcend any particular musical content, thus allowing the scene to continue over time, even as the music changes. This also means that very different musics may exist in very similar scenes. The logic of a scene can be described along a variety of dimensions. For example, we can describe different taste-cultures according to their sense of history: Is there a "canon" that is incorporated into the present, thus denying a sense of change? What is the role of covers? We can also look to the various sorts of practices that are valorized: What is the meaning of "authenticity"? What is the perceived relation between recording and performance? between music and lyrics? What is the status of lip-synching? What sorts of instruments and performances are tolerated or required? We can also differentiate scenes according to the ways particular sounds and practices are articulated to different structures of social differences: for example, the perceived relations between race and hard rock or gender and heavy metal.

Straw, in his important article on rock scenes, distinguishes between alternative rock and dance music; whatever Straw's intentions, I want to read his description of these as logics of consumption. While such labels certainly operate in the logic of production describing different apparatuses, we cannot assume that they would refer to precisely the same structures, since both their boundaries and their specific characteristics would be significantly different. According to Straw, the logic of alternative rock is canonical (the past is constantly present); it places great emphasis on the individual career (earning your way); it has little sense of progress (rather there is a lateral expansion through what Straw describes as "generic exercises"); and the local scene is always at the center, where it functions to reproduce the logic of the scene in its entirety. On the other hand, Straw characterizes the dance scene as polycentric, emphasizing spatial diversity, so that each local scene is a unique part of the whole rather than merely a repetition of the larger whole. Moreover, this geographically based sense of musical diversity is represented as a teleological temporal sequence. The result is that, while there may be a canon of sorts, it does not exist as part of the present except insofar as its songs can be covered and reworked into this narrative of movement.

But while Straw only describes these two logics, it is reasonable to assume that there are other logics of consumption, defining other scenes. And these logics need not correspond to critical genres or the apparatuses of production. For example, in a list of the logics of consumption of the rock formation, we might want to include the following: Top 40, oldies, hard rock, underground, hip mainstream, avant-garde, and world music.

Operational logics, or logics of effects (which are always made manifest in specific alliances), describe the place of musical practices and relations in people's lived realities *understood socially (as a context of determination and power) rather than psychologically (as a context of experience).* Within this stratum, rock's history cannot be reduced to that of its sonic register. There is no necessary identity between particular musical practices and the identity of rock as a cultural formation. That is, rock cannot be defined in purely musical items, although we cannot ignore its musical textuality, its sonorial presence. Rock is more than just a conjuncture of musical and lyrical practices. Moreover the identity, meaning, and effect of rock—as a singular cultural formation or in its various local articulations (alliances)—is always contextually produced. Rock's musical practices always already exist in specific and complex sets of relations that articulate their meanings and effects. Consequently rock's musical and lyrical practices, while often taken from other traditions and cultural formations, are almost always received as if they were already part of rock's conventionality.

Operational logics involve more than just the relationships between logics of production and logics of consumption. They define particular ways of navigating the spaces and places, the territorializations of power, of daily life. That is, they define the empowering and disempowering possibilities of the rock formation or at least of its different alliances. They articulate rock's political possibilities, its effectivities.

II

The following remarks, then, are meant to describe something about the changing operational logics of the rock formation. I will begin by briefly describing the conditions under which rock emerged and the ways rock was shaped by its attempt to respond to those conditions, but always within the constraints they imposed. This will lead me to an equally brief discussion of some of the basic characteristics of the operational logic that defines the rock formation as a specific, determined, cultural event.

I want to identify four of the historical conditions of rock's possibility. First, rock emerged within a particular social and economic context. The postwar years were a time of economic prosperity and relative affluence, although this was unequally distributed. This prosperity was funded through a continuing war economy (increasingly funded through deficit spending) and an exploding consumer economy. Whatever redistribution of wealth took place was funded through taxation and government spending rather than through real economic restructuring.

At the political level, the postwar years embodied a powerful ideological contradiction. On the one hand, a particularly American version of liberalism took shape, which celebrated America's difference from the rest of the world based on its acceptance of an internally differentiated society (although these internal differences were assumed to have no political significance). On the other hand, it was a time of political quietism: America had won its well-deserved place as leader of the free (capitalist) world and it was no time to rock the boat. Any protest or even criticism was taken as a threat to America's sense of its own uniqueness and identity. Thus this quietism was itself articulated to a celebration of America, whether a conservative celebration in the 1950s or a utopian one in the 1960s. These two conflicting impulses—liberalism and quietism—were reconciled in an ideology of mobility and ameliorism; the trajectory of this mobility was defined by its supposed universal access (through hard work) and its speed (or more accurately, its gradualness).

The second condition of rock's emergence was sociological: the emergence of a large youth population distributed broadly throughout the population (the so-called baby boom). This youth population had to be disciplined, which called forth new investments, institutions, and strategies to shape youth, to police and control youth's practices and mobilities, its places and spaces. Yet at the same time youth, first as a generation and increasingly as an attitude, was privileged and even celebrated. In a sense, youth itself was identified as the embodiment and the potential realization of the American Dream.

The third condition was the appearance of a certain structuring of experience, the emergence of a "postmodern" structure of feeling. By this I mean the disarticulation, at specific sites, of the relationship between affect and ideology, of investment and meaning, as two intertwined constitutive dimensions of human experience. "Affect" here refers to the quality and quantity of energy invested in particular places, things, people, meanings, and so forth. It is the plane on which we anchor and orient ourselves into the world, but it is neither individualistic nor unstructured; it is not some pure psychological energy erupting through the social structures of power. Moreover it is complexly articulated and structured, producing configurations not only of pleasure and desire (through economies of repression and satisfaction) and of emotion (through narrative economies), but also of volition (or will), of moods and passions. These latter describe the organization of what matters; they point to the fact that people experience things, live different identities, practices, relations, to different degrees and in different ways.

The postmodern structure of feeling describes the partial but increasing lack of fit between mattering maps and maps of meaning, between the organization of what matters and the social languages of signification, representation, and value. The result is that, at particular sites, it is apparently impossible to invest in those meanings that supposedly make sense of life. And similarly it is apparently impossible to find a structure of meaning that makes sense of what matters. For the most part, during the immediate postwar years this postmodern disarticulation, always and only local, partial, and temporary, was lived privately, as a psychological experience of alienation. It was lived with a very real sense of seriousness and ressentiment (negativity). And it increasingly became a signifier of a generational difference that separated the baby boomers from their parents.

The fourth condition of possibility involved a series of developments in the cultural domain. Technological developments changed musical practices at every point in the cycle of production: amplification in performance; magnetic tape in recording (allowing sophisticated intervention between production and recording); and transistorization in consumer reception. The result was the increasingly sophisticated manipulation of both the sound and the musical commodity. At the same time, the music industry was undergoing serious changes and reorganizations: the "majors," reorganized as multinational corporations centered in the United States and Britain, gained substantial control of the market. And the market itself changed, as the major source of profits for the music industry shifted, from the sale of sheet music and the stocking of jukeboxes to the sale of records to individual consumers. In this context a particular structure of relations developed between these major corporations and the so-called independents: on the one hand, the independents were left to service markets deemed too small or too marginal by the majors; and on the other hand, there was a good deal of hostility between them, as the majors simply outbid and outdid the independents whenever one of the latter's markets suddenly seemed significant enough for serious exploitation.

This cultural context was also characterized by what might be called a particular "media economy," that is, a particular relationship or ratio between sight and sound, between visual and aural discourses. More concretely, for the postwar years, this is a question of the relative weight and impact of the two relatively new media of entertainment: television (and here I would include film) and music (records and radio). The former belonged largely to an industrial-domestic set of relations, especially within the lives of youth, so that the latter was naturally constructed as the locus of authenticity. This implied a particular relationship between fandom and participation (for instance, the importance of concerts), one that was very different from what existed around Tin Pan Alley sounds and styles.

Finally, the cultural context made available particular images of rebellion. For the most part, these were images of alienation in the form of the Beat poet (via the black hipster) and the juvenile delinquent or punk (largely through myths of urban and motorcycle gangs). These images defined a particular relation to marginality and, I would argue, in particular to black culture. There was no assumed identity between being black and being young, or even necessarily between black and white youth, but there was "a structure of imaginary desire" between them. (One can think of the appropriation involved in the 1960s slogan "student as nigger.") This may help to explain the unique relation between rock and African American sounds and rhythms, a crucial relation that nevertheless often occludes rock's relations to other sources, including country and western, swing, Tin Pan Alley, folk, and Latino sounds. It also helps to explain rock's constant tendency to both appropriate and reject black musical practices.

Having laid out some of the parameters of the context of rock's emergence and existence, let me try to describe the operational logic that rock defined and that, in turn, defined rock. First, rock is an affective machine. It operates on the plane of affect and its primary effects are affective. Rock is about the production of moods and passions and the organization of will. It constructs temporary mattering maps. For the most part, and most of the time, rock simply ignores ideology. Or to put it another way, it remains within the broad terms of the ideological mainstream. It does not (or only rarely) challenge the major dimensions of American ideology; it is largely liberal and ameliorist.

Second, rock is a differentiating machine. It continually separates Us (those within the space of its logic) from Them (those outside the space of its logic). A generational difference (a matter of the logic of consumption) becomes a social difference. And the differentiation continues even with the space of rock, for that is the nature of differentiating machines: they proliferate differences. But unlike liberalism, rock's logic says that differences do matter. In the terms of rock, this becomes a struggle over authenticity (where authenticity must be understood as an affective term). The history of rock is marked by a continuous struggle over what is really authentic rock and which groups are really invested in it. To be clear here, I am not saying that there really is such a difference; rather it is an effect of rock's differentiating work, the operational logic's construction of the relations between different scenes, different apparatuses, and, most importantly, different alliances. In this way, rock is continually restructuring itself as a field, reconstituting its "center"—or actually, its centers (since there are always competing definitions of and investments in "authentic" rock).

Third, rock defines a politics of fun (where fun is not the same thing as pleasure, nor is it a simple ahistorical experience). In privileging youth, rock transforms a temporary and transitional identity into a culture of transitions. Youth itself is transformed from a matter of age into an ambiguous matter of attitude, defined by its rejection of boredom and its celebration of movement, change, energy; that is, fun. And this celebration is lived out in and inscribed upon the body—in dance, sex, drugs, fashion, style, and even the music itself.

Finally and most importantly, rock is a deterritorializing machine that defines a politics of everyday life. Let me begin to explain this by elaborating on my use of "everyday life" here, which I take from Henri Lefebvre (1984). Everyday life is not the same as daily life. It is a particular historical organization of the space of daily life, an organization based on principles of repetition and recurrence. It is daily life becoming routinized, without any principle that can define its unity and meaningfulness. Everyday life is predictable, and, paradoxically, that predictability is itself a kind of luxury and privilege. At the same time, as Lefebvre points out, everyday life is a form of control: in Foucault's (1977) terms, a kind of disciplinization or, in Deleuze and Guattari's (1987) terms, a politics of territorialization. I think it is safe to assume that in postwar America everyday life had already been or was rapidly being put into place.

In this context it is important to begin by admitting the obvious but painful truth that rock rarely challenges the political and economic institutions of society (and when it does, it is usually either marginal, utopian, or hypocritical). It does not even challenge or attempt to negate the political and economic conditions of everyday life. It remains largely within the privileged space of everyday life, although it often imagines its romanticized other—its image of alienated rebellion, its black musical sources—as living outside everyday life.

Rock's politics are defined by its identification of the stability of everyday life with boredom. Consequently, it can only operate as a deterritorialization. It draws or produces "lines of flight" which transform the boredom of the repetition of everyday life into the energizing possibilities of fun. It creates temporary and local places and spaces of mobility and deterritorialization. It challenges the particular stabilities or territorializations of the everyday life within which it exists by producing and celebrating mobilities. Thus all rock can do is change the rhythms of everyday life. It restructures everyday life by articulating its lines of flight into new mattering maps. Although it cannot break out of everyday life, the trajectory of its mobilities at least points to (even if it cannot define) a world beyond, an alternative to, everyday life. It is as if it imagined that Saturday night was outside the discipline of territorialization and projected a world in which every moment could be lived as Saturday night.

As I have said, rock's lines of flight have rarely led to other planes of political, social, and economic existence. When it does connect to such issues (for example, Vietnam), it is usually because political or economic realities (the draft) have suddenly appeared within the everyday lives of its fans. But rock does articulate the possibility of investing in a universe of diminishing opportunities. If it cannot offer transcendence, it can at least promise a kind of salvation. If it does not define resistance, it does at least offer a kind of empowerment, allowing people to navigate their way through, and even to respond to, their lived context. It is a way of making it through the day.

III

Hopefully by this point it is clear that there is at least a sense in which it might be empirically meaningful to talk about the death of rock without merely reproducing the logic of the rock formation (that is, without confusing the level on which such a claim is operating). It is also possible that some of the same musical practices that existed within the rock formation might be relocated in a new, emergent, popular formation, also organized largely around popular music, with a different operational logic. It is in light of this possibility that I want to rethink the nature and effects of popular music in the 1990s.

In order to make sense of the current state of popular music, we have to make sense not only of what differences make a difference, but of how they make a difference. I propose to continue, then, by considering the context of contemporary popular music and by looking at how rock's conditions of possibility have been transformed so radically as to suggest that rock's operating logic might no longer be either effective or possible.

I think most people would agree that the political and economic context of the United States has been drastically restructured. Not only have liberalism and the liberal state been methodically eroded, but the "quietist" construction of conservatism has given way to active, even aggressive, fundamental-ist, and popular conservatisms. Consequently the reconciliation afforded by the ideology of mobility has become unnecessary, allowing the very notion of mobility to be refigured, so that it is increasingly signified by images of crimi-nality and chance.

Similarly even the appearance of economic prosperity has disappeared into an increasingly visible and publicly accepted disparity of wealth, result-ing in the impoverishment of significant portions of the population, both nationally and globally. That has gone hand in hand with the transformation of the military/consumer economy into a global corporate economy aimed increasingly at privileged enclaves around the globe, willing to resort to the most exploitative sorts of practices to extract profit at any cost.

Given the havoc and pain that has been wrought by more than twelve years of conservative rule (and one year of neoliberal rule), it is not surprising that the optimism and faith in progress that characterized postwar America through most of the 1970s has all but collapsed. Nor is it surprising that the celebration of America has been inflected into an empty and sometimes fa-natical patriotism.

Adopting a sociological perspective, I want to point to the changing pres-ence, power, and status of youth, the result in part of the aging of the baby boomers who, continuing to invest in their own "youth"-fulness, are engaged, with the complicity of the Right, in an ideological struggle over the meaning of youth. At the same time they are increasingly involved in and supportive of explicitly repressive policies aimed at policing and controlling the ac-tivities and practices of young people (for example, attacks on music and drugs, use of medical incarceration, depriving youth of civil rights and of a public voice). And in many instances, at the very least, they tolerate the very real material impoverishment of young people.

All of this has further depended on the fragmentation of "youth" as a chron-ological and social category into multiple generations, crossed by class and race, in complex relations. Two of these fractions have become the object of rather intense scrutiny: first, a generation of preadolescents who apparently do not want to grow up to be teenagers because they perceive adolescence as too dangerous. And second, a fraction that has come to be called, in an un-precedented debate over their identity or, more accurately, their lack of iden-tity, Generation X (or alternatively, the baby busters, the Brady boomers, and so on).[3] These names refer to those born between 1961 and 1981; they are the children of the pre-baby-boom silent generation and the earlier parts of the baby boom. And they are presented as marking a new generation gap, one defined against the baby boomers. Their identity crisis seems to be defined not within their experience (for within their experience they have no identity crisis) but rather within the experience of the baby boomers, who seem to have a desperate need and a total inability to identify them. Generation X seems to exist in a space of a common terror at the inability to name, to understand the next generation. This is the Reagan youth, but it is also the grungers, the rappers, and the American punks!

What I earlier called the postmodern experience has become a *dominant* structure of feeling, especially for the post-baby-boomers. Now everything has come under the antiaura of the inauthentic; everything is already co-opted, already an act. The result is that one's responsibility is only located within a realm of affective sovereignty and individual choices where it does not matter what you invest in, as long as you invest in something. Consequently there is a tendency to keep everything at a distance, to treat everything ironically, with no investment in one's investment. Moreover this structure of feeling is now lived publicly, on the surfaces of popular culture, not as an alienation but as a taken-for-granted context of everyday life. The often noted rise in the acceptance and practice of dishonesty can be seen as based in a postmodern redefinition of ideology:[4] from "They don't know what they are doing but they are doing it anyway" to "They know what they are doing but they are doing it anyway." Students cheat (and feel guilty) because, after all, no one—even those who demand honesty—is honest.

Regarding the cultural domain, the transformations have been even more remarkable. There has been a technological revolution in the past ten years as great as that of the postwar years, and it has affected every site of musical and popular cultural practices (as well as inventing new ones); and the "revolution" is accelerating: from synthesizers and samplers to digital recording to laser disks and CD-ROMs. But already the music industry is investing in digital distribution systems (using the new "information highways") that will not even require the mediation of prerecorded commodities.

Similarly the music industry has been and continues to be reconfigured. The majors have become multinational media and leisure corporations no longer based on North Atlantic capital. The relations between these transfigured majors and independent record companies have become less hostile (even while it has become more difficult for the latter to survive economically) as the majors increasingly come to view the independents as their own "minor" league. At the same time, the source of profits is shifting: at the moment it still depends heavily upon the sale of CDs, but that is largely because of the trade practices that have attempted to increase their price even while the actual cost of production decreases. On the other hand, a greater share of the profit depends on selling secondary rights across media and on secondary merchandising. All of this is, of course, taking place in the context of the shifting distribution of the market for music across age and geography, and the changing relative importance of different media (from radio to television) for introducing new music.

Similarly the particular media economy, the particular structured relationship between aural and visual imagery that characterized the rock formation is changing. As Tony Parsons has recently written: "Pop culture [read here the rock formation], though it lives on in the hearts of those of us between the ages of 30 and 50, has largely been replaced by game culture. But any industry that still generates around [$25 billion] worldwide every year is alive and kicking. Pop as culture is dead. Pop as industry is thriving" (Parsons 1993, 14).

Leaving the question of game culture aside, I do want to suggest that the ratio of sight and sound has already changed significantly. The visual (whether MTV or youth films or even network television, which has, for the first time since the early 1960s, successfully constructed a youth audience) is increasingly displacing the aural as the locus of generational identification, differentiation, investment, and occasionally even authenticity. The result is that new visual formations of youth culture speak, often in the space of rock and sometimes even against rock, of a kind of salvation without the necessity of authenticity. As a result the rhythms of both visual imagery and music have changed, the music, as it were, having adapted to television's beat.

Finally, I would suggest that there is almost a complete absence of any compelling, viable images of rebellion. All that is left is the fact of marginality and the struggle for identity. This has resulted, I think, in a kind of deromanticization of blacks, who are no longer imagined to exist outside of everyday life, and a more immediate and affective identification between whites and blacks (consider the images of various white rappers). One interesting result of this transformation is that, while the popular formation is still strongly linked to national identity, it is no longer involved in a celebration of America.

Now it is perhaps possible to speculate—and I emphasize that, at the moment, speculation is all it is—about the operational logic of the popular music formation that is emerging in this context. I am not claiming that the rock formation has disappeared, only that we may be witnessing its transformation; or perhaps it is better to say that the rock formation is giving ground to something else. Once again, it is necessary to emphasize that this new formation cannot be defined in purely musical terms. This new formation cannot simply be identified with, for example, rap or house/dance, although these are clearly central to it. But so is the experimentation so powerfully illustrated by rap's relation to other forms of music (including heavy metal and jazz). The new formation would certainly include a lot of techno-pop and even hard rock, especially some alternative scenes and apparatuses. And these may all be brought together around apparatuses and scenes like the Lollapalooza tours. But it would also include, more centrally than the rock formation, televisual and filmic texts and practices (as well as a wide range of other cultural imageries).

While I believe that the operational logic of this new formation is still affective, the other three features of rock's logic seem to be significantly different. While the new formation still manifests an obsessive self-referentiality that somehow equates the music with the identity of its audiences and producers, making the visual signs of marginality the condition of authenticity, there is a change not only in the way scenes and alliances are formed, but also in the forms of mobility between them. In other words, differentiation—the production of differences—seems not less important or less effective, but rather to have a different sort of effectivity and a different sort of importance. Such differences have become the crucial markers (billboards) of certain kinds of investment. Consequently apparatuses, scenes, and alliances are proliferating and, more importantly, the relations between them are becoming more fluid and temporary and less exclusionary. If rock responded to the assumption of 1950s' liberalism that differences do not matter precisely by making them matter, the pluralism of contemporary music seems to echo the 1950s' image of differences without any power. But this is not quite accurate, for they do matter, as the public face of the last site of individual affective agency. There is a new tolerance across differences, and the only exclusionary function of these differences seems to be to exclude those for whom the music matters too much (those still in the rock formation?). As Simon Frith puts it, "the rules of cult exclusion no longer apply—there is no musical taste that guarantees distinction" (1987). This doesn't mean that fans do not still make judgments about authenticity, but that such judgments are not invested in the same ways. Nor do I mean to deny that there are still fractions that invest in rock and continue to articulate its differentiating power, but even those investments are no longer capable of totalizing themselves across the entire field.

All of this can be interpreted as pointing to the changing place of the music, not only in the social formation, but in people's lives as well. It reflects a change in the quality and quantity of people's investment in the music—a change not only regarding its place on their mattering maps, but also in its ability to articulate mattering maps for them. Again, to quote from Simon Frith (while he is describing British youth, I am confident that similar trends are observable in American youth):

> A new Gallup survey of Britain's 14- to-16-year-olds found that the average teenager now listens to pop music for 4 hours a day, 3 times more, it's claimed, than teens spent listening to pop in the mid-1970s. The poll also reveals that pop is "very low" on a list of "the most important things in life" (after, in order, education, home, friends, money, sex, appearance, work, going out, sport, hobbies and football) . . . This is the postrock generation gap. The young listen to more and more, and it means less and less. The old listen to less and less, but it means more and more. The young are materialists; music is as good as its functions. The old are idealists, in search . . . of epiphany. (1991, 88)

Thus the various post-baby-boomer generations seem barely able to use the music to mark any generational difference and totally unable to mark intra-generational differences. While the music matters, it matters in not quite the same way. Rather than being the affective center and agency of people's mattering maps, music's power is articulated by its place on other mattering maps, by its relation to other activities, other functions. Rather than dancing to the music you like, you like the music you can dance to. Thus the music's popularity depends less on its place within specific alliances than on the construction of hyperalliances as venues for other sorts of affective relations and activities.

Similarly, while this new logic continues to foreground fun and the body, sexuality and dance, fun has been "depoliticized," since it is no longer defined by its antagonism to boredom and no longer built upon a vision of the permanent celebration of fun embodied in youth. Rather fun is apparently celebrated for its own sake, as the party due (not just) youth before the responsibility of the rest of their lives, before the likelihood of an early death. Fun is no longer defined against adulthood. To return to Parsons's image of a game culture, we now see that the games, mediated through computers, are matters of skill that define a new and different difference from adults. And yet these games prepare youths for adulthood (sometimes a particularly vicious kind) and sometimes even define them as already more adult than the adults.

Let me now come to my moment of optimism, for I do not think that the politics of this new formation remain constrained to deterritorializing the spaces of everyday life, which is not to say that it escapes the "prison" of everyday life. In a way, in fact, it no longer has the power to restructure everyday life. So its politics are, to borrow a phrase from Certeau (1984), polemological, predicated on the constant reassertion of the fact that we (they) are getting screwed. In this sense, it is more ideological than rock, and this may be reflected in the reemphasis on lyrics (almost always only in relation to the rhythm).[5] This new formation keeps trying to name the power, to identify those who are doing the screwing, so to speak, and thus its lines of flight constantly take it to the boundaries of everyday life. The real question is: Can or will such a polemological politics take its own conditions, the conditions of everyday life, into account as the enemy, or will it constantly return to everyday life, reinscribing its own privilege? If we can "fabricate" the future, the answer may be ours—fans', critics', and academics'—to give.

2 IN SPITE OF . . .

(POSTMODERNITY)

The Indifference of Television, or, Mapping TV's Popular (Affective) Economy

SPEED LIMITS

A theoretical framework for interpreting television—its specific textual practices and forms, its active insertion into real historical formations, and its appropriation by audience formations—has to recognize not only that television includes a wide range of discourses and textual practices, but that it reshapes and reinflects them by incorporating them into its own practices and contexts.

I want to look at one line of contemporary cultural discourse, sometimes referred to as "postmodern," that is increasingly active in different genres on the television screen. Its most popular televisual sites at the moment include *Miami Vice, Moonlighting, The Max Headroom Show, Pee Wee's Playhouse,* and perhaps *L.A. Law.* But it is not limited to "fictional" series; it increasingly enters television's relationship to certain "real events." Recent examples might include a sportscaster's excursion to a *real* Boston sports bar that turned out to be the set, in Los Angeles, of *Cheers;* or Geraldo Rivera's documentary on drugs—*American Vice*—which was built around live coverage of *real* drug busts that had obviously been timed and orchestrated for their visual power on the program; or the recent network coverage of the congressional hearings on the Iranian arms sales and the contra connection, containing hours of the witnesses' preannounced refusals to testify. Such "postmodern" texts have not emerged ex nihilo; they operate in other media and have their own historical precedents. But their incorporation into popular television does suggest that they have moved on the contradictory terrain of common sense, what Gramsci described as "traces without an inventory." If such practices are increasingly taken for granted, the question is precisely what is being taken for granted and how it is being effectively articulated. If these "postmodern" texts are increasingly visible in a wide range of media and forms, the issue is precisely how television articulates these structures. How can we make sense of such texts as televisual practices within a broader historical configuration of the popular?

Television theory needs to operate at the intersection of three models of cultural interpretation or, more accurately, in the spaces won and lost by each of them as they have responded to Althusser's theory of ideology and the social formation. *Film theory*'s poststructuralist and psychoanalytic focus on subject positionings foregrounds the specificity of the medium and its apparatuses. Yet it fails to radicalize this commitment because it privileges particular apparatuses as a result of its assuming an engaged subjectivity concentrating on and absorbed into the film world. *Cultural studies* uses Gramsci's theory of articulation to foreground notions of struggle and contradiction in the economies of power and to undermine assumptions of historical necessity and critical elitism; yet it continues to confine questions of cultural power to ideological struggles over the double articulation of signification and representation. Its notion of culture remains flat and passionless, and its theory of articulation remains abstract and unmotivated. Finally, *postmodernism* attacks any manifestation of structure (or difference) in the name of multiplicity and dispersion. Its radical contextualism emphasizes historical specificity, pointing to the emergence of new historical events, structures, and experiences. Yet by absolutizing the historical breaks, it fails to describe the specific configurations—the partially continuous contexts—within which these emergent practices are effective.

It is within this theoretical space that I propose to examine how television appropriates certain "postmodern" practices and what their popularity says about the current struggles and relations of power on the cultural terrain. Consider *Miami Vice,* in some ways the most interesting current program, if only because it has so easily divided the audience into fans and enemies. *Miami Vice* is, as its critics have said, all on the surface. And the surface is nothing but a collection of quotations from our own collective historical debris, a mobile game of trivia. It is, in some ways, the perfect televisual image, minimalist (the sparse scenes, the constant long shots, etc.) yet concrete (consider how often we are reminded of the apparent reality of its scene). The narrative is less important than the images. In *Miami Vice,* the cops put on a fashion show (not only of clothes and urban spaces, but of their own "cool" attitudes) to a Top 40 soundtrack. (Importantly, it incorporates into the dominant Top 40 sounds many songs that are less likely to be recognized by the general audience.) They spend their lives not so much patrolling Miami as cruising it, only to rediscover the narrative as an afterthought in the last few minutes. Narrative closure becomes a convenience of the medium more than a demand of our lives. And the spectator as subject all but disappears in the rapid editing and rather uncomfortable camera angles. In a recent ad, it appropriated the very criticisms that have been made of it ("It's wall to wall style"). But of course it has always flaunted its absolute indifference to its content. When asked what was the basic rule for producing the program, the producer responded "No earth tones." Similarly, his recent suggestion to change the color scheme (abandoning its pastels) is a more radical threat to the program than the declining quality of the scripts.

Of course, the gestures of such irony are historically part of the media, both technological and discursive (e.g., Ernie Kovacs, *Saturday Night Live, SCTV,* and David Letterman). Yet it is often missed by those who condemn *Vice* for its representation (and celebration?) of a particularly luxurious lifestyle. After all, the lifestyle of the two cops is a pose and, in some real sense, the style but not the life is theirs. Two actors posing as cops posing as "players" (or poseurs). Crockett's famed boat and car are the property of the Miami Dade Police Department, despite the fact that he seems to go into withdrawal when confronted with the thought of losing them. And when he almost loses his car to the budget cuts, it takes an act of god (or in this case, Lt. Castillo) to restore his right to possess it. In fact, the show makes a great deal of the problematic line between the two levels of performance. As viewers we are never really sure which one is talking, cop or player. Moreover the two lead actors often refer to the line, marking it as both decisive and undecidable, the only site of reality and yet ultimately ironic. But this explains neither its popularity nor the vehemence of those who attack it. Why is dressing "like *Vice*" any different than the sense of style embodied within rock/youth subcultures? If the latter encodes some moment of resistance, why doesn't the former? Is it merely the fact of its origin—TV—or its success—the size of its audience—or the commercial sources of the clothing that render it somehow inherently less capable of marking some struggle?

Such ironic gestures are common across a wide variety of programs. What once were taken as signs of seriousness—a kind of self-reflexivity about the relationship between image and reality—has become an almost requisite but still clichéd gesture. Let me just give one more example. *Moonlighting,* a sort of film noir video version of *Miami Vice,* regularly incorporates such moments into its script but without any sense they need be jarring; for example, the male lead, Addison, rushes in to the police office to "save" his female boss. Although both are detectives, his image of "saving" in this context has apparently demanded that he become a lawyer (he performs as a lawyer, within his performance as hard-boiled detective, within his performance as a surprisingly well-educated, witty, and sensitive "male chauvinist pig," within his performance as an actor). Whether any of these performances are credible seems irrelevant or undecidable; the cop seems unable to decide, his partner is unconvinced. The cop says, "Hey, you can't just break in here like that," to which Addison responds, matter-of-factly, "Tell the writers." In another episode, Addison is made the star of his own TV detective series. And in the final episode of the season, the crew dismantles the set before any narrative conclusion. The lead actors simply walk offstage, trying to decide whether to finally enter into the sexual relation that has been a subtext all season. But once again, the audience is uncertain as to whether the choice is posed in their role as detectives or as actors.

I point to these rather common events in order to suggest that their power and impact cannot be found if we treat them as texts to be interpreted. I propose to take them as billboards to be driven by, roadmarkers that do not tell us where we are going but merely advertise or, better, announce (because they comprise and mark the boundaries, they are both the inside and the limits of) the town we are passing through. Of course, billboards do more than advertise; they are a space in which many different discourses, both serious and playful, appear. They are also sites of struggle, both institutionalized and tactical. The billboard telling us that the New York Deli is two miles left at the next turnoff does not mislead us into thinking that we are in, or even remotely near, New York. Its direct appeals, its inscribed meanings, its specific message, seem oddly irrelevant and rarely useful (whether because we are driving too quickly or because we see them everyday). It doesn't really matter whether it is another billboard for McDonald's, an anonymous bank, Pepsi, a PSA, or a political organization. It is not a sign to be interpreted, but rather a piece of a puzzle to be assembled.

I want to suggest that interpreting the effects of popular culture, and its politics, is less like reading a book than like driving by the billboards that mark the system of interstate highways, county roads, and city streets that is the United States. (This is not to offer the street as the only reality, for there are real events taking place off the roads—in houses, factories, jails, etc. Further, if one wants to understand the United States, a balance must be struck between the local detail and the national structures. The United States is neither New York nor Texas nor Main Street. It is, somehow, scattered among all of these.)

We might say that any individual billboard is indifferent. It is neither built upon a radical sense of textual difference nor does it erase all difference. The billboard's identity and power somehow depend upon its own indifference to its apparent lack of difference. It is different only because it is indifferent to difference. Indifference describes a particular historical structure of autorelationship enacted in the contextual play between identity and difference. It is this notion that I wish to explore here. If semiotics teaches us that identity is constituted out of difference, and postmodernism that identity has disappeared with the erasure of difference, I want to argue that the effectivity of TV is precisely the complex effects it generates by operating, in specific ways, on the line of indifference. TV practices function in part within a larger context that is reshaping (1) the powers and pleasures of identities and differences, and (2) the relationship between ideology and affect. Together these define an affective economy around television. As a response to a particular historical set of events, at least a part of TV's functioning involves rearticulating what we might describe as the social structure and power of difference within an affective democracy. In the present paper, I want only to lay out the theoretical and critical framework for such analyses, for it is necessary to get some sense of the cultural landscape before one can begin to locate particular events within it.

POST NO BILLS

The most compelling example of a critical theory that responds to the specificity of a popular medium is film theory. But film theory rests on the assumed privileging not only of a particular apparatus, but also of a particular form of engaged subjectivity. Despite Benjamin's descriptions, film theory (and even most popular critics) act as though viewers were engaged in a concentrative act in which they are absorbed into the world of the film.

It is irrelevant whether this is empirically accurate (what about all those kids who go to films on dates, sometimes explicitly as an occasion for making out: are they absorbed into the film, or is the film absorbed into their context) or whether it is itself constitutive of the ways we expect people, ourselves included, to behave while watching films.[1] Such theories do little to explain the popularity (and reaction against) diverse media events, whether *E.T., Rambo, Back to the Future, Out of Africa, The Color Purple,* and so on, or *Dynasty, Hill Street Blues, Cagney and Lacey, Miami Vice, The Bill Cosby Show,* MTV, megaevents, reruns, game shows, particular ads (which are hyped and watched with the same intensity as programs), wrestling, and so on, not to mention the various clones—good and bad, usually bad—that have emerged. Moreover if we try to untangle the audiences for these, we will find a complex series of overlapping sympathies and antagonisms. And we will find little help in preexisting sociological or political positions (e.g., the left-wing critic who, like so many fans, knew he had to hate *Rambo* but loved it "once the shooting started," or all those who recognized how manipulative *E.T.* was and yet still enjoyed it). Recent work, even within film theory, has attempted to move beyond the original position's (e.g., the classic *Screen* theory) inadequate assumption that its reading of the text describes the necessary effects of the text on the audience. That is to say, film theory finds itself facing much the same dilemma as its sometimes nemesis, cultural studies: the problem of the gap between productive interests, textual practices, and consumption effects or, in simpler terms, the gap between encoding and decoding. This problematic is now inscribed into the heart of cultural interpretation (in a variety of disguises—e.g., intertextuality).

However, the problems of cultural interpretation are, if anything, magnified to an unprecedented extent by the functioning of the mass media apparatuses. Not only is every media event mediated by other texts, but it is almost impossible to know what constitutes the bounded text that might be interpreted or that is actually consumed. It is absurd to think that anyone watches a single television show, or even a single series, just as it is absurd to think that only by watching it is one brought under its intertextual filigree. But there is even more to the intertextuality of TV, for it defines an "indifference of content." There is, in fact, a significant difference between watching a particular program (which we all do sometimes) and watching TV (which we all do most of the time). That is to say, the specifics of the episode are often less important than the fact of the TV's being on (e.g., one form of viewing involves TV fans as "couch potatoes" who often "veg out" in front of the tube rather than pay any sort of normal concentrated attention to it), or the fact of the latest installment (repeat or not) of a particular series. (*Hill Street Blues*'s effort to have the audience determine which episodes would be repeated was an interesting recognition of this dilemma.)

Film theory correctly recognized that it was not defining a particular medium but rather an entire apparatus defined by particular contexts of production and consumption, as well as by the technological appropriations of the medium. The very force and impact—the presence, if you will—of any medium changes significantly as it is moved from one context to another (a bar, a theater, the living room, the bedroom, the beach, a rock concert—all of these are occasions of TV's delegated look and distracted glance). Each medium is then a mobile term, taking shape as it situates itself—almost always comfortably—within the different roadside rests of our lives. That is, the text is located not only intertextually, but in a range of apparatuses as well, defined technologically but also by other social relations and activities. Thus one rarely just listens to the radio, watches TV, or even goes to the movies: one is studying, dating, driving somewhere else, partying and so on. Not only is it the case that the "same" text is different in different contexts, but its multiple appearances are complexly intereffective.

This implies two further practices of indifference as constitutive of the media: the indifference of context and of form. The first refers to the fact not merely that people use or consume media in different ways, but that the media are themselves inseparable from the diversity of contexts within which they are identifiable. The second marks the way that the mobility of the media constantly undermines any attempt to define them apart from and as different from particular cultural forms. What is the medium and what the form of television? What is its relation to film or video or even music? Is radio the medium and rock and roll the form? But then what is the relationship of rock and roll on records, on television, "live," and so forth.

In fact the indifference of the media displaces the problematic of cultural theory from that of coding (encoding, decoding, transcoding) to that of the apparatus itself (articulation). Television makes this displacement particularly obvious and disconcerting, if only because the apparatuses are so complexly interrelated and so rapidly changing (e.g., larger screens, higher-quality resolution, VCRs and remote controls, stereo, cable, the incorporation of TV into public places like discos, bars, and concert stadiums—where the choice of what to watch becomes self-consciously problematic). There are nevertheless some things that cut across the majority of TV apparatuses. Television viewing is a large temporal part of our lives, with prolonged viewing periods that suggest the formation of viewing habits. Certainly this has partly determined its ordinariness, its taken-for-grantedness, its integration into the mundanities of everyday life, and simultaneously its constant interruption by and continuity with our other daily routines, activities, and social relationships. One rarely makes plans to watch TV—although it is on occasion a social event to be shared with friends. Not since the fifties has it been privileged in anything like the ways in which "going to the movies" is. Moreover one rarely intently gazes at TV, allowing oneself to be absorbed into the work, but rather we distractedly glance at it or absorb it into our own momentary mood or position, or treat it merely as a framework of another reality (when only the character types and narrative facts are important, as in daytime soaps). Its taken-for-grantedness makes it appear trivial, an unimportant moment of our lives, one in which we certainly invest no great energy. And yet its power to restructure the temporal and spatial aspects of our lives remains unquestionable. And it continues, across a broad spectrum of people and programs, to continuously fascinate us. TV makes the trivial into the important; again, the structure of indifference appears. TV is empowered precisely because we are comparatively indifferent to it even as it is indifferent to us (it doesn't demand our presence, yet it is always waiting for us). It is this "indifference of the fan" that makes even the idea of a television *fan* seem strange.

We might also point to the fragmentation and interruption of the discourses constantly appearing on and disappearing from the TV screen.[2] There is no doubt that this is an accurate description, both textually and phenomenologically. This does not mean, however, that segments, of whatever size, do not take on some meanings for the viewers. Television is constructed from intersecting discourses; it is an assemblage of segments that need not (but can) bear an obvious relation to their most immediate context. Yet they always do have relations to other displaced segments, and particular segments can regularly or momentarily take on relationships to one another. These connections, however, are neither necessarily part of the phenomenology of viewing nor dependent upon the ability to read such intertextual interpretations from the screen. This fragmentation is only magnified by the interruptions built into the viewing contexts, and it is obviously increased by the emerging technological capacities to zip and zap within the programs and around the channels. This fragmentation is also evident in the secondary status TV assigns to narrative continuity, preferring to establish a limited continuity by repetition (of scenes, of issues, of images) and a broader continuity by its unique relation to itself. In that relation, television creates its own history and its own reality (as a CBS ad recently offered, "Come into our world") within which programs and characters increasingly refer to each other (Nick at Nite now defines its viewers by their media history). This is an intertextuality that requires no elite knowledge or even actual viewing history. It is history inscribed upon the screen, history as and within its own images. And yet it is a history that, increasingly, is the proof of our own existence.

Television criticism has yet to confront the problems posed by the determinations of TV apparatuses; it either ignores the problem entirely or else depends upon limiting itself to a small assumed set of apparatuses defined by the conjunction of a primitive video technology (small screen, low-quality reproduction, both visually and aurally), a particular domestic context (usually in a semipublic private space like the living room), and a capitalist imperative (to sell bodies and thus to hold the viewer's attention). The conjunction of these features is taken to explain the peculiar signifying practices of this supposedly dominant apparatus: the importance of sound (it makes sense to listen to TV on a radio; a similar connivance for cinema would be absurd, although the changing source of revenues for a film increasingly requires adjusting the ratio of image to sound); the minimalism of the image; its constant domestic framing and appeal; its ability to become "a relay of a reality already there," that is, its apparent status as a "live" window on the world. TV becomes our representative; we do not identify with the position of the camera so much as "delegate" (J. Ellis 1982) our look to it. It is this lack of voyeurism that explains why everything becomes fictionalized by the cinematic apparatus while everything appears real in the TV apparatus.

But such descriptions, however insightful, still fail to question the limits and effectiveness of this apparatus, nor do they explain the fluidity with which television has moved into different apparatuses, both less and more private, both higher and lower technologies, both larger and smaller screens, and so forth. Further, they fail to face the consequences of the fact that viewers rarely "pay attention" in the way that sponsors want, and there is little relation between the TV's being on and either the presence of bodies in front of it or even a limited concentration or interpretive activity invested in it. (Nevertheless we continue to speak as though all of the values we can read in the text are somehow magically inscribed upon the minds of the viewers.) Nor can this descriptive/interpretive framework question the actual effects of the television or of particular viewing habits, unless it simply blames televi-

sion (through conscious or unconscious practices) for what we too often take
to be the sorrowful state of political and moral consciousness in the world
today.

On the other hand, approaches that attempt to understand the particular
decoding or transcoding practices by which particular audiences appropriate
the texts into the contexts of their own discursive competences fall prey to
the ever-diminishing return on sociological differences. In fact they end up
largely ignoring the determining power of the apparatus in favor of the signifying networks of connotation. That is, such theories cannot escape the
problematic of meaning and representation. Their sophistication lies in the
recognition of the gap between the two terms (requiring either a double articulation or a process of subject-positioning; both of these serve to describe
how some meanings become empowered as representations or how some
signifying practices are also ideological). Nevertheless, they still fail to take
into account the radical implications of the gap between text, meaning, and
representation (or, more broadly, the gaps between production, texts, and
consumption or between interests, practices, and effects). They fail to recognize that "people making history but in conditions not of their own making"
is as necessary an insight in the field of culture as it is in political economy.
People are constantly struggling, however naïvely and ineffectively, to bring
what they are given into their own contexts, to make something out of it that
would give them a little more purchase on their lives, a little more control,
that would enable them to live their lives a bit more as they see fit (i.e.,
according to their images and desires—moral, ideological, and affective).

MAPS FOR SALE

If not every meaning is a representation and not every text has representational effects, it may also be true that texts may have effects other than
meaning-effects, and meanings themselves may be involved in relations
other than representational. That is, the connection between a particular cultural practice and its actual effects may be a complex multiplicity of lines or
articulations. But even this is too simple, for it suggests that articulations are
themselves individually simple or straightforward links. Instead we must
recognize, on the one hand with Hall (1985), that articulation is always a
struggle and, on the other hand with Deleuze and Guattari (1981), that such
lines are themselves fragmented and rarely proceed in what might be represented as a straight line. A text may, in some or all contexts, have meaning-

effects, but it may have others (e.g., TV is rearranging the physical space of the house; laws against drugs give shape to the commodity structure of that market; lower speed limits contradict the design practices of highways); and in some contexts, meanings may have representational effects, but they may also have other effects (e.g., on our mood). Effects are always intereffective, on the way from and to other effects. That a particular meaning-effect also has a representational effect may in part be determined by other articulations (e.g., subject-positionings).

This increasingly complex and convoluted description offers the possibility of placing the media in a context of effects that are not necessarily defined or completed by signification (i.e., it is not merely a matter of recognizing the difference between representation and fantasy) and that cannot be guaranteed in advance. One might perhaps add that meaning-effects are not a simple category: there are different forms of meaning (e.g., narrative, connotative, evaluative, reflective). The ways in which the meaningfulness of *Miami Vice*, *Hill Street Blues*, and *The Bill Cosby Show* are defined by and matter for the fan (i.e., are effective) are quite different. This becomes even clearer if we compare such "traditional" forms of programming with MTV or wrestling. Yet in any program or form, we have to leave open the possibilities of different effective meaning-forms (e.g., a large number of people claim not to like wrestling but to watch it because they like Hulk Hogan; what then are they seeing?).

This model presents what I take to be the postmodernism of theory in Deleuze and Guattari (1981) and Foucault (1981) (Grossberg 1982). One can describe it by four assumptions: (1) anti-essentialism (radical contextualism, overdetermination, no necessary guarantees); (2) a "monism of pluralities" (heterodoxy—otherness rather than difference, a theory of practices as effectivity); (3) wild realism (a materialism that recognizes the multiplicity of planes of effects); (4) articulation (the historical specificity of and struggles over structures of identity and difference). Each of these assumptions has both a theoretical and a political inflection. For example, the last points to the need to move, theoretically, between different levels of abstraction and, politically, between different levels of structures (hierarchies) of power relations.[3] On the other hand, the first challenges any theoretical hierarchy and demands, politically, that one not seek the high ground of elitism but always the quicksand of the masses.

Postmodern theory also requires us to reposition ourselves in the contexts we are describing (for we are always doing more than describing), which is not the same as, but might well include, problematizing our relationship to them. Nor is it merely a case of, as Foucault might have said, "taking sides." It rather involves moving through the complexity of social positionings and social identities (which, while not the same, are closely connected), of recognizing that any individual position (including that of the TV fan) is actually mobilely situated in a fluid context. Thus being a fan does not guarantee how one watches TV or even a particular program; there is a complex set of practices and identities that are differentially distributed within particular apparatuses. They do not simply vary with the program, although that is sometimes determining. (In particular contexts, one cannot talk during *Hill Street Blues,* while conversation during *Miami Vice* is often allowed if it is related to the program, and during the Super Bowl talk is requisite and not necessarily related to the game. But that all changes when one moves the TV into a different social context.) It is not merely that individuality is fragmented, but rather that it functions as, and is articulated out of, a nomadic wandering through ever-changing positions and apparatuses (dance fever). The critic has not only to map out the lines of this mobility but also recognize that only by entering into this nomadic relation to the media can he or she map the complex social spaces of media effects. We need a vocabulary to describe the shifting and contradictory partial relations of nomadic subjectivity, a subjectivity that is always moving along different vectors and changing its shape, but always having a shape.

Nomadic subjectivity describes a posthumanist theory of the subject. Rejecting the existential subject who has a single unified identity that somehow exists in the same way in every practice, it proposes a subject who is constantly remade, reshaped as a mobilely situated set of vectors in a fluid context. But also rejecting the poststructural deconstruction of the subject into a fractured, fragmented, and ad hoc discursive production, it proposes that it does matter who is acting and from where, that the subject is the site of struggle, an ongoing site of articulation with its own history. The nomadic subject is amoebalike, struggling to win some space for itself in its local context. While its shape is always determined by its nomadic articulations, it always has a shape that is itself effective.

There are, however, at least two other ways in which the term "postmodernism" is used: as a cultural description and as a historical description. Without directly engaging the enormous variety of discussions that have taken place on these issues, let me propose alternative terms for these (if only to avoid the temptation to slide from a common signifier—"the postmodern"—to an assumed or necessary relationship between the domains, as if one could easily move from Jameson's [1984] convincing descriptions of cultural practices to Baudrillard's [1983a] simulacrum to structures of late capitalism): pose-modernism and hypermoderism (admittedly ugly terms). "Pose-modernism" refers not to some constitutive textual structures or meanings, but rather to a set of discursive practices that are only visible in the complex articulations within and among the various cultural media. It is the media's performance of particular poses—and a pose, however artificial and local, is never constituted merely by a single instance or image. Many of these practices are, in fact, modernist, but they are articulated differently as poses within the context of the media. But if they are poses, they also relate problematically to the real (that reality is nothing but poses is, of course, a pose: nothing matters and what if it did). Thus the fact that certain media practices clearly challenge the line between the real and the image does not tell us what its effects are, or even what the practices themselves are, in the broader contexts of different media apparatuses or social formations.

"Hypermodernism" points to the fact that many of the historical structures and experiences that so-called postmodernists describe depend upon the continuation, although perhaps rearticulation of, many of the structures and experiences of modernity. This is not to deny the emergence of new historical events (e.g., the destructibility and disposability of the earth; significant redistributions of wealth, population, and power; new structures of commodity production such as infotech; and new media of communication)[4] and of new historical experiences (e.g., that there are no transcendental values capable of giving shape and direction to our lives, a decreased faith in progress, new kinds of pessimism and cynicism). To draw upon Hall (1986b), if reality was never as real as we have constructed it, it's not quite as unreal as we imagine it. If subjectivity was never as coherent as we imagine it, it's not quite so incoherent as we would like it to be. And if power was never as simple or monolithic as we dream it (reproducing itself, requiring giants and magical subjects to change it), it's not quite as dispersed and unchallengeable as we fear. The specificity of the contemporary social formation is more complex than simple descriptions of the simulacrum or late capitalism suggest, although these are both real events and have real effects. I want to use postmodern theory to help explicate the uneven and even contradictory relations between the pose-modernism of the media and the hypermodernism of contemporary life.

HITCHHIKING ACROSS AMERICA

It is time to return to billboards, although the task is qualified in the context of postmodern theory. It is important not to confuse the project of looking at cultural practices as billboards to make visible particular levels of effects, structure, and struggle, with the postmodern theoretical practice. The conflation of these two seems to be a fundamental flaw in much postmodern criticism. In the first place, one is operating at a more abstract level than that of concrete media contexts involving concrete individuals. The postmodern critics often mythologize America—they have the comfort of distance—by confusing its highways (certainly a real part), its surfaces, for its concrete social life. There is no guarantee that effects on one level will appear in a corresponding form at another level; on the other hand, they must presumably be having effects, and those who would ignore the effectivity of surfaces fail to adequately confront the media. Thus what I am proposing would be only part of a constant struggle to describe and articulate the relations of the media to social life and history.

In the second place, while the image of billboards (perhaps like that of the simulacrum) seems to collapse reality into its surface, postmodern theory reminds us that the surface is itself plural. That something does not immediately appear on the surface neither denies its reality nor prevents it from appearing on the surface at another place, from another set of positionings. But no structure is necessarily and always "deeper" or somehow more real than that which appears on the surface. If we want to understand something that we intuitively recognize as American culture, which exists, without any essential identity, in many different local forms and contexts, then the commitment to localism is likely to either lead into indeterminacy or some sort of phenomenological attempt to reconstruct the locale. That is, without any maps we have no idea about how to begin moving through the local contexts. Obviously we are not entirely without maps: economic relations, ideological relations—semiotic and psychoanalytic, psychological effects, phenomenological structures. Each potentially enables us to chart a particular set of effects and to locate particular sites of power and struggle.

But none of these seems to explain the enormous power and popularity of the media, especially TV. In contemporary America, young children seem to favor their televisions over siblings and friends, often over their fathers and sometimes even over their mothers. The "popular," whatever its economic and ideological effects may be, seems to work at yet another level (the affective),[5] and in fact the very notion of popularity (which entails certain kinds of investment of energy, e.g., enjoyment) seems to signal the unequal—and perhaps even unusual—weight of the affective. I want to read, across the broad landscape of American popular culture, television as billboards for certain affective structures that emerge from and impact upon every level of contemporary social life. Rather than talking about particular programs or episodes, I want to talk about certain practices, gestures, or statements (Foucault) that appear, in numerous forms, across different media and forms. The question is how they function in the affective economy of the popular, what they are "announcing" to us on TV once we begin to follow the highways.

In fact, I want to talk about three related sets of such gestures: irony, repetition, and excess, and the three forms of indifference that they announce. The gesture and the annunciation are inseparable on the billboard. I have already said some things about the indifference of television. To put it most bluntly, TV is indifferent to differences even as it constructs differences out of the very absence of difference. I have also said something about the first of these billboards: the particular forms of media irony by which the media declare the indifference of reality.[6] In a certain sense, everything becomes equal on TV (e.g., the late-night talk show) by apparently erasing the line between image and reality. But it is not the case that everything is appropriated to become a media object; rather its reality depends upon its already being such an image, speaking the discourses of TV. The A-Team can bring together, all battling on the side of justice (and America), B. A. Barrakas (aka Mr.T., as a quasi-guerrilla), Hulk Hogan (a wrestler), and William "the Refrigerator" Perry (a football star). And at the end of the episode, as if to remind us that the line between TV and reality is problematic, "Refrig" gives that week's victims (now saved by the A-Team, Hulk, and Refrig) a Chicago Bears hat, but B. A. and Hulk are quite annoyed at not having received their own. Moreover, in a few weeks all of them will appear in a closed-circuit, internationally broadcast wrestling extravaganza. More radically, consider the list of guest stars from programs like Miami Vice, which has included not only rock and roll stars but politicians (negotiations are under way with Bush, and Kissinger and Ford have already appeared on Dynasty), criminals (G. Gordon Liddy), business figures (Lee Iacocca), columnists (Bob Greene), artists (Julian Beck), and so on. The intersection of TV and reality, TV's indifference to reality, is marked everywhere on the screen (wrestling, comedy, the popularity of Bill Cosby, Reagan) but nowhere so beautifully as by contemporary advertisements: in one particularly apt commercial for caffeine-free Pepsi, we are shown scenes of life in TV-land while the voice-over says, "For those whose life is already exciting enough." The point is not that the line has disappeared or that TV is somehow erasing it, but rather that its effectivity is being changed by television's indifference to it.

A second moment of television's indifference, an indifference of identity or meaning, is announced over and over again in the various forms of repetition that TV practices. It is the peculiar way in which television deals with the difference between the same and the different. One can recall Andy Warhol's attempt to distinguish his enjoyment in seeing the exact same thing over and over from the everyday pleasures of seeing almost the same thing over and over. But the distinction quickly collapses. At every level, television seems to be structured on repetition: episodes, character types, narratives, program genres, programming (e.g., reruns and repeats), ads. Television is, at all these levels, the most predictable set of images one can imagine. Yet there are differences: whether one prime-time soap looks just like another, whether one episode of *Miami Vice* says the exact same thing as every other, somehow the pleasure of the viewing depends upon the ability to renegotiate the difference that difference makes. Baudrillard (1983a) has pointed to the implosion of difference in the media and argued that, as a result, the media are indifferent to meaning. This is an argument against those who attempt to see reality represented in the media, or who attempt to understand the media's power in its repetition of (what is apparently almost always) the same message. Rather I would argue that TV is indifferent to meaning, that is, that meaning is necessary but irrelevant: that TV moves through meaning to get somewhere else, and it doesn't particularly matter what meanings it uses. Its minimalism, its often cartoonish sense of reality is quite allowable because the point is not to communicate particular meanings as if they were structures to be lived in and experienced. Moreover television does not need to worry about the line between realism and fantasy; it presents images of the indifference of meaning, fantasy, and reality (which is not to say that the viewer confuses these domains).

If the popularity of TV programs is not immediately dependent on ideological issues (e.g., a recent Feiffer cartoon of a woman in front of the TV: "Ronald

Reagan talks to me on television. No nonsense . . . and sincere. Who cares if he's lying?"), perhaps we can get some grip on it by looking at a third set of gestures common not only to TV, but to the range of popular media, namely, excess, which announces an indifference of the norm (even as television constantly reinscribes it). Televisual excess takes many forms: visual excess, stylistic excess, verbal excess, imagistic excess (especially in its images of violence, wealth, and sexual titillation), and so on. But perhaps most important is what one might call the emotional excess, which is made possible by TV's indifference to meaning and reality. Current TV's most powerful annunciation is its emotionalism, the fact that it is structured by a series of movements between extreme highs and extreme lows. In fact it presents an image of an affective economy marked on the one side by an extreme (postmodern) cynicism ("Life is hard and then you die") and on the other by an almost irrational celebration of the possibilities of winning against all odds. Often these two are combined, as in the *Miami Vice* genre. While it is hard to know whether TV or reality is crazier and more unreal, it is clear that TV is the site of emotions more "real" and more intense than those we can comfortably claim for ourselves. It is almost as if, in various ways, TV viewers get to live out the emotional highs and lows of their lives on TV, as if they just want to feel something that strongly, no matter what it is ("I'd rather feel bad than not feel anything at all"), to feel what it's like to believe in something that strongly regardless of what it is ("I believe in the truth though I lie a lot"). And this does not require any simple identification, either with the camera (for we allow it to move, as if by proxy), the characters (for they are typical and yet unlike us), or the narrative uncertainty (for one always knows how it will end).

Baudrillard (1983b) argues that, with the implosion of difference, the indifference of meaning, reality too has collapsed into its model. The subject, the social, the political—all have become simulacra, located in a logic of deterrence that has redefined the operation of power. But Baudrillard confuses the collapse of an ideology of the real (including its various scenes) with the problematizing of the link between ideology and reality. Again, it is not the social that has imploded but a particular ideological structuration (private/public) that seems no longer effective. Baudrillard makes the real into nothing but an effect of meaning so that when meaning collapses, the real must as well. But if, as I have argued, reality is more than meaning ("wild realism"), and if in fact meaning has not disappeared but merely been rearticulated into different relations within certain historical structures, then Baudrillard is less an analyst of our historical condition than another of its many billboards. Increasingly, reading Baudrillard is no different from watching *Miami Vice* (as one friend told me, "I dress like *Vice,* I talk like Baudrillard"; again, there is no guarantee that this signals the commodification of knowledge rather than the emergence of new forms of popular intellect). The social may not be meaningfully invoked (it may have lost its "existential" meaning), but that doesn't mean it is not still effectively constituted through other discursive effects. It is easy to lose sight of this gap when reading Baudrillard, just as it is when watching *Miami Vice,* because his writing, like the world he celebrates, moves so quickly that nothing is allowed to impinge upon it, nothing can break its slippery surface.

In particular, the televisual practices of excess point to an emerging historical contradiction between affect and ideology. If the relation between the two is normally anaclitic, the postwar years have seen it broken. That is, at least a part of the structures of hyper-modernism is marked by a series of events that challenged our ability to make sense of our relationship to our world and ourselves, to normalcy and the future. Not the least important of these events was the incorporation of such apocalyptic images into the mass media and popular culture. While history seemed to demand a different structure of affective investment, there seemed to be no way of making sense of the emerging struggle.

What appeared was a crisis in the relationship between common sense and faith. Within this gap, it is not the case that one doesn't live ideological values (or that nothing matters) but that these seem not to speak to our affective mood. It is as if one were to experience and in certain ways live values without actually investing in them (it doesn't matter what matters), because our affective investments seem to have already been determined elsewhere, in another scene. This structure—whether it has its own tradition or not—seems to have become increasingly dominant, a common announcement on our cultural billboards: images of the contradiction between contemporary affective organizations and the ideological appeals that attempt to articulate them. Thus happiness becomes an impossible but necessary reality (a bit like déjà vu with amnesia), or rather its possible ideological relevance collapses into its extreme affective images. It is as if our ideological maps and our "mattering maps" were unable to intersect, unable to articulate one another. Each continues to exist with its own autonomy, although our sanity apparently demands their integration. It is no longer a matter of seeking, in culture, to articulate the new organization of our affective relations to reality (as in much of high modernism), but rather of locating the site of the contradiction itself (pose-modernism).

Television announces that site in its own performance of indifference, in its practices of irony, repetition, and excess. It does more, however, for it also offers, in the apparatuses of its viewing, a strategic response to the contradiction between affect and ideology by placing the nomadic subject within an affective democracy that is, I believe, constitutive of almost all of the televisual apparatuses. In this particular economy, every image is equally open to affective investment because everything is a media event, a style, a pose. This doesn't mean that we don't live certain poses, or that we don't have to. But it also does not mean that we necessarily live in their ideological spaces even though we might speak some of their languages. The particular democratic form of this economy responds to the broad ideological demands of subjectification and commodification. Both, as constant social positionings with their own pleasures and pains, negate the indifference of affect and thus ultimately the power of affect itself. TV reestablishes a site of and source for affective living within its democratic economy. It does this by constituting an empowering form of identity: the mundane exotic. It celebrates the ordinariness of the exotic and the exoticism of the ordinary. It locates identity in the absence of any difference by affectively investing in the difference of the same. Thus the televisual star system is radically unlike the classic Hollywood version, for the contemporary star is, in most cases, necessarily like us in ways that violate the code of the Hollywood star system. His or her fantastic difference is affectively empowered (as style and chance) and is effective only at that level.[7]

It may be useful to briefly contrast the affective economies of TV and rock and roll (Grossberg 1984b). While both, as popular media, operate in what I call an affective economy determined largely by the postwar contradiction between affect and ideology, the forms of their economies are radically distinct. If TV responds to the general structure of subjectification/commodification, rock and roll responds to the narrower structure of terror/boredom. If TV constitutes an affective democracy within which the mundane exotic relocates identity, rock and roll constitutes an affective elitism built upon investments in "fun." This is not to deny significant overlaps between the two economies; for example, TV may be fun at times and rock and roll may build mundane exotic identities (e.g., Elvis Presley and Bruce Springsteen: Is it for this reason that they are, respectively, the "King" and the "Boss"?), but they are not dominant or determining in quite the same ways. Moreover one can see the interaction of the two economies at various sites of the media apparatuses, for example, lip-synching on TV and in bars.

Obviously the economy I have described is precisely that which is often attacked by many of television's ideological critics. But I have tried at least to imply that this economy may be an empowering one for many of its viewers precisely because it is not ideological. It is by now a common critical defense to argue that TV's economy is a domestic one, built upon structures of security and comfort. TV is a domestic medium; but it need not constantly domesticate every image, nor is it already domesticated, without any role in ongoing cultural struggles. TV is domestic in that it is indifferent to the difference between subordination and resistance. It is both immensely public and intensely private and, once again, its power lies precisely on the line that marks the indifference. Television is not often an active site of struggle, but that does not mean it is not involved, in important and constant ways, through indirection, in active struggles.

Postmodernity and Affect: All Dressed Up

with No Place to Go

INTRODUCTION: A MODEST PROPOSAL

The discourses of postmodernism are undoubtedly both too anxious and too immodest. Simply amassing historical events (atomic warfare, televisualization, computerization, etc.) or texts (whether in galleries, streets, cinemas, or televisions) does not justify the fascinating and ultrarapid leap into such highly charged abstractions as the "disappearance of the real" or the appearance of the schizophrenic subject. In the attempt to control our anxiety, we might inscribe above our desks Nietzsche's admonition that when studying monsters, one must take care not to become one oneself. Similarly, in an effort to be more modest, we might add his observation that what is important is not the news that god is dead, but the time this news takes to have its effects. The first reminds us that differences that are politically as well as theoretically significant continue to exist; a narrative that makes the impossibility of narrative into an apocalypse is still a narrative. The second reminds us that history is complex; it is produced as events move through it, along different vectors, at different speeds.

Yet while I am critical of the various attempts to talk *about* the postmodern, I do not want to abandon the effort to understand contemporary cultural practices in light of the question of historical difference and specificity. To put it in this way is, I hope, to offer a more modest way of locating the postmodern within contemporary political and intellectual work. Correlatively I want to suggest a more modest strategy of theorizing around concrete events and effects without fetishizing them and without abandoning the gains that have been made by theoretical critiques of essentialism. Anti-essentialism should not be confused with a fetishism of the particular. I want to distinguish anti-essentialist arguments from antitheoretical arguments. While we must begin by approaching contemporary practices and events as statements to be, as Donna Haraway (1987) has phrased it, "taken literally," we must not abandon the "detour through theory" that Marx (1973) thought necessary to transform the empirically available into the concretely understood. We must attempt to move, slowly and carefully, between different levels of abstraction, from specific events (any description of which is always an abstraction) to the most decontextualized categories and concepts, and back again. This is a way of recognizing, first, the complexity of social realities, and second, one's own socially determined position within the history one describes, and yet not abandoning the possibility of realistic and value-laden political intervention. Will Straw recently characterized the "style" of many of those who write about the postmodern as "a discourse of cumulative anecdote . . . signifying the epic/epoch" (1987, n.p.). This leap, which confuses accumulation as the construction of a text within its interpretation, constitutes a powerful ideological moment in which any (politically) demystifying impulse is abandoned. The accumulation of fact, even when framed within a narrative, may offer some semantic sense, but it constitutes neither an account nor a theory.

Still there is something extremely compelling about such anecdotal logics, and so let me begin by simply recalling a few examples of postmodern statements, drawn from a very narrow range of discourses: the recent emergence of a style of television ads that can be described as cynical, if not nihilistic, and superrealistic (by which I mean that they offer the grainy and gritty details of everyday life with no sense of transcendence, not even that of the grandeur of meaninglessness): Jordache's film-noir scenarios of despair and the imminent collapse of our lives, constructed through images of a girl running away from home, a boy trying to make sense of his parents' divorce; Honda's many fragmented scenes of urban life and decay or, more powerfully, an ad that offers a series of graffiti-scrawled questions—from the existential to the mundane—and then suggests, "If it's not an answer, at least it's not another question"; Converse's image of a couple breaking up in which the assertion that they can and will remain friends is greeted with an ice-cream cone in the face, followed by the order "Take a walk"; the self-conscious irony of Nike's commercial using "Revolution"; Levi's commercials predicated on the assumption that after everyone and everything one has loved has left, you still have your jeans; a Volkswagen commercial in which the young driver readily admits to his mother that "It's not supposed to be a nice car. [After all,] it's the eighties." These are successful advertising campaigns, but what are they sell-ing: depression? reality?

Such statements are of course to be found all across contemporary cultural production. On television, consider USA Network's moment in which direc-tor Terry Gilliam describes how he likes the idea of thinking he can change the world and of fighting as hard as he can to do it but knowing all along that it's a lot of nonsense; MTV's self-promos; post-holocaust films like *River's Edge* (where the holocaust has already happened) and *Mad Max* (where the high-tech utopian future resembles the contemporary image of a war zone). In fiction: for example, however classist the yuppie culture of *Less than Zero,* statements resonate beyond their class: "But you don't need anything. You have everything." "No I don't." "What don't you have?" "I don't have any-thing to lose" (Ellis 1985: 189–90). Or in slogans and humor: a recent Tufts University newspaper that offered the following two statements as the "best philosophy of life": "Don't sweat the small stuff. It's all small stuff."

But if we are to understand such statements, it is not a matter of looking for the formal practices that mark their textual difference. If anything, the vari-ous postmodern texts often betray themselves as "modernism with a ven-geance," magnifying and multiplying many of the formal practices consti-tutive of various modernist movements. This is, of course, not to deny a significant difference between them: what was a crisis for the modernists has become common sense, if not the occasion of celebration. If one makes an effort to construct such a postmodern aesthetics, the generic diversity is over-whelming. One would have to include, or at least justify excluding, a wide range of texts: not only the hyperfragmented, the hyperrealistic, and the neo-historical (in which the real history of the audience provides the codes, e.g., Keith Haring's Jetsons-inspired graffiti or Stanley Kubrick's use of "The Mickey Mouse Club Theme" in the closing to *Full Metal Jacket*) but also the neofantastic; one would have to include not only the self-consciously ironic and deconstructive (Max Headroom, Pee Wee Herman) statements, but neo-nostalgic ones (*Rambo, Top Gun, Back to the Future, E.T.*) and cynical ones (*Blue Velvet, The Life and Times of Molly Dodd*); one would have to include not only the new horror and gore movies, but the various "New Age" texts as well. And of course part of the very structure of the assemblage of "postmod-ern texts" is precisely that a text need not appear postmodern to be appreci-ated as such (e.g., the appropriation of various reruns and styles and, in some cases, the instant appropriation of a text as "intentionally doublecoded": *Dragnet,* superhero comics).[1]

The point is that neither such individual statements nor the formal categories we construct can be separated from the context within which their particular effects are articulated. They are not texts to be interpreted nor merely embodiments of, nor microcosmic representations of, a postmodern world. They are, as Deleuze and Guattari (1977) would have it, point-signs always imbricated in contradictory, complex, and changing rhizomatic contexts. They take great pains to differentiate such a "linguistics of flows" from the "linguistics of the signifier," even from one in which the transcendence of the signifier is established only by its withdrawal. Point-signs have no identity, no difference; they are merely the intersections and fissures of flows and breaks along vectors of effectivity.

One response to the impossibility of finding meaning intrinsic to a particular text has been to suggest that our understanding of cultural statements must depend crucially on how they are decoded, used, and even enjoyed by particular audiences. For example, what makes the above examples of advertisements so striking is that probably the most common response is "Of course. So what?" What seems obviously "commonsensical" and, at the same time, ironic today would have been considered only thirty years ago, within the terms of modernism, to be the mark of either insanity or poetic genius. But once again, we must tread cautiously, for while the practices of appropriation, interpretation, and consumption are significant aspects of the concrete effects and articulations of these statements, these practices are no less problematic than the statements themselves. Again, while they have to be taken literally, that only defines the beginning of our work, not its conclusion. They are in fact part of the context we are constructing that is then in need of some accounting. The surfaces of everyday life—whether in practices and relations of production or consumption—may be the site of important struggles, but they are not the totality of the social formation nor of the determinations of everyday life.

Appeals to neither encoding nor decoding can define the answer or even the language of the answer. Whether we begin with observations of, for example, the increasing formal and self-conscious fragmentation of cultural texts, or the tone of certain texts as they seemingly speak the ultrarapid languages of obsolescence and fascination, we have only begun to define the problem. Similarly to take account of the ways in which people appropriate, decode, and enjoy these texts only continues the necessary work of constructing the complicated space within which the question of interpretation has to be asked. One can only begin to understand how these postmodern statements are functioning, to move beyond the fact of their existence, if we look at both their trajectory and their mode of existence (i.e., their plane of effectivity). We have to examine their movement into the center of popular culture and everyday life and their emergence along, and construction by, multiple vectors or codes constituting the social and cultural space of our advanced capitalist formation. Thus one can only speak of an emergent assemblage of statements, a complex array of cultural formations and intersecting codes which exist within the larger contradictory terrain of contemporary history, economics, ideology, pleasure, and so on—in fact, the terrain that is articulated as everyday life.

The very postmodernity of these formations is marked by contradictory semiotic and political tendencies and effects. It is not enough to collect "postmodern statements," although it is fun to do so; rather the increasing presence and power of such statements must be taken seriously, not only in the worlds of art and media, but in everyday life as well, as an emergent aspect of the popular. There *is* something anxious, even terrifying, about such statements, just as there is something pleasurable (and even funny) about them. We may laugh at statements like "Life is hard and then you die" even as we are horrified and condemned by them. It is only if we begin to look at the complex ways in which these statements are inserted into and function within the social formation that we can offer effective political responses to the contemporary demands of history.

I want to begin with a rather simple observation: that much of what is talked about as "the postmodern" is predicated on the perception that something "feels" different not only about particular aesthetic practices, but about a wide variety of life experiences and historical events. Yet it is not clear what the status of this "feeling" or experience is, in what planes of our existence it is anchored. Moreover there are two inseparable but different perspectives one can take here, two different questions one can ask, two different ways of entering onto the same terrain: First, what are the complex determinations or conditions of possibility of this "feeling," and second, what are the effects that we are trying to describe as an emergent historical "feeling," what conditions does it make possible? My main concern here is the latter, and my argument is that we should not too quickly recuperate it into either a phenomenological transcendentalism or into a deconstructive theory of the ideological production of experience. That is, there is no reason to assume that it is necessarily and primarily operating within either a signifying or representational economy. While not denying that it is partly ideological and always articulated to ideological positions, one need not assume that its most significant effects are located on such planes. There is even less justification for assuming that descriptions of its ideological effects provide a sufficient account.

THE SPECIFICITY OF THE POSTMODERN

I want to speculate on the popularity of these postmodern statements for, in fact, they are not only increasingly obvious but also increasingly popular; there is, in fact, nothing weirder than mainstream television today. What is the effectivity of these postmodern statements? What is it that we "hear" in them as we place them into the context of contemporary life? What do they evoke or invoke? It is not a "structure of feeling"—as a phenomenological description of the lived—but rather a particular attitude or mood—"empowering nihilism" or an "indifference to indifference"—embodied and enacted, in part, in a particular set of discursive strategies—"authentic inauthenticity" or "realistic irony." (I will return to these concepts later in the argument.) This discursive maneuver is neither wholly ideological nor simply semiotic. It is "communicated" through a different mode, in a different plane of effects: the "affective."

The affective is one plane of everyday life, one form of communicative economy. If we recognize the diversity of communicative economies, then we can recognize the truth in Baudrillard's description of the postmodern as "a virus" that leaps across social organs and domains (1985, 13), and my own claim (Grossberg 1987b) that it functions like billboards providing the imaginary unity and continuity of America:

> The pleasure of fashion is certainly cultural, but doesn't it owe more to that immediate consensus, shining through the game of signs? The styles also go out like epidemics, when they have ravaged the imagination, and when the virus gets tired, the price to pay, in terms of wasted signs, is exactly that of the epidemics in terms of lives: exorbitant. But everyone agrees to it. Our social marvel is that ultrarapid surface of the circulation of signs (and not the ultraslow one of the circulation of meaning). We love to be immediately contaminated, without thinking about it . . . Fash-

ion, like many other processes, is an irreducible phenomenon because it takes part in exactly the sort of senseless, viral and in some way asocial mode of communication, which only circulates so fast because it side-steps the mediation of reason. The logic of difference, of distinction, could not alone explain that: it is too slow. (Baudrillard 1985, 13)

However, unlike Baudrillard, I do not want to give up the possibility of struggle and the reality of contradiction. Nor do I want, in the name of anti-essentialism, to establish a new essentialism that would isolate this affective communication from, or substitute it for, the complex processes of the determination and articulation of the social formation. The social formation is characterizable only in its historically specific complexity. And although that complexity (or difference) is always structured in historically specific ways, its structuration is never completed and secure. The contradictions are never finally "stitched up" into a singularly coherent structure. Moreover the history of such struggles to disarticulate and rearticulate social, cultural, and political relations is precisely the history of the continuing establishment and reshaping of multiple regimes of power. It is within such struggles that the concrete effects of any practice are determined. Although such regimes are themselves not reducible to a single plane of determination, their autonomy is always limited by the ways they themselves are linked together into specific relations. For example, although systems of power organized around gender and sexual difference cannot be explained in terms of economic and class relations, their specific historical forms cannot be understood apart from the ways they are articulated into specific economic and class relations.

There are two implications of this conception of the social formation worth pointing to: First, there are no guarantees in history. Practices, relations, and social positions are not inherently identified with each other, nor are their politics, meanings, and effects determined outside of the real social context within which people can and do struggle—not necessarily in ways that are intentional or resistant—to "make history in conditions not of their own making." As Hall (1985) puts it, although such correspondences are always real, they are never necessary. Second, there is no secure knowledge, no position outside of the social formation from which anyone, including critics and intellectuals, can survey the entire terrain. Consequently critics cannot assume the validity of their own interpretations, nor of their political agendas. More importantly people are not cultural dopes who are totally unaware of their own interests and needs and subordinations. One cannot tell people where or how to struggle, but that does not mean one cannot intervene, in intelligent and effective ways, into the space of everyday life. It does mean that such interventions depend not upon judgments critics bring from their own social position, but upon a real effort to map out some of the complex and contradictory vectors operating at specific sites in the social formation. But I also want to emphasize the limits of both the lack of guarantees and anti-elitism. On the one hand no social practice, no cultural text determines its own effects or speaks its own truth. On the other hand not every effect or articulation involves real struggle, not every struggle is won, not every victory is resistant, and not all resistance is progressive.

As Stuart Hall wrote in 1960, "The task of socialism is to meet people where they are—where they are touched, bitten, moved, frustrated, nauseated—to develop discontent and at the same time, to give the socialist movement some direct sense of the times and the ways in which we live" (1). The terms of Hall's description echo Raymond Williams's (1965) structure of *feeling*, although to a certain extent both authors failed to theorize the added depth that the notion of "feeling" brings, as well as the historically specific forms of this socialist project. Still, Hall's statement offers us rich advice, for it makes three demands upon us: first, that we enter onto the terrain of the popular in order to make intelligible when, where, and how people live. This is not the phenomenological task of discovering the forms of consciousness that people have of their existence (although that is certainly a part). The second demand is that we recognize the complexity and multiple determinations of such positions. Finally, it demands that socialism's task be understood not as defining the place, time, and form of revolution and change, but rather as prising open already existing contradictions and "thereby renovating and making critical an already existing activity" (Gramsci 1971, 331).

Thus we neither celebrate nor panic in the face of contemporary developments and tendencies, nor do we merely stitch them (and history along with them) into our already defined theoretical and political positions. The task of understanding the postmodern, to return to my beginning, can only proceed by theorizing from and around the concrete and can only proceed toward opening up a more explicit "politics of the possible" (Chambers 1985) and "finding another way of imagining the future" (Hall 1987). Such a position establishes a sharp difference between marxist efforts to come to grips with the postmodern and what Guattari describes as "the deplorable conclusion to which many intellectual and artistic groups have come, especially those who claim the banner of postmodernism . . . that [it is] inevitable that we remain passive in the face of the rising wave of cruelty and cynicism that is in the process of flooding the planet and that seems determined to last" (1986, 40). But even Guattari here takes too much for granted, namely, that it is obvious that there is a link between contemporary forms of cynicism and of cruelty, and that these are "flooding" the planet.

STRATEGIES OF THE LEFT

Let me briefly turn to the question of how the Left has responded to the challenge of the postmodern and the dominant interpretations and frameworks it has put forth. The first and most influential marxist response to the emergence of the postmodern—derived from literary theory—reads it as a new ideological formation in which postmodern statements are ideological texts. For example, Jameson (1984) assumes that the structures of various discourses are direct expressions of the structures of our experiences, which are, in turn, directly determined by our insertion into the economic relations of late capitalism. It is as if ideology's determination of experience were immediate and causal. Apart from the theoretical objections that can be raised to challenge this view, it ignores that there is something different, something "postmodern," about the way ideology works today.

Let me explain by turning to the question of mystification: How do we hold on to such a critical notion if we renounce theories of false consciousness? Part of the radical solution that both Gramsci (1971) and Althusser (1971) offered was to argue that ideology is a matter of practices rather than beliefs or, if you prefer, that belief is a matter of practice. As Slavoj Žižek (1987) recently argued, the best description of the working of ideology is "they don't know it but they are doing it." That is, ideological activities are always characterized by the fact that illusion structures real social activities. When Marx claimed that the ideology of capitalism was Hegelian idealism—the belief that particular entities (commodities) were the expression of universal abstract value—he was not claiming that people hold such a belief. Common sense is not Hegelian; it is on the contrary nominalist. People believe in the reality of the concrete particular. But people act as if an ideal universal value existed. People know how things really are, but they act as if they had mystical beliefs. This distance—between belief and action—is crucial, for it allows both the reality of mystification and the possibility of a space for critical work and struggle. But Žižek goes on to argue that this critical space has disappeared in the operation of what one might call a postmodern ideological formation. There is instead a cynical irony operating in the realm of ideology. People know what they are doing, but they continue doing it anyway. They are aware of ideological mystification but enter into it anyway. Thus contemporary ideological practice already assumes the distance toward the dominant ideology that had defined the possibility of critically responding to it. Thus the very need, if not the possibility, of a critical relation to the dominant ideology is apparently undermined. This cynicism, the collapse of distance, is also ironic: it operates by refusing to take its own ideological positions—or anything, for that matter—too seriously. In fact, within this cynical reason, the real evil is taking any ideological belief too seriously, regardless of whether it is dominant or oppositional. But this analysis, however accurate, leaves the crucial question unanswered: Why has this cynical irony, which has certainly had a long history, suddenly become part of the popular attitude?

The second strategy of the Left, derived from art criticism, argues that in the contemporary context, all of culture—including the production of meaning and consciousness—has been incorporated into capitalist commodity relations. For example, Frith and Horne (1987) talk about the "equation" of art and commerce, as a result of which the "aesthetic effect" of texts cannot be separated from their market effects. Further, they argue that the desires they address cannot be separated from their market effects; increasingly, art situates the viewer as spectator-*cum*-consumer. While I do not want to entirely disagree with this position, I do want to raise two objections to too strong an interpretation of it. The first is historical: after all, art (and culture in general) was incorporated into the capitalist economy long before the contemporary era, in terms of its mode of both production and distribution. Its location within the market economy is not new. What is new is the mass availability of cultural commodities. The second objection is conceptual: if the difference between art and commerce has, in some significant way, collapsed in recent times, it is important that we try to identify the specific dimension in which this indifference (the apparent irrelevance of the difference) is manifested. It does not follow, necessarily, that art can be reduced to a commodity if we situate it in people's lives. That it is a commodity does not deny that it still may be other things as well. Moreover the concrete complexity of the practices of consumption suggests that such artistic practices, even if they situate the audience as consumer, may also situate them in other contradictory subject-positions.

Another way of saying this is that there is a tendency to treat the commodity as a simple and transparent, ahistorical concept, forgetting that, for Marx, it operates on a very general level of abstraction. On the one hand the concept of the commodity implies a relation between use value and exchange value; on the other hand it implies a contradiction between the forces and relations of production. These two equations are not only mapped onto each other in historically specific ways but are also each articulated in historically specific ways. It is only as we begin to examine the complex nature of the relation between sign and commodity, and recognize the multiplicity of communicative economies within which various texts operate, that we can begin to unravel the outlines of everyday life.

The third strategy is the most complex and amorphous: the "politics of transgression and pleasure." Such a strategy views pleasure as a second dimension of the effectivity of particular textual practices and, following Chambers, assumes that pleasure operates "on the immediate surfaces of everyday life" (1985, 211). It "transforms the seeming 'obviousness' of popular culture into an imaginative conquest of everyday life" and serves as "an affirmation of your right to inhabit the present." Such views are often deconstructive in that they assume that structure and the singularity of meaning are always repressive; it is only through the explosion of the signified, and the ascension of the signifier, that the threatening possibilities of anarchic libidinal gratification are liberated. They often celebrate such deconstructive orgasms as the positive face of the postmodern, ignoring the fact that, in the popular media, even the most fragmented texts and images often offer new forms of identity and coherence; fragmented identities are still identities although they incorporate new forms of fragmentation into identity (e.g., cyborgs like Max Headroom and Robocop). I do not mean to equate all such views of pleasure and transgression. There are significant differences among left views of pleasure, ranging from an ultrapositive, elitist view (e.g., Barthes's distinction between *plaisir* and *jouissance* [1975]) to Jameson's negative vision of pleasure as "the consent of life in the body" (1983) to Baudrillard's image of fascination as an indifference "at least as great" as that of the simulacrum (1986).

Let me briefly identify three problems with the attempt to locate the politics of the postmodern in the regime of pleasure. First, such theories ignore the complexity of "pleasure" itself: they fail to distinguish between desire, emotion, satisfaction, need, and enjoyment. They also fail to note the ambiguity that arises from the different discursive economies within which pleasure has been theorized: as the satisfaction of need, the avoidance of pain, the dissipation of tension, and pure positivity. They often end up ignoring the complex relations that exist between forms of pleasure and ideological formations. As a result, pleasure is often reduced to an ideological process (despite their protestations to the contrary, e.g., Jameson [1983] and C. Mercer [1986]) or to the ideological determinations of libidinal displacements (as in *Screen* theory). Neither of these positions adequately analyzes the complex and often contradictory relations that exist between ideological and libidinal economies as different planes of effects.

Second, such theories often ignore the fact that pleasure is never inherently, essentially, or necessarily a form of resistance, nor even of empowerment. Pleasure is only empowering within specific contextual determinations. That the very assertion of pleasure may be, at a particular moment, a political statement does not guarantee the political effectivity of pleasure in any social conjuncture. As Judith Williamson (1986) has argued, after we acknowledge and even describe the pleasures of popular culture, we have still to return to the question of its concrete political articulation.

Finally, like theories of the postmodern as ideology, such theories fail to notice the postmodern ambiguity of pleasure, an ambiguity captured in such statements as "Seek small pleasures; big ones are too risky," or, Sex is "nothing but thirty seconds of squelching noises" (Johnny Rotten).

AFFECTIVE COMMUNICATION

I want to turn to the question of Baudrillard's "other mode of communication" (1985) in order to make some brief suggestions about the modality of its communicative economy. Then I shall turn to the question of its historically specific place within the social formation, that is, the question of its determinations and determinants within a postmodern formation. Again, we might begin by taking a lesson from Guattari in order to simply acknowledge effectivities other than those we are used to dealing with: "concrete social formations . . . stem from something more than a linguistic performance: there are ethological dimensions and ecological ones, semiotic and economic factors, esthetic, corporeal and fantasmatic ones . . . a multitude of universes of reference" (1986, 41). Guattari's last phrase is particularly significant: we are not in the (post)structuralist's refusal of referentiality (in the name of the primacy of the signifier), but rather we are in the realm of the multiple planes of effectivity and referentiality.

I want to introduce a fourth term into the already crowded relations of signification, economy, and libido: "affect" or "corporeal attitude." In order to begin to explain this notion, let me turn to two figures who have made important efforts to theorize what I take to be similar (but not identical) concepts. Such discussions make clear the need to constantly return to the problem of historical specificity and determination. In the context of debates around postmodernity, no figure is more important than Nietzsche, and his theory of the "will to power" (as read by Deleuze [1977]) provides important insights into what I am calling "affect." For Nietzsche, the notion of force (or power) always assumes not only a multiplicity of specific forces, but also a principle that "brings forces into synthesis." Such a "genealogical principle" is, at once, differential and genetic; it produces simultaneously the *quantitative* difference between forces and the *qualitative* identity of each force. This quantitative difference is the measure of power; in Nietzsche's terms, it constitutes the difference between dominating and dominated forces. The qualitative difference defines the directionality of the vector of each force as either active or reactive. It is, according to Deleuze, only in this complex economy of relations, that the "will to power," as the source of value, can be either affirmative or negative. One final point needs to be made lest we falsely assume that this genealogical principle—the Will to Power—is universal. It is always contextually specific; it is, echoing both Althusser and Foucault, determined by what it determines. It is itself always the concrete product of the *field of forces on which it operates.*

The second figure I want to introduce here is Freud (as interpreted by Laplanche and Pontalis [1973]), from whom I have taken the term "affect," used by him to refer to psychic energy. Psychic energy could be either bound to a specific idea or unbound; hence there is the possibility of affect without an idea and ideas without affect. Since Freud, the notion of affect has been lost, either in the psychoanalytic substitution of sexual energy—libido—for affect, or in the nonpsychoanalytic reduction of affect to universal principles (as in Jung and Reich). (It is, after all, important to remember that one of Freud's attacks on Jung was that he had collapsed the difference, desexualizing libido into every "tendency towards.") Nevertheless, if we are to understand the notion of psychic energy, we have to ask how it has been erased and where it has been lost. Freud's metapsychology depends upon the necessity of holding together three perspectives that are, in a sense, contradictory but are not, as is sometimes assumed, mutually exclusive: the topographical, the dynamic, and the economic. The topographical perspective constructs a structural model of elements as relations: usually ego-id-superego. The dynamic perspective constructs a battleground of conflicting forces: the conscious versus the unconscious. And the economic perspective, finally, constructs a machine or space defined by the circulation and distribution of energy: an economy of cathexis.

One can read the history of psychoanalysis, although this is obviously an oversimplification, as progressively making each of these perspectives less important than the preceding one (e.g., in ego psychology, the conflict is defined topographically; on the other hand, Lacan's return to Freud was, in part, a recovery of the dynamic model, with its dynamism now defined by the semiotics of the unconscious). But for Freud, psychic conflict is also located, albeit in transformed terms, within the economic model—for there is always an other to libidinal energy. The libido is never the only form or organization of psychic energy. More importantly, it is never originary; it arises anacliticically, leaning upon other instincts or drives. Libido, the energy of the sexual instincts, is always located in a larger economy of difference. Of course the project of describing the terrain of this larger economy occupied Freud all his life, as he increasingly recognized its complexity and contradictions. Thus on the one hand the sexual instincts are opposed to the ego instincts (the instincts of self-preservation); this difference is closely related to that between the pleasure principle and the reality principle. On the other hand both of these instinct sets are part of a larger apparatus—Eros, or the life instincts—which is in turn connected and opposed to another apparatus—Thanatos, or the death instincts. As one moves to this even higher level of abstraction, the proliferation of psychic "principles" becomes increasingly difficult to unravel. But it is here that we discover at least one of the major ambiguities of "pleasure" in psychoanalytic theory: pleasure is located in both the constancy principle, which seeks homeostasis, and the Nirvana principle, which seeks to reduce all tension to zero. Pleasure is thus describable, on the one hand, as the total absence of tension and, on the other hand, as the discharge of excess tension and the maintenance of a state of balance.

It is interesting that both Lacanians (e.g., Laplanche and Pontalis) and anti-Lacanians (e.g., Deleuze and Guattari) agree that one cannot define this energy except in its effects and transformations without falling into various metaphysical ideologies. Both sides seem to recognize its connection with notions of life-force, will, preconstitutive life-world, and Heideggerian mood, but are unwilling to follow these traditions because they conceptualize and recast the problem as one of origins. Affect or psychic energy is the very existence of tension, of a relationship that is always a difference, marked upon larger contradictory fields. Moreover affect is not a homogeneous category: one need only think of Deleuze and Guattari's distinction (1977) between three kinds of psychic energy: libido (as the connective synthesis of production); numen (as the disjunctive synthesis of recording); and voluptas (as the conjunctive synthesis of consumption). Finally, affect is both qualitative and quantitative. It can be characterized quantitatively—as a measurable "quota" (in Freudian terminology)—and qualitatively—as a state of mood (or what is often expressed as an emotional attitude).

By citing Nietzsche and Freud I do not mean to equate my use of "affect" with either the will to power or psychic energy. I merely intend to demonstrate that there is a history of attempts to theorize economies other than those of value, ideology, and libido. In fact, I want to distinguish between libidinal economies of desire and affective economies of mood as two different planes on which psychic energy is organized. If desire is always focused (as the notion of cathexis suggests), mood is always dispersed. While both may be experienced in terms of needs, only libidinal needs can be, however incompletely, satisfied. Moods are never satisfied, only realized. If desire assumes an economy of depth (e.g, in the notion of repression), mood is always on the surface (which is not to be equated with consciousness). It is the coloration or passion within which one's investments in, and commitments to, the world are made possible. Finally, affective economies empower difference while libidinal economies do not. Pleasure and desire operate within a structure in which it is their own satisfactions—however infinitely deferred—that define the operation of the system. They are systems replete with content. Affect is contentless; on the contrary, it is precisely aimed at constituting not only the possibility of difference, but the terms within which such differences are possible in a particular affective economy. Consider for example the affective need for security and intimacy, both psychically and materially, in home and relations. Such a need is never satisfied by particular relationships but only by a more general attitude or mood within which any particular relationship has its effects.

In ending this discussion of affect, let me draw four conclusions. First, affect produces systems of *difference* that are *asignifying*. Affect constructs a difference, both quantitatively (as a measure of the degree of energizing) and qualitatively (as a particular mood, within which other differences function). The very form of affective difference—not only the "conditions of its possibility" but the very ways in which such differences are mapped—are not necessarily the same as those that construct other more typically discussed systems. Only if we recognize the different economies operating in everyday life can we come to terms with both the specificity of various social practices and the contradictory terrain of everyday life. Thus for example if the unconscious is like a language, it is also not like a language; the specificity of its effects depends in part on the differences between libidinal and semiotic economies. This does not deny that affect, and affective difference, may themselves be implicated directly in systems of power. Nor does it deny that such affective differences can be and are articulated ideologically and libidinally into other structures and forms of social difference and power.

Second, affect describes historically specific modes and organizations of *material* attitude or orientation. Although it always involves vectors into the materiality of the social world, affect is the intentionality neither of consciousness nor of the lived body (understood phenomenologically). Third, affect describes not a subjective property, but the historically specific processes in which the subject is defined by the intensive qualities (the affective states) through which it passes. That is, the subject is constituted nomadically, by its movements across the fields of affective difference. The affective subject is always transitory, defined by its qualitative and quantitative trajectories.

Finally, the form of *empowerment* operating at the affective level involves something other than control, direction, or meaning. The very possibility of struggle depends upon an affective empowerment, what Gramsci (1971) referred to as an "optimism of the will." Benjamin (1968) recognized that the strongest ideological position would entail an organization of pessimism in which a sense of the lack of power to change the world operates not only in our maps of intelligibility but also in the most basic sites of our impassioned relation to the world. This of course does not answer the question of the politics of such affective economies; it is open to struggle and articulation. Affect defines, then, a condition of possibility for any political intervention; it is, however, ideologically, economically, and libidinally neutral except as it is articulated into these systems under specific historical conditions.

POSTMODERNITY AND AFFECT

To bring these remarks to a close, let me return to the question of the nature or status of the "event" of postmodernity, or at least to the nature or status of the sorts of postmodern statements with which I opened this paper. If we are to understand their real effects and significance, we have to locate them within the changing historical relations in the social field of forces. When Gramsci (1971) talked about the "war of positions," he had in mind something other than my model of the complexities and contradictions between and within the historically specific formations and economies of affect, libido, semiosis, and value. Yet I think it is not unfair to appropriate this image to describe the way in which particular cultural statements are positioned within the social formation and their political effects determined. In this context, I want to talk about the affective force of such statements in terms of a "crisis" of the historical form of our dialectical or dialogical (in Bakhtin's sense [1981]) relation to the social world (which includes words as well as things).

It is possible to identify two vectors in this crisis. The first was already operating—both historically and semiotically—in a great deal of modernist cultural practices. It involves an increasingly problematic relation between affect and ideology, in our very ability to invest in the meanings—and meaningfulness—of the world, to locate any meaning as a possible and appropriate source for an impassioned commitment (in whatever qualitative state). We could describe this as the dissolution of what Foucault (1970) has called the "epistemological doublet." It is an increasing inability to live on the border of subjectivity and objectivity. This becomes semiotically coded, in many modernist texts, as the reduction of subjectivity to objectivity and of objectivity to subjectivity. It is lived as an increasing sense of horror or terror, not only in the fact of objectivity but in the fact of subjectivity as well. Thus if we consider contemporary experience, we can suggest that the affective poles of boredom and terror are organized in a nonlinear way around the possibilities of the absence (in pure objectivity) and uncontrollable excess (in pure subjectivity) of affectivity. This becomes, in recent history, an even more powerful determinant when language and meaning are themselves rendered objective through theoretical work and when such theoretical positions begin to enter into "common sense." But even in this "crisis" there remains an investment not only in libidinal relations but in an ideology of libidinal gratification (e.g., in the counterculture of the '60s).

The second vector of this restructuring of the field of forces that I am referring to as the crisis of the postmodern is defined precisely by the increasingly problematic nature of the relations between affect and libido. To put it crudely, structures of pleasure are themselves, increasingly, only problematically cathected. There are no doubt many events that can partially explain how pleasure itself came to be mistrusted if not seen as threatening: for example, the apparent failures of the counterculture of the sixties and of its obvious attempt to create and invest itself in an ideology of libidinal pleasure; the important successes of feminism in pointing out that libidinal as well as gender relations are overcoded by relations of power; the major redistribution—sometimes involuntarily enforced—of the relations between labor and leisure. It has become increasingly obvious that leisure—both as a space within everyday life, the site of our "private" and privileged identities, and as specific forms of activities—is intimately implicated in broader relations of power.

To live in the space of this growing gap between affective and libidinal economies—or perhaps, more accurately, of these mobile and growing gaps— is to be suspicious of any object of desire, as well as of desire itself: "This is the generation that inherited the cry, 'I can't get no satisfaction.' And they live its contradictions, grabbing at satisfaction while rejecting the possibility itself" (Aufderheide 1986, 14). Contrary to popular wisdom, this is not a cultural space in which people seek risks or seek to live on the edge. Rather it is a space in which people seek to feel the thrill without the reality—because the reality of the edge threatens to make the thrill itself too real and too dangerous. As Glenn O'Brien (1987) has recently suggested, it is enough to know someone who is only a phone call away who lives life on the edge. Libido has become the enemy—not only for the neoconservatives who seek to attack such pleasures but for those who are drawn to those pleasures as well: "Sex is now a conceptual act; it's probably only in terms of the perversions that we can make contact with each other at all. The perversions are completely neutral, cut off from any suggestion of psychopathology—in fact, most of the ones I've tried are out of date" (Ballard 1985, 63). One need only consider the viral, ultrarapid proliferation of sexually transmitted diseases: sex *has* become a terminal illness. The current campaign by the Right against pleasure is not simply manipulative; it does connect into real changes in the affective economy of contemporary life.

The postmodern signals a shift in the complex economy of everyday life; as a crisis, it points to significant changes in what one might call the "anchoring effects" through which different communicative economies are related to one another. The contemporary formations of the ideological and libidinal economies, however specifically and historically defined, continue to anchor themselves within the affective in terms of the commitment to difference: all that matters, in terms of their conditions, is that something specific and different matters. Affective difference, then, must always be anchored in the differences constituted by other economies. On the other hand, within the conditions of affectivity it doesn't matter what matters. What does matter is precisely the quality and quantity of the mattering (the mood, the passion) itself. But if the very possibility of anchoring affect in nonaffective differences is problematic, then, literally, nothing matters. Affect becomes, temporarily and locally, free-floating. Affect can only construct difference from indifference; its difference must be defined without an economy of difference. The crisis can be described in terms of the need to make something matter (to care, in whatever form—to make a commitment) without the possibility of connecting the various economies (of difference). Affect (or mood) itself in those circumstances becomes increasingly suspect, available to the articulations of the same structures of power: caring about anything is always either too easy (to be significant) or too difficult (to be possible). But moods, like ideologies, are unavoidable and so, like the cynical irony of postmodern ideology, there is a cynical logic of moods as well (what I have called "authentic inauthenticity")[2] in which only the quantity of affect becomes relevant. What matters is how much you care, not how you care ("I'd rather feel bad than not feel anything at all") or about what you care. Our postmodern heroes—most recently, Oliver North—are those who are different only because of the quantity of affect, only because they are able to care so much about something (whether we agree with it or not) that they make themselves different (even though they don't make a difference) and, not coincidentally, achieve some victory. That they become our "heroes," if only for a brief moment, depends on the fact that their only difference is affective. In all other respects they are like us: their transformation depends upon their impassioned relations to goals and/or ordinary skills.[3]

In a recent Bloom County cartoon depicting "the premature arrival of the future" (Toffler 1971), Binkley finds himself "all dressed up with no place to go." Binkley, whose narratives often involve his being visited by his night-mares coming out of his closet, is confronted with his worst nightmare yet: he is visited by his future self and shown his future:

Young Binkley: We married Lizzie "The Lizard" Blackhead??
Old Binkley: We call her "Queen Elizabeth." Now come . . . follow me into your future world, younger self . . . This ugly little dwelling is our house. We call it "Binkley Manor." We moved here in 1998. That's our '93 Volkswagen. We call it our "Little Lamborghini." It's all a way of some-how dealing with the mediocrity of our adult life . . . And the failed dreams of our youth. *Your* youth.
Young Binkley: Hey . . . There's a gopher wetting on my foot . . .
Old Binkley: *Bad dog, Rambo . . . Bad dog!*

There is in this, as in the ads I cited earlier, something that rings depressingly true. Binkley will have to face the next morning and, despite the terror and pessimism, find a way of affectively negotiating his way through everyday life. The commonplace has, after all, become dangerous (e.g., driving to work in Los Angeles). Whatever the historical facticity, everyday life feels threaten-ing, and we are all worried that Freddy or Jason is, in fact, our next-door neighbor.

If there is a political crisis implicit in this situation, it is a crisis not of a particular politics (the rise of neoconservatism), nor of anomie (as aliena-tion), nor of apathy (as disinterest). It is a crisis of the very possibility of politics, not in a form that negates the very real and continuing construction of ideological, economic, state, and libidinal regimes of power. It is rather a problematization of the very ability to articulate these structures (which we increasingly recognize and acknowledge) to the site of our own sense of how and where we can be empowered and our sense of difference constituted. However, the point is not merely to accede to the crisis but to articulate new forms of affective empowerment by which people are able to construct and invest in difference. But even that is perhaps misleading, for it seems to suggest that there is a kind of totalized affective disempowerment or nihil-ism. The increasingly rapid move of a postmodern cultural formation into the center of the field of popularity suggests that its statements serve, in part, to offer strategies for affective empowerment in the face of the postmodern crisis.

Thus the postmodern cultural formation is not, as Baudrillard might have it, the celebration of nihilism and indifference. It is not the production of nihilism as the site of empowerment but the production of forms of empowerment in the face of the possibilities of, and to a certain extent the reality of, nihilism. There is a truth to the notion that the only certainty today is ambiguity because it is less constraining: reality is, after all, "too constraining as a lifestyle." Postmodern statements are not empowering *because* they are nihilistic (nor merely in spite of it); they are both nihilistic and empowering.[4] Thus the interpretive task facing us is to identify the strategies and sites of affective empowerment made available in the contemporary cultural forms of popular mood or attitude. If the Left fails to recognize the reality of affective empowerment and fails to identify the particular sites that are currently and widely available, then it will not be able to recognize that a space for struggle can be, and is already being, fashioned. Nor will it be able to identify the sites of empowerment that have to be rearticulated to different political and ideological projects. That means that the response of the Left to this crisis cannot be to define new goals or new moralities but rather, in a historically specific way, to enter the contradictory terrain of everyday life on which this postmodern formation is only one vector, to rearticulate it, to reconnect it, to the real concerns, needs, and struggles of people.

Postmodernist Elitisms and

Postmodern Struggles

Culture is never abstract: it always involves particular practices of production and consumption and concrete connections between such practices and everyday life. Therefore let me begin with a number of contemporary media events. Perhaps you have seen the bumper sticker that declares "Now that I've finally lost all hope, I feel better." Or the T-shirt that says "If you love someone let them go. If they don't come back, hunt them down and kill them." Or the ad for the Brookfield Zoo that presents a picture of a tiger and the caption "When was the last time you took the kids to see something real?" Perhaps you saw a recent episode of *Valerie* in which a child wonders why his real life (which is, of course, TV life) never works out as well as the image of TV life that is presented on his television. Perhaps you have seen *Moonlighting* (ABC, 28 October 1986), from which I've taken the following dialogue:

> Maddy: David, what's going on in the world?
> David: In the world, well, you got your arms race, you got your assorted diseases, you still got your apartheid down there in South Africa. What were you referring to?
> M: Maybe it's not the world, maybe it's me . . . Maybe I'm the only one who gets upset about seeing a secretary laying a man across her desk like a blotter, or chasing him around the office . . . Maybe I'm the only one who finds it strange when a married woman walks in and tells us she wants to stop an affair she's having through the mail.
> D: Can you blame her? Those little envelopes kinda limit the possibilities.
> M: Oh David, nothing makes sense anymore. What's happened to all the rules? You meet someone, you flirt with them, you go out with them, you flirt some more . . . What's happened to romance?

D: Have you looked at the calendar lately?

M: What's that supposed to mean?

D: It means this is the eighties, Maddy, and in the eighties you take your romance where you can find it. And if that means a twenty-two-cent postage stamp, fine. And if it means a buck to rent an adult video, that's fine too. Maybe it's a two-dollar toll call to someone you never met who would say things you would never utter to someone you know. It's all romance.

M: That's not romance. That's dirty solitaire.

D: Yeah. These are great times we're living in. It no longer takes two to tango.

Perhaps you remember *Davy Crockett,* presenting one of the first images of the hero appropriated by the baby boom generation. It was also the first sign that this generation would preoccupy Madison Avenue for decades. However silly it was, *Davy Crockett* provided both kids and businesspeople with the unassailable assurance that here was a generation with its own identity, or at least its own need for an identity. In seven months it grossed over $100 million, the price of raccoon skins increased sixteenfold, and four versions of the song were recorded, all of them making the Billboard charts and three of them in the top hundred records of the year. Current research suggests that Crockett did not die heroically at the Alamo but surrendered and was killed only after having denied his actual role. Even worse, he did not wear a coonskin cap until he saw it used in a play lampooning him. The heroic myth is, at worst, a fabrication of historians and, at best, a fabrication of Crockett himself. The celebration of the latter possibility apparently makes "disinformation" a positive practice. But that is precisely what is at stake when Paul Andrew Hutton describes Crockett as "perhaps the first American hero to make a living portraying his own fanciful image" (1986, 130). Does this negate his evocative power? Hardly. "But even as the myth began to unravel, I found myself liking Davy Crockett. He is that rarest of American icons—a legendary hero who turns out, after all, to have been more or less a decent, admirable human being" (123–24). A strange recuperation of heroism, to say the least.

Perhaps you watched the pregame show of NBC's broadcast of one of the World Series games from Boston. The host announced that he had gone to a Boston "sports bar" and talked to the patrons. The tape, however, quickly revealed—at least to the television cognoscenti—the scene and cast of *Cheers* (in Los Angeles). The "deception" was never announced—it was taken for granted. According to Bob Greene, it "felt more real than if [the host] had gone to a genuine Boston bar. Because *Cheers* is seen in millions of American homes every week, the pregame bit had a warmth and familiarity that would have been lacking in a real Boston bar" (1986, 1).

ARTICULATING THE POSTMODERN

Something new has entered the cultural terrain: the postmodern. It is as real as the sometimes frightening forms of cynicism and ironic juxtapositions that constantly announce their pervasive presence within everyday life. This is not to claim that it has no precedents or that it is the only or even the dominant element in our lives. But it is to register the importance of an emergent set of practices and statements that increasingly saturates and colors our lives not just in our cultural forms but in historical events and interpersonal relations as well. The cultural critic asks what the postmodern is, and what it is doing in our everyday lives.

1. Understanding the postmodern is not the same as seeking to identify the boundaries that differentiate forms of cultural practices (e.g., mass, popular, and high), whether located in their relations to the economic system (in their forms of production and consumption) or to the sociological system (in their origins in particular social groups). Such efforts are always articulated into binary systems of power, whether they are conceptualized vertically (as domination and subordination) or horizontally (as the incorporation of the resistance of the margins into the mainstream).

Nor is it merely a question of recognizing that the construction of the popular is itself the site of an ongoing struggle, of arguing that the popular "consists of those cultural forms and practices—varying in content from one historical period to another—which constitute the terrain on which dominant, subordinate and oppositional cultural values and ideologies meet and intermingle, in different mixes and permutations, vying with one another in their attempts to secure the spaces within which they can become influential in framing and organizing popular experience and consciousness. It consists not of two separated compartments—a pure and spontaneously oppositional culture 'of the people' and a totally administered culture 'for the people'—but is located in the points of confluence between these opposing tendencies whose contradictory orientations shape the very organization of the cultural forms in which they meet and interpenetrate one another" (Bennett 1986, 19). Such a view correctly displaces the relation between culture and economy as well as the relation between cultural practices and preconstituted social groups existing outside of the struggle: "Just as there is no fixed content to the category of 'popular culture,' so there is no fixed subject to attach to it" (Hall 1981, 239).

Yet simply making the popular into an abstract site of struggle, an empty signifier, does not tell us precisely what the struggles are about and how they are organized in any historical moment. Although there is no necessary content to, or boundaries around, the popular within a social formation, there are always boundaries already defined and content already inserted. We may struggle against what we are given, but we also struggle over and within it. The postmodern, then, points us to particular structures and struggles within popular culture and everyday life.

2. What is it that marks the break of the postmodern? What is it that is constantly foregrounded in these diverse statements and practices? What is it that the postmodern ushers onto the stage of everyday life? After all, there are real stakes in the question: the politics not only of particular practices, but of their insertion into everyday life and the possibility, if not the necessity, of the construction of new forms of popular politics. The issue is precisely what these cultural statements portend. Is Greene correct when he writes that "the important thing to take away from this [is that] television has become more real than real life" (1986, 1)? Does the postmodern erasure of the difference between TV and reality mean in fact that television is the new locus of the real? Is the baby boom in fact "the transition generation into the media-mad world where image is reality," so that we experience everything as "a kind of movie, real yet depthless" (Aufderheide 1986)? How do we make critical choices between those who would argue that such postmodern texts reproduce "the qualities which constitute the dominant cultural form of commodity aesthetics under late capitalism" and those who maintain that they are "endowed with a skeptical spirit which is truly threatening to the protocol of art viewing as visual consumption"? Or are we left with our own nihilism: that these are merely "signs of the times that we can't decipher" (K. Mercer 1986)?

Interpretations of culture are never offered in a vacuum: they always involve taking particular positions within a field of political possibilities. No event—textual or historical—speaks its own truth; its meaning, its relation to reality, its politics are never guaranteed in advance. Its truth—its effects— have to be struggled over and won. Any discourse that claims to represent reality functions ideologically; as it slides across its own surfaces, it naturalizes certain linkages, conflates differences, and constitutes the necessity of certain connections and correspondences. The postmodern names the real relations and practices we are attempting to describe. But our descriptions inflect them onto particular political terrains and into particular political positions. On the other hand, although the postmodern is always shaped by the ways we articulate these practices and relations, it is never merely constituted by our articulations.

Cultural critics, like people in their everyday lives, are engaged in struggles with, within, and sometimes against real tendential forces and determinations. People struggle to appropriate what they are given and to define practices that will enable them to win some greater purchase on and control over their lives: sometimes they win, sometimes they do not; sometimes they struggle where one might expect them to and in ways that fit already defined models, sometimes their struggles remain unrecognized, perhaps even unrecognizable. People are not merely the passive products of external conditions; they are never merely the colonized dupes of dominant systems of power. This means that cultural practices can only be described in their complex and active insertion at particular sites of everyday life. And this means as well that we must understand how debates about the postmodern and popular culture are themselves important sites of struggle.

3. There seem to be only two ways in which the question of the politics of popular culture can be framed in contemporary discourse: either it is celebrated as the almost inevitable site of resistance that locates all struggle within an equally inevitably incorporated metropolitan politics of pleasure, or it is attacked as merely reproducing the existing relations of subordination and domination. Condemnation or celebration, neither position enters onto the terrain of the popular to understand the ways in which it struggles not merely by difference or negativity (as critique and resistance), but by constructing and opposing its own positivity, its own forms and sites of celebration. Only by operating from within the postmodern, by understanding the very domains and structures that it valorizes, can we understand the material

it offers for the articulation of a popular politics within everyday life. What is at stake, then, is the historical positivity of contemporary culture and the notion of positive opposition itself. If we are to understand the way it opposes particular dominant positions, we must begin by understanding what it offers in its place, what it celebrates, where it locates its own investments in reality. It is this "sensibility" of mass culture that has remained uninterrogated; when it is raised, it is too quickly glossed as a matter of "taste." But taste merely opens a field of questions; it does not provide the necessary concrete analyses.

This project was recognized in the first editorial of *New Left Review:* "The task of socialism is to meet people where they are—where they are touched, bitten, moved, frustrated, nauseated—to develop discontent and at the same time, to give the socialist movement some direct sense of the times and the ways in which we live" (Hall 1960, 1). (Note the particular affective status of the adjectives that are used to describe popular reality.) On the other hand, Judith Williamson has decried the tendency on the Left to simply "grovel before a popular culture we would once have tried to create some alternative to." She continues, "Many left intellectuals are not only fed up; they are, in a sense, bored. It gets draggy to keep on repeating all that left-wing stuff when the nation is busy waving plastic flags at Fergie . . . All these people on the left . . . are in fact rediscovering popular culture as really quite good fun. However the vast majority of people knew it was quite good fun all along" (1986, 14–15).

If the terrain of popular culture is increasingly the site of political concern, it is precisely because of the increasing necessity for power to enter into and structure the domain of everyday life or, in Gramscian terms, of common sense. If processes of consumption have become increasingly determinant, it is because the new media have brought the vast majority of the population into relations of cultural consumption even as they have rendered the effort to control the ways in which such consumption is enacted increasingly difficult. Yet even those contemporary arguments that ground themselves in Gramsci's notion of hegemony (1971) too often fail to take account of the difference between the ideological moment of the construction of leadership—an ideological struggle within which opposition is always constructed negatively—and the affective moment of the construction of the popular itself—with its own positivity.

Here the more positive understandings of the possibilities of mass culture found in Benjamin (1973) are significant. Benjamin understood that the terrain of popular culture is contradictory and that the masses have a complex relation to the new forms of cultural production and consumption. The masses bring new forms of historical agency and political struggle onto the historical stage. Their relationship to power, and to culture, is always double-sided: always inside and outside of its organizations, always its subjects and objects, always appropriating it as strategies of evasion and control, always manipulating and manipulated. New cultural forms of fragmentation and dispersion in the new media signal not only changes in the status of culture and its forms of appropriation, but also new possibilities for a modern politics defined by their positivity, by the forms and content of their celebrations more than by their negation of dominant structures of relations and practices. Are such positivities necessarily oppositional? Hardly. Can they be articulated to such political positions? Yes, but that requires us to enter onto the terrain of popular common sense in order to open up its contradictions, thereby "renovating and making 'critical' an already existing activity" (Gramsci 1971, 331).

POSTMODERNIST ELITISMS

1. Such a reading of the postmodern, one that would open up its political horizon, must first disarticulate postmodern practices and statements from those interpretations that are already becoming taken-for-granted truths, defining a new common sense about contemporary reality and experience. It must break the assumed identity of the postmodern with the various postmodernisms that have attempted to interpret it. We have to begin by struggling against those who would articulate it in ways that inevitably deny its positive possibilities within everyday life, those who would construct it within their own systems of elitism and negativity (Adorno 1976).

There is a significant gap between what is at stake in the postmodern as it functions within popular culture and everyday life and in postmodernism as a set of discourses. The latter assumes an already accomplished, qualitative break or difference in social life and practice. Their project is to determine—in advance—the politics of this "other side" of history. The operation of "postmodernism" as a master signifier makes it possible to slide across registers in order to constitute its own political positions as both real and inevitable, even as it erases the effective positivities, contradictions, and popular struggles of everyday existence.

Further, in their attempt to interpret the relations between contemporary cultural practices and the social formation, postmodernists have too often surrendered the ground that has been won in cultural theory itself. They often fall back upon simple models of textuality and textual politics, within which texts embody their own essential identity that is necessarily related to (a reflection or expression of, without contradiction) the "deep structures" of the social formation. Postmodernism offers a series of conflationary juxtapositions that are both inflationary and inflammatory. We need to deconstruct postmodernism if we are to understand the celebration of the postmodern.

Nietzsche warns us that when we study monsters, we must take some care to avoid becoming monsters. But the postmodernists have sought to construct the world, and people, in their own image of monstrosity; they have expunged the contradictions, positivity, and possibility of popular struggles and denied their own everyday existence as witnesses, if not fans, of the postmodern. And this process cannot be viewed outside of the contemporary relations of power and struggles for survival. My argument is quite simple: The postmodern is too real and too important to be left to the postmodernists, whether artists, historians, or theorists. The postmodern is part of the fabric of reality. And if we are concerned with structures of power and the possibilities not only of opposition but of positive struggles, we must navigate the space within the popular between utopianism and nihilism. We must understand how the apparent loss of a certain set of critical positions and oppositional differences in various domains of our lives may yet point to new critical and oppositional possibilities.

2. By postmodernism, I mean all of those discourses that claim that the contemporary social and cultural formation is marked by the collapse of difference as an effective historical structure. This claim—whatever its particular force—needs to be distinguished from the Derridean notion of *différance,* which still operates within an economy of identity and difference. The postmodern places the possibility that difference makes no difference on the agenda of contemporary life. The postmodernists construct a set of features that are taken to constitute the postmodern, features that are the necessary signs of the disappearance of any effective difference between the signifier and the signified, the image and reality, the original and the copy, identity and difference, the part and the totality, surfaces and deep structures, truth and politics. In various combinations, the postmodern is described, negatively, as the denial of totality, coherence, closure, expression, origins, repre-

sentation, meaning, teleology, freedom, creativity, and hierarchy; and posi-
tively as the celebration of discontinuity, fragmentation, rupture, effects, surfaces, interventions, diversity, chance, contextuality, egalitarianism, pastiche, heterogeneity (without norms), quotations (without quotation marks),
and parodies (without originals). Despite the variations that may appear in
particular descriptions, the list remains fairly constant as the register of cultural practices that have emerged in the last twenty-five years.

Yet postmodernism's description of a practice of reflexive fragmentation
only renders it available in its purely negative aspect—as anti-essentialism—
since all these practices are all present in if not partly constitutive of the
modernist project. (This often leads to the addition of a second—ad hoc—
"feature": namely that the particular postmodernity of a specific practice can
only be understood in its negation of a narrowly constructed tradition of
modernism. This avoids the more complex question of the relations between
the postmodern and various forms of modernist sensibilities.) Within postmodernism the celebration of the local, the contextual, the fragment only
functions as negation. But postmodernism does assign these features a specific positivity, for it assumes that they are inherent within and self-evidently
available upon the surface of the postmodern, whether text, medium, or
event. This recreates a kind of self-sufficient realism of the fragment. In the
end postmodernism assumes that the postmodern speaks its own truth, a
truth that is not constructed but merely reported—postmodernism reports the
obvious—as if one could read the "postmodernity" of reality off its surfaces.

3. If we are to deconstruct postmodernism's articulation of the postmodern
and to make visible its negativity and elitism, we have to begin by considering the various forms of postmodernism. We can distinguish between those
versions that take the postmodern to define an ideological discourse within
late capitalism and those that take it to be the sign of the irrelevance or
disappearance of ideology in late capitalism. Within each we can construct
two alternatives, depending upon whether they remain within the realm of
discourse and inscribe an "elitism of frontiers" or enter the realm of the social
formation and inscribe an "elitism of the vanguard."

First, consider those theories that argue that postmodern features constitute specific ideological texts, that make the collapse of difference into an
ideological strategy. Such interpretations claim that texts that deny meaning
and reference and hence the possibility of ideology function ideologically by

either challenging or occluding the place of ideology. As a description of ideological texts, postmodernism identifies a difference in their formal constitution. Apart from the self-contradictory nature of the claim that a text's "status" can be read outside of any local context (who is the audience that is assumed in such descriptions?), such theories also ignore that whether and how any particular feature is registered and effective is always open. For example, notions of fragmentation are only constituted against particular ideologically constructed notions of unity. Unity is not an abstract and universal category to be singularly negated, but rather is always the expression of specific concrete unities that are themselves historically determined.

The result is that the position of the critic is reinscribed within new forms of elitism. In an elitism of an "internal frontier" (e.g., Foster's attempts to distinguish between "a postmodernism of resistance and a postmodernism of reaction" [1983, xii]), a distinction comparable to the claim of an aesthetic difference between high and mass art is reinscribed, albeit elsewhere. The canon is revised without the absolute hostility to or romanticization of the popular arts and the mass media (although some critics remain hostile). The difference is displaced into an ideological gap between authentic work (which necessarily resists or negates the commodification of art and life) and hegemonic work (which allows its own incorporation and even celebrates its own commodification). The difference is located within a particular experience of the text, in how the text determines its own consumption and whether it allows itself to be inserted into the various cultural economies of capitalism (galleries, museums, collections, media, advertising, art critics, etc.). Insofar as this difference cannot be read off the mode of production, there is a necessary discontinuity between politics and origin. But insofar as it can be attributed to the text itself, the frontier is reinscribed within discourse. While postmodernists may refuse to equate this difference with that between the avant-garde and the mainstream, the difference is reconstituted in the same form, as an internal frontier within discourse. Cultural texts are defined by their position within an already constituted set of political oppositions and possibilities: a text either challenges commodity culture or succumbs to it. And since such judgments require, at the very least, a privileged understanding of the economy of culture and the critical reception of particular artists, it is only the critic who can make the judgment, just as it is the artist who provides the model of resistance as negativity. An aesthetic elitism is reconstituted within the political; politics is relocated along the internal frontier of discursive difference. There is no positivity possible within these alternatives. There can be no celebration except of the pleasure of resistance itself; celebration itself is only worthy of being celebrated as negativity.

4. An elitism of the vanguard is predicated upon an interpretation of the postmodern that locates the break in a history outside both ideology in general and the specific forms of postmodern ideological practices. It thus seeks the "truth" of the postmodern not on its own surfaces, but in its relationship to a deep structure (a metanarrative) of real historical processes, for example, the transformation from monopoly to "late" capitalism, multinationalism, and the saturation of everyday life by the commodity form. Postmodern texts are the displaced signs of the new political-economic context. The displacement is accomplished by the mediation of experience. Textual practices are not merely the reflections of economic structures, they are the expressions of how we experience such structures, experiences already contaminated by ideology. Textual fragmentation is a sign of the real fragmentation of our subjectivity, which is itself a sign of the fragmentation of space in multinational capitalism.

If an ideological theory of frontierism assumes that the meaning and politics of discourse are determined internally and are written upon its surfaces, vanguardism assumes that they are determined elsewhere and written within their homologous relation to an equally transparent experience of reality. It is the critic's already taken-for-granted understanding of political and economic structures, of the historical narrative, that defines the ideology and politics of the postmodern. There is no space for contradictions; the postmodern refers to reality and defines the possibility of the true form of political struggle. (For Jameson [1984], for example, we need new cultural forms to provide maps enabling us to understand the organization of space in late capitalism.) In the end the masses remain mute and passive, cultural dopes who are deceived by the dominant ideologies, responding to the leadership of the critic, who is the only one capable of understanding ideology and constituting the proper site and form of resistance. At best we succeed in representing our inability to respond. Without the critic, we are unable even to hear our own cries of hopelessness. And hopeless we are and shall remain, presumably until some vanguard comes to provide us with the necessary maps of intelligibility and critical models of resistance.

5. The second category of postmodernism rejects concepts of ideology (and hence of experience and of the epistemological problem of subjectivity). It argues that power operates somewhere else or, more accurately, that the (always ideological?) construction of meaning, the very binary form of difference, is itself the locus of power. It rests upon the radical difference between difference and otherness in which the other (fragment) has neither a positive identity nor an identity constituted in relationships. There is, in Hall's terms (1986a), a "necessary noncorrespondence," which negates the reality of any constitutive or determining relationship. The other's "identity" is always established somewhere else, where its effects are. Again, we can distinguish between a discursive form that constructs an elitism of frontiers and a sociohistorical form that constructs an elitism of the vanguard.

The first makes the postmodern into the form of theoretical practice; in some readings of Foucault (1980), the collapse of difference becomes a theoretical strategy that challenges the status and form of theory itself.[1] Because it rejects difference as inherently hierarchical, it collapses reality into the local fragment and theory into the politically determined description of reality. Its radical contextuality denies the reality of structures, tendential forces, contradictions, and a history of determinations (even as "traces without an inventory"), for such real correspondences would reassert an economy of identity and difference.

The apparent positivity of otherness, however, is really a smoke screen since the fragment can only be realized as the negation of anything but the local. Because postmodernist theory cannot privilege any term, its only practice is the negation of any identity, relation, or structure, the endless subtraction of essences or unity (Deleuze and Guattari 1984). What appears as a positivity—the multiplicity of otherness, the reality of effects—must deny any particular other its identity except as a refusal of difference, as an increasing isolation from relations. What appears as a positive practice—the addition of fragments (politically, the construction of alliances)—is always merely an accumulation (gathering more rhizome) since what is added is never allowed to impinge upon the radical otherness of the fragments gathered together. Politically this means that there can be no vision of alternative structures, nor any recognition of the possible oppressiveness of the local. There is only an ongoing battle between the forces of structuration (which organize identities and difference) and the forces of radical otherness as negativity. Local negativity is the only form of political struggle. The celebration of possibilities gives way to the pure celebration of the possibility of otherness, without continuity and without any possible purchase on the larger structures that organize everyday existence (a politics of terrorism?).

Because postmodernist theory negates the possibility of difference (in the form of any binary logic) it leaves itself no position from which to theorize (or criticize). By so radically affirming the category of otherness, it undermines the possibility of ever occupying an other position. And yet it continues to do so. How? If the local is always constituted in terms of its difference from the impossible unity of a larger context, such a theory must always reprivilege its own position, allowing it to construct a boundary, an external frontier, circumscribing the local. This descriptive elitism ignores the fact that the concrete is always constructed in a detour through theory and inscribes an absolute principle of resistance as the other of power; it (and it alone) constructs the difference between power as territorialization and resistance as deterritorialization. But the ability to make this absolute distinction is only possible because of the particular elitist relationship that the critic establishes with those who are struggling (Spivak 1988).

While postmodernist theory seems to acknowledge the reality of people's struggles (and thus avoid both an internal frontier and vanguardism), such struggles are allowed only insofar as they speak their otherness, that is, insofar as they speak their radical negativity. In fact, such struggles are never allowed to speak; if they do, the positivity and contradictions that exist within their speech cannot be acknowledged. But nothing ever simply speaks its own truth. Its speech is always partly determined, partly negative and partly positive. Precisely because it denies the positive function of structures and the differences among structures of power (as well as any ability to choose between them), postmodernist theory denies the reality of struggles in favor of its own practice, which becomes the only viable form and measure of politics.

6. The second variant of anti-ideological postmodernism makes the collapse of difference into a description of historical reality (Baudrillard). The fragmentation of the postmodern has become the only reality—a hyperreality—available to us. Difference is no longer effective; every difference has imploded, rendering both terms within any binary construction ineffective. This postmodernism rejects not only the difference between signifier and

signified (which might still allow for the primacy of the former) but the very positivity of the signifier as well. Similarly the fact that the difference between reality and appearance and between reality and meaning has collapsed (the former in the nineteenth century, the latter as a result of the media's negation of their own mediation) means that appearance, meaning, and reality have disappeared; reality can no longer be the site of power or the origin of its own effects. In the simulacrum, "reality" no longer exists outside of "the compulsive repetition of the codes"; it is merely that which can be modeled or which fits a model. Even desire and power are no longer salvageable, for they reconstitute the real: we live in "the age of events without consequences" (Baudrillard 1984, 39).

Power can only be located in those processes that deny the disappearance of reality by reinscribing the real, or structures of meaning, within the operational codes of the simulacrum. Power exists in the binary codes that continue to construct differences (between the image and the real, surface and depth, subject and object, individual and social, power and resistance, activity and passivity) as if they were still effective. But their only effect is to occlude the fact that they are no longer effective, that the simulacrum needs them only as an "alibi." Power is not in reality but in the continuing appearance of the real. Power has disappeared, collapsed into its simulation.

Disappearance and implosion define the only point of celebration within such a postmodernist description. It defines a pure negativity of nihilism or indifference. The only possibility that remains is the hypersimulation of the very operations that define the simulacrum as a system of disappearance. Such a nihilism cannot even be oppositional or critical; it can only be fascinated with the neutralization, the nihilism, of the simulacrum itself. It can only seek to make indifference into "a stake, a strategy: [to] dramatize it" and thereby to institute a "disappearance beyond disappearance" (Baudrillard 1986, 39). Within such a postmodernist description, the only response to the collapse of difference is the celebration of an indifference "at least as great." We can only stand in the place the simulacrum offers us: indifferent to the absence of reality, amusedly living the media hype, fascinated by the forthcoming catastrophe of disappearance. Implosion is an ecstatic possibility and a catastrophic inevitability, a control system and a system of fascination. There is, after all, no difference. Nihilism is the only reality, celebrating the postmodern collapse of difference that has already happened.

There is, then, no struggle possible except that which would move with the simulacrum, pushing it beyond where it already is. Any struggle would rest upon the reality of a power that has already disappeared, and so it would, in the end, not struggle. It is, then, precisely the indifference of the masses, their refusal to struggle, to be represented or even to speak, that defines the postmodernist strategy. This is, obviously, a reverse vanguardism in which the masses—already operating within the simulacrum—become the leading edge of history, living the disappearance of agency and activity. Yet this negative vanguardism is also a ventriloquism, in which the postmodernist critic is the only voice that speaks in history. Although they claim to speak on behalf of the masses, they deny that the masses speak, or even care to. Baudrillard becomes the director of a postmodernist drama that has been placed upon the stage of history by the media, a theoretical Wizard of Oz hiding behind a history that has been reduced to the simplicity of Before and After, with neither cause nor effect. Contradictions disappear into the geometry of postmodernist indifference.

POSTMODERN STRUGGLES

1. Postmodernism makes the collapse of difference real. And it makes the postmodern into a sign of that reality—the reality of indifference—in texts, experience, and/or history. Postmodernism—perhaps because it exists largely within the empowered dominant ideological apparatuses—has emphasized its existence within the various forms of aesthetic practices. In fact, many of the practices of so-called postmodern art—that which we are warranted to take seriously—involves the appropriation of strategies—often without the fun or the enormously powerful investment—that have become the norm of popular culture in the age of the mass media. This is not to deny that many of these practices emerged within modernist art, but rather to affirm that their trajectory into contemporary art is mediated by the quotidianization of such practices, their incorporation into everyday life and common sense. However, it is not a question of constructing the ultimate text of the postmodern. How would one go about constructing such a text? Would it have to be less narrative than music videos, more of a spectacle than rock and roll wrestling, more disconcerting than Penn and Teller's "comic" routines, more stylized than *Miami Vice,* more parodic than *Moonlighting,* more meaningless than the *Wheel of Fortune,* more nihilistic than David Letterman, more camp than *Dynasty?* Perhaps it cannot be approached analytically but only through its absurdly real juxtapositions: an episode of *Miami Vice* in which Crockett must face down—probably in a clothing store—Jean Baudrillard, who plays a Frenchman trying to manipulate the American drug supply from behind his theoretical curtain. Or a game show on which Bruce Springsteen and Ronald Reagan compete, before a panel of ordinary celebrities, to see who will be the new president of CBS News.

In fact it is here that we can see the appropriation of the postmodern into postmodernism, for it is impossible to separate postmodern statements from their impact, that is, from the ways they are consumed and appropriated into the everyday lives of their fans. In fact the postmodern is, potentially at least, everywhere. I propose rereading the postmodern[2] as a popular sensibility, an attitude, if you will, providing a set of strategies of consumption within a larger context of needs[3] that appropriate practices and treat statements as billboards rather than signs. A sensibility describes particular modes by which objects are appropriated into configurations and inflected into a context of needs and empowerment.[4] Billboards are not signs of a displaced meaning or reality; they are not signifiers functioning within larger maps of intelligibility. We drive past billboards without paying attention because we already know what they say or because it doesn't matter, because we are driving too quickly to get somewhere else or because we see them everyday.

It is postmodernism's incessant shift from consumption back to production that reinscribes traditional forms of elitism. Self-consciously postmodernist texts are perhaps better conceived of as second-order constructions of the postmodern: attempts to make the structures of the text itself guarantee that this particular mode of appropriation will be reproduced. But they are unlikely to succeed because postmodernism appropriates the billboards of a popular sensibility into the "legitimated" aesthetic disposition or mode of perception that capitalizes on "the capacity to consider in and for themselves, as form rather than function, not only the works designated for such apprehension, i.e., legitimate works of art, but everything in the world, including cultural objects which are not yet consecrated . . . and natural objects" (Bourdieu 1984, 3).

A sensibility involves more than the struggle over meaning and art; it defines forms of investment, strategies of appropriation and expropriation, mattering maps, and organizations of taste, all of which cut across and relate diverse practices in our lives: "music and food, painting and sport, literature and hairstyle" (Bourdieu 1984, 6). Moreover, there are always competing sensibilities within the social formation, in relations of domination, subordination, and resistance. Bourdieu describes a "popular" sensibility "based on the affirmation of the continuity between art and life, which implies the subordination of form to function" (4). This sensibility refuses the refusal of the dominant aesthetic: it recognizes that detachment and indifference really involve the "refusal to invest oneself and take things seriously" (34). The dominant sensibility neutralizes any affective interest in the object, reducing life to art. The popular sensibility incorporates art into the material structures of everyday life. The popular sensibility therefore shifts the emphasis from difference to the positivity of celebration.

But there is also not a single popular sensibility, and no sensibility is without contradiction. The popular sensibility is always multiple, contradictory, and conditional, not only because of its subordinate position but also because of its primary commitment to the positivity of everyday life. The postmodern then is one version of such a popular sensibility. It is not the same as that which Bourdieu finds in the contemporary French working class, with its emphasis on narrative realism and ethical relevance, although the two share many features (including commitments to repeatability and ornamentation). But the postmodern sensibility does not operate within the realm of signification and representation, the realm controlled by the dominant dispositions and occupied by many subordinate sensibilities. It neither consumes an object as meaningful, nor attempts to bring meaning to bear upon everyday life.

Insofar as the postmodern constantly announces itself in media texts, it is because the media exist as part of the materiality of everyday life, not as its representation. The postmodern sensibility refuses to take the media as statements about reality, even about an absent or constructed reality. Rather they are appropriated into the temporal and spatial organization of everyday life. (How much of our physical reality—from houses to jeans—is marked by, if not as, media practices?) Because such media billboards are inseparable from everyday life, they are always part of a network widely available in popular histories. Moreover, they cannot be appropriated apart from their complex connections to social relations and activities that are both continuous with them and continuously interrupting them. The complexity of billboards' insertion into everyday life defines structures of mutual control locating our relation to them somewhere between absorption and distraction. If the dominant sensibility can confer aesthetic status on objects that are banal, even common, by treating them formally as signifying practices, the postmodern sensibility treats everything, even the most legitimated objects, as equally

common and banal. It appropriates anything—images, signs, realities—as
postmodern billboards.

2. What is it that such billboards mark and announce for us? What is the
strategic place of the postmodern sensibility in everyday life? Obviously we
cannot appeal to such statements as if they spoke their own truth. They never
do. Nor can we assume that, because they constantly announce fragmentation, reality or experience is correspondingly fragmented. Truth is never that
simple and, in part, it always has to be won. If we are to understand the
postmodern as a set of strategies within contemporary life, we have to enter
its terrain in order to understand its conditions of possibility, what enables
such strategies and what they in turn enable, what is invested in their material existence and what they in turn are invested in, how they empower their
fans and how their fans empower them. Postmodern billboards take us beyond the critical insight that identity can't be read off surfaces, that there are
no necessary correspondences. They seem to construct a necessary noncorrespondence, making it impossible to find connections between surfaces and
identities. But this is a historical strategy within the postmodern sensibility.
Billboards exist within contradictory structures of omnipresence—they are
everywhere and nowhere, entirely integrated into the mundanities of our
lives—and omnipotence—they are simultaneously trivial, threatening and re-
deeming. Every billboard is equally memorable, equally forgettable. This entails neither social amnesia nor the construction of a generally shared popular memory, for such issues fail to recognize that billboards work affectively
rather than ideologically. They are "tags" (as in graffiti) marking sites of investment. The postmodern appropriates billboards as boasts that announce
their own existence, much like a rap song boasting of the imaginary (or real, it
makes no difference) accomplishments of the rapper. The positivity of contemporary popular culture is located, in part, in the specific context within
which such affective investments have become problematic.

  If we are to understand how such a form of appropriation is empowering,
we have to specify the particular site at which it is positioned in the structures of everyday life. One of the features often tied to the postmodern is "the
waning of affect" (Jameson 1984, 61–62). But what is involved is not the
absence of intensity and investment (the realm of excitation, energy, and
activation for Freud, the realm of mood for Heidegger, what we might describe as a nonphenomenological theory of feeling) but the fact that intensity

is "free-floating," that it cannot be articulated to or experienced as alienation, that it is not effectively stitched into the structures of subject-positions and signification. This is not to suggest that such correspondences between the affective and the ideological are ever finally accomplished without contradictions. The historical difference is certainly not apocalyptic; it is quantitative and involves only part of our everyday lives. But its effects are real and increasingly visible. The postmodern operates at the site of the absent relation between affect and ideology, the fragmentation of at least a part of the constructed anaclitic unity of everyday life (and experience) into the indifference or otherness of mattering maps and the available maps of meaning. Each has become autonomous, but this does not make the rupture necessary or inevitable. Contemporary ideologies seem incapable of making sense of or articulating the intelligibility of certain affective structures. It is not that one doesn't live ideological values but that they are unrelated to—neither identified with nor differentiated from—our affective relations to the world. (Consider our increasingly contradictory relation to notions of happiness and love.) If modernism often attempted to reinscribe the disappearing possibility of this articulation, the postmodern operates within its absence.

But this absence—one that became increasingly dominant after the Second World War—exists within the context of another, earlier historical change. The postmodern is situated as well at the site of the indifference of subjectification and commodification. Their indifference does not mean that they are not different but rather that they bear no relation to each other, that they slide past and across one another, that, in the end, their difference doesn't matter. This is, according to Benjamin (1973), the condition of the masses. The space between affect and ideology is inserted into the everyday life of the masses as an almost schizophrenic failure to live what Foucault called (1980) the "epistemological doublet." The result is that everyday life is simultaneously constituted as unpredictable and totally predictable, uncontrollable and totally controlled, full of meaning and meaningless.

Ideologically this is like trying to make sense of the fact that life makes no sense, to understand why it matters that nothing matters. Affectively it involves living with and within the indifference of terror and boredom. These poles have become the most powerful and pervasive affective relations in everyday life, but they have also lost any historically constructed guarantees of where they are to be located, of how they are connected to specific events (e.g., think of their relations to subjectification and commodification: which is more terrifying? more boring?). Similarly they have lost any historically constructed position in an economy of meaning that could define their difference. The result is that our affective existence is increasingly defined by the collapse of the difference between the extremism of terror (as the uncontrollability of affect) and the nullity of boredom (as the absence of affect), between the terror of boredom and the boredom of terror. The postmodern offers strategies that open up the possibilities of terror and boredom as occasions for empowerment (e.g., as fun) and empowerment as the occasion for terror and boredom. (The counterculture of the 1960s may have been the last time one thought one could represent—and hence live [or experience]—this affective economy.) It is, specifically, within this complex economy that the postmodern is empowered and to which it offers itself as a response empowering its fans.

3. As soon as we begin to consider the politics of contemporary culture and the possibilities of a popular politics, we cannot help but note that the postmodern seems to operate as an obstacle. It throws us into a realm of non-contradictory identifications with the likes of Rambo, Springsteen, Madonna, Reagan, and Vanna White. One is confronted with people's increasing willingness to enjoy images by denying their political connotations. The obvious example: the large number of people who support Reagan despite their ideological opposition to his positions. A student recently struggled to find the terms that would allow him to define his distance from Reagan: "He's a great TV star, but I just can't watch his show" was all he could say. The same week that Reagan's campaign of disinformation against Libya was "uncovered" in the news, *Miami Vice* featured a show on the contras that ended with the government's explicitly lying to the American people. My students could organize their anger in response to *Vice* and they believed the news stories about Reagan and Libya, but they were unable to find a way of linking the two events and responding to them together.

Consider at this point what may be the most glaring contradiction of the postmodern within everyday life: that billboards that apparently represent the collapse of difference actually announce and enable us to continue struggling to make a difference, despite the fact that we take it for granted that such struggles are against all the odds. It is as if "the motive of this scavenging is to go on; not to progress, because we no longer believe in progress . . . [it is] the desperate determination to go on at any cost" (Schjeldjahl 1986, 23). But is this all that is at stake?

The empowerment of the postmodern depends precisely on its ability to open up the possibility of the positivity of affective investments or, in other words, to establish difference within indifference. The postmodern relocates otherness into relations of difference by celebrating identity; although it operates on the signifiers of ideology, it remains within the register of affect. It connects the two distanced economies although it cannot reintegrate them. Instead it uses the criteria of an affective economy to define its ideological relations or, more accurately, it appropriates ideology into affect. Difference is constituted not within ideology, but as a question of the distribution and the differential investment of energy. It is not merely a matter of making selected sites of the ideological feel good (for they can as easily feel bad) but of differentiating them by their possibilities of relating to our mattering maps. The postmodern empowers affect, bringing reality and ideology into its economies. Insofar as it is within pop culture that this affective economy is organized, it appears reasonable that it is pop that matters; whether and how particular ideological elements matter is not determined by their meanings but by how they can be incorporated into the mattering maps of pop.

Thus the postmodern makes irony, the celebration of excess and of outlandish surfaces into the billboards of the positivity of affective difference. These strategies are positioned in relation to the demand/threat of subjectification and commodification, but in an other place, for they slide from the ideological to the affective, locating themselves between the absolute loss of control and identity and their partial recuperation at the level of an affective mastery. As soon as we attempt to live again in ideological spaces, we are thrust back into the determining economy of terror and boredom (life is "a rat race at a snail's pace"). Alternatively, affectivity is stitched into reality without the mediation of ideology, although it is always the ideological whose surfaces provide the sites of the real. The postmodern circumvents the gap between ideology and affect by using the ideological merely as the raw material with which it can organize its maps of what matters. In ideological terms it doesn't matter what matters, but in affective terms it makes a real difference. This strategy—however politically problematic—provides a way of living "in a war zone" despite the fact of the impossibility of a representation that would enable us to respond to it in more traditional political terms. The postmodern becomes the paradoxical site at which we live an impossible relation to the future. By shifting from the ideological to the affective, it transforms the terror of the absence of the future (for which one must seek an ideological answer that is simply not available) into the impossibility or even irrelevance of any framework that could make sense of that absence. (Similarly it is the everydayness of the apocalypse that is boring and banal.) Postmodern "celebrations" of violence and destruction are predicated upon their meaninglessness, a meaninglessness that frees them to be relocated and identified affectively.

The postmodern articulates moments of affective positivity within the apparent reality of the indifferent and it marks their possible sites with its billboards; it appropriates these possibilities from various ideological organizations of reality, but it always removes them into its affective economy. In these terms, the privileging of an economy of "fun" becomes an empowering form of celebration. Although it is not the only postmodern moment of positivity, it reshapes the ways in which we organize our investments in the world; it struggles against the debilitating pessimism (if not nihilism) of that indifference, an indifference that exists not in reality but only within ideological articulations (and increasingly, one that is appropriated by the dominant ideologies). In response, the postmodern sensibility offers a strategy of indifference, a nomadic wandering through difference. Indifference points to the construction of identity, not by the negation of indifference but precisely by remaining indifferent to the question, to both difference and the collapse of difference. In fact, in a wonderfully ironic reversal, it asserts that there is no difference between an economy of difference and one of indifference.

By its indifference to significant difference, the postmodern relocates identity in a different dimension, as a matter of pure intensity, a question of asignifying investments. Identities are constructed within affective maps, implicated in constantly mobile affective relations, producing new empowering sites and reempowering old sites within its own terms. What appears ideologically mundane (because still caught in an economy of difference and indifference) is appropriated and reconstituted as affectively exotic. The postmodern allows us to assert and celebrate, simultaneously, our own ordinariness and our fantastic (even if fantasmatic) difference. It makes the ordinary extraordinary, establishing identity without negating difference. It creates difference in the celebration of its absence (e.g., Elvis as the self-made king; Springsteen as the star because he is just like us).

But this strategy is only available to the fan. For it is of the essence of such popular postmodern strategies that they encapsulate individuals within their own fluid affective investments. Fans locate themselves in an affective formation that is the only reliable statement of their condition, the only viable strategy for their survival, the only real index of their identity. The postmodern as a popular sensibility is exclusive; it dictates both generally and specifically that not everyone can exist within the same affective economy. It forces those (perhaps like myself) who would speak for and about it to vacate its terrain. It denies that mainstream popular culture is an amorphous and homogeneous incorporation machine engulfing all those who would resist it. Or rather, as an affective economy, it sacrifices the negativity of resistance for the positivity of its own celebration and survival. The mainstream then becomes a constantly changing configuration of encapsulated "elites"; each moment of affective identity assumes a privileged status for its own positivity, assumes that its own affective extraordinariness justifies, if not consecrates, its ideological ordinariness.

It is obviously the last move that must be challenged if we are to find ways of mobilizing the energy of the popular and articulating its positive celebration into negative opposition. This is not to suggest that the Left must create an "alternative" popular culture, but it is to recognize that contemporary popular culture maintains the possibility of opposition only by giving up its place within the domain of ideological resistance. Its oppositional status— when and where it may be realized—is an affective one, offering alternative maps of the organization of energy, concern, and desire. The task then is to win back its empowering positivity for progressive political investments, to reestablish a connection between ideological difference and affective identity. Nor is it a matter of merely moving our politics onto the terrain of pop culture, but of recognizing the power of this postmodern sensibility operating upon the terrain of an affective economy, and of realizing that such strategies may themselves be "necessary forms of appearance" in contemporary everyday life. And the only way we can accomplish that is if we connect to it, if we take on the task proposed twenty-five years ago, "to meet people where they are, where they are touched, bitten, moved, frustrated, nauseated" (Hall 1960), if we understand what it feels like to be alive in the modern world (which is not the same as the privileging of experience). We need to construct a politics of everyday life that begins with popular sensibilities, including the postmodern. That is the final boast of the postmodern billboard.

3 MYSELF . . .

(POLITICS)

▌t's a Sin": Politics, Postmodernity,

and the Popular

🔳

I want to begin by looking at the relationship between the Left—a set of progressive political positions—and cultural studies—an attempt to answer the question, What's going on? (or more accurately, What's going wrong? since that is usually the context in which "what's going on" becomes a pressing issue). The urgency of the issue, at least in the United States, I believe is demonstrated by the almost total inability of the Left to actively and strategically intervene into the discourses within which people's political positions are constructed and linked with support for systemic (structural, institutional, pragmatic, "real") politics.[1] For the past ten years, the Left has largely bemoaned the population's apparent support of the government's race to the Right. Suddenly, with Reagan out of the picture, optimism is running rampant, often based on the flimsiest of evidence: for example, an American[2] journalist writing in *Marxism Today* (July 1988) of "a new mood emerging in the United States that portends a fundamental political shift in post-Reagan America." The accompanying photograph shows four black children in front of the Lincoln Memorial with the caption, "Is America's youth returning to its founding principles?" The evidence offered consists of a single movie (*Wall Street*), a best seller (*The Bonfire of the Vanities*), and a rather dubious interpretation of the appeal of Dukakis.

My assumption, no doubt too forcefully argued because of my professional intellectualism, is that a theoretically rigorous and historically responsive analysis of the ways popular culture has helped to shape the vectors of political change in America over the last decade (at least) might enable more effective political struggle. I do not claim to be able to offer such an analysis, but I want to begin to think about its possibility and to offer some suggestions for what it might find. In fact, whatever the outcome of the next presidential election, I am not optimistic about the defeat of the New Right, because I am uncertain that its most powerful project actually requires control of the state.

I will begin by arguing that the "scandal" of cultural studies is not, contrary to some critics, that it cannot talk about systemic politics, but rather that it cannot talk about the increasingly important connections between such political struggles and popular culture and tastes. This "roadblock" is not the result of personal choice but of the concrete ways in which cultural studies has been determined by its social and historical circumstances. If its theoretical positions are always offered in part as strategic responses to those circumstances, then it must continuously question its positions in the light of emergent political and historical challenges. Second, I want to argue that we must extend recent work on "hegemony" to take account of the specific hegemonic struggles being waged in distinct national formations. Contrasting the rise to power of a conservative alliance in Britain and the United States enables us to see that at least one of the struggles of the American New Right involves a project aimed neither at the control of the state nor at redefining the contents of "common sense" (ideology), but at restructuring the terrain of the "national popular." This involves more than just the revival of a popular nationalism or a changing definition of the nation, for it entails a new relationship between the people and the nation.

This hegemonic project "uses" the very strategies of popular culture that empower its fans. These popular practices are not produced by or for the Right; they are the product of the real changing needs and desires of postwar generations on the one hand, and of late capitalism on the other. Yet they can serve to construct a certain structure of hegemonic power. In particular, I want to talk about "postmodernity" as an empowering sensibility that responds to real historical experiences and offers its fans strategies for gaining some measure of control over their lives. And yet at the same time, this set of strategies can and is being rearticulated to engender a significant, and significantly dangerous, restructuring of our relations to the meanings and politics of the nation.

THE SCANDAL OF CULTURAL STUDIES

The In-stall-ation of Cultural Studies. In the United States, cultural studies is a success; in fact, its recent rise has all the ingredients of a made-for-TV movie. Its success can be measured economically: publishers seek manuscripts and journals that can be framed and nominated as cultural studies. It can be measured professionally: it now enters into job descriptions and the titles of academic centers. And it can be measured discursively: it appears to be the latest signifier of what was called "critical theory" in a variety of academic organizations. The increasing appropriation and power of "cultural studies" often make it difficult to know what positions are being specified; nevertheless, even amidst this constructed ambiguity, there remains something like a center—to be precise, the tradition of British cultural studies, especially the work of the Centre for Contemporary Cultural Studies. In my own field of communications, cultural studies is no longer merely tolerated as a marginal presence; it is courted and even empowered—within limited parameters—by the discipline's ruling bloc. It is, in some ways, the first intellectually marginal and politically oppositional position to be legitimated by and incorporated into the mainstream of this relatively young discipline. (And of course, this has made it problematic for those in other still marginalized positions, some of whom have begun to construct it as an imperialistic "devil" worship.)

Yet, as Springsteen would say, there is a price to pay, and it is ironic that cultural studies has been installed into the American academy at just the moment when its work—especially in the United States—seems to be stalled. Or, perhaps more accurately, it has been hijacked by an alliance between the apparent demands of intellectual work (which would always condense it into a theoretical position), the exigencies of the distribution of its work (which has functionally erased its history, its internal differences, and its continuous construction through ongoing debates), and its own success as a politically committed and theoretically sophisticated body of work. The power of cultural studies has always been its refusal to construct itself as a theoretical position that can freely move across historical and political contexts, its refusal to define its own theoretical adequacy in academic or even epistemological terms. Theory in cultural studies can only be measured by its relationship to—and its enablement of strategic intervention into—the specific practices, structures, and struggles of its place within the contemporary world. Cultural studies has always been propelled by its desire to construct possibilities, both immediate and imaginary, out of its historical circumstances. As Hall (1986b) puts it, the purpose of theory is "to help us get a bit further down the road." Cultural studies does not surrender the epistemological question, rather it historicizes and politicizes it; a theory's ability to "cut into the real" (to use Benjamin's image) is measured by the political positions and trajectories it enables in response to the concrete contexts of power it confronts.

The irony is not merely the result of failing to recognize the complex ways in which the work of the Birmingham center was determined by its place within a specifically British topography and history. The irony I am thinking of is more alarming, and it threatens to undermine the relevance and cred- ibility of cultural studies. It has to do with the erasure of systemic political struggles at the very moment (perhaps the first since the postwar years) when there is a significant struggle over the structure of the relations between the state, the economy, civil society, and culture. In John Clarke's terms (1991) (although I am not sure they work as well in the United States), cultural studies seems unable to address the significant return of "political ideology" and the very real redistribution of political, economic, ideological, and cul- tural resources and power that is taking place. Consequently even its de- scriptions of "everyday life" fail to consider the devastating effects of these changes on the lives of individuals, including members of both subordinated and traditionally more privileged social groups—for example, the feminiza- tion of poverty, the increasing economic gaps, the almost hopeless position of black men (as well as that of other racial and ethnic minorities), the erosion of civil liberties and cultural freedoms, the impact of American international terrorism, and so on.

Let me add that while my comments are directed out of, and back into, a specifically American context, I think that much the same argument can be made about much of the current work in England, with some notable excep- tions. But even those exceptions—for example, Hall's interventions (1988) into debates about Thatcherism and hegemony—have ignored the changing relations between popular culture and systemic politics within the context of a hegemonic struggle. Others, like Hebdige, who do seem to address the ques- tion, reduce the relationship between hegemonic politics and popular cul- ture to a difference between abstract cultural logics that guarantee either domination or resistance. Thus in his most recent efforts, Hebdige (1987) distributes cultural practices onto a binary map in which there is a formal correspondence between cultural practices and political positions, deter- mined by the social location of the consumer. Power, however dispersed, is always articulated into a struggle between the popular—represented by Lon- don's street-styled and economically marginalized male youth—and the (evil) other of Thatcherism and official culture. Culture is differentiated according to a single dichotomous vision of contemporary Britain and of the possibilities of British identity. The answer to the question Which side is a cultural practice on? is always to be read off the social position of the consumers who intertextually articulate the text. Compare the following, first, on official culture: "All too often the packaging of product lines descends into designer cliche. All too often the 'revolution' in shop interiors means the installation of standardised fillings: the creation of the 'americanised' postmodern space that Jameson describes in which consumers drift like the zombies in George Romero's *Dawn of the Dead* . . . The effacement of regional differentiae beneath the hyper deluxe chic which has become synonymous in some quarters with the very word 'design' forms part of that englobement of the real by uniform solutions underpinned by uniform exchange values, part of the onward march of commodification" (Hebdige 1987, 52). And now, on the "casual style" as an exemplar of the popular: "The 'casual style' of dress which since the early to mid-80s has functioned as a uniform for 'street wise' inner city youth of whatever ethnic origin represents a similar appropriation [i.e., similar to other marginal and subcultural uses of music and style] . . . The various combinations of expensive designer label sportswear . . . are at once a repudiation of the rhetoric of wasted youth and of subcultural 'costume' . . . The casual style asserts the right to be relaxed, at home on Britain's windy streets . . . Despite its upward aspirations—its fixation on status—there is a democratic inference underneath this—on the surface—yuppie style. The casual look displaces attention away from the question of ethnic origin onto the question of how to build affinities on a shared cultural and aesthetic ground. It is focused on a set of common preferences rooted in the experience of the contemporary realities of city life" (47). What is the difference here? Hebdige's critical practice assumes that the articulation of texts depends on little else besides the social location of consumers (and in the case of official culture, the producers) within the binary difference between official culture (Thatcherism, Americanism, capitalism) and the culture of urban streets (the site of style and appropriation as resistance). There is an assumed necessary correspondence between social position, lived experience, cultural practice, and political significance.

Strategies of Cultural Analysis. Contemporary analyses of the politics of popular culture often operate with a limited repertoire of strategies, which almost guarantees our inability to come to terms with the relationship between popular culture and the rise of the New Right. Moreover, many of these strategies are reconstructions of older practices that have already been judged to be theoretically inadequate. Let me briefly, then, lay out the possibilities of this repertoire. At one extreme, cultural analysis reembraces a politics of domination in which cultural subjects are either actively and intentionally manipulative or passively manipulated. Such a strategy reinscribes a linear relationship between production and consumption by substituting a mediated, formal correspondence between cultural images and social imaginaries for older causal models. Cultural politics is defined by ideological frames and/or homologies that, in the end, guarantee how cultural formations are delivered over to political positions. Despite the complexities of the analysis, in the end the popularity of Rambo evidences the xenophobic and militaristic anticommunism of the American public, just as the success of *The Bill Cosby Show* traces out the public's nostalgic return to a conservative domestic economy (not to mention racism). On the other hand, specific marginal (or subcultural) subjects can and do produce their own alternative and resistant frames or homologies. But such moments are always quickly reincorporated into the passively received and dominantly constructed mainstream. The result is that the critic is condemned to being nothing more than the witness and chronicler of the impending, if not continuous, victory of the dominant forces.

At the other extreme, cultural analysis reinscribes liberal and conservative efforts to depoliticize (and aestheticize) popular culture. The "end of ideology" is recast as the disappearance of the political scene and the celebration of apathy as the "hypersimulation of politics" (as if it were an intrinsically active refusal). Similarly the aestheticization of politics is transformed into its discursification, as if the entire substance of political differences was defined by discursively produced subject positions. In the end, political critique is reduced to the deconstruction of any political claim, difference, or position. But since such reflexivity can never be completed, it merely reproduces those positions of power that the critic has failed to, or refuses to, or is unable to deconstruct. Such strategies end up by willingly and often dispassionately vacating the historically specific and lived terrain of cultural and political struggle.

One of the most common strategies of cultural analysis is located between these two extremes. While refusing to continuously rediscover the effective presence of essentialized transhistorical relations of domination and subordination, and abstract structures of our own ideological inscription—for example, patriarchy (or feminism), or commodification and consumerism (or socialism)—this strategy continues to read texts as if they enacted political theories in the form of abstract structural logics: fetishization, hierarchy, fragmentation, and deconstruction.

But the most compelling strategies of contemporary cultural analysis are those that address the politics of everyday life. Unfortunately this often entails adopting traditional strategies (as above) to address the question of difference and power within individuals' lived reality and the construction of popular pleasures, forms of empowerment, and local resistances. In some cases cultural practices are seen as texts: the critic seeks the contradictions, the empowering gaps within its ideologically dominant positions (e.g., Modleski 1984). In other cases cultural practices are defined formally: the plurality and fragmentation of popular practices are read as a struggle against the dominant hierarchically organized modes of modernist cultural power (e.g., Chambers 1985). In still other cases cultural practices become the modes of popular consumption by which people appropriate the resources of their cultural environment to their own ends, to construct their own meanings and pleasures (e.g., Fiske 1989). The recognition that there is a politics operating within everyday life is an important advance, which further enables us to talk about the complex effects of cultural practices in multiple domains. But such strategies too often reduce the politics of culture to the terrain of the quotidian; they fail to rearticulate the forms of empowerment and survival with which people maintain some control over the construction of their own differences, their own lives, and their own possibilities, to the structures and tendential forces of the social formation. They construct the everyday as if it were absolutely autonomous, and its practices as if they were always forms of empowerment, resistance, and intervention. This simply answers too many questions ahead of time: it negates the fact that there are moments and formations of ignorance and passivity within everyone's cultural relations. Empowerment by a single practice is, after all, never total, never available to everyone, never manifested in exactly the same way, and moreover its success is never guaranteed. A text may be polysemous, even to the point of constructing its own contradictions, but that need not erase the reality of dominant, "preferred" meanings. Furthermore, not all "negotiated" readings or uses of a text[3] are oppositional, or even resistant. By whom are particular practices or pleasures seen as empowering or subversive? And as Judith

Williamson (1986), Meaghan Morris (1988a), and others have recently argued, the fact that specific cultural practices are pleasurable, even empowering, does not tell us anything about the political valences of such pleasures or the possibilities of articulating such empowering moments to explicit political positions. It is too easy for these strategies to become little more than the fantasy of politically correct (guilty) pleasures. Cultural analysis has to acknowledge not only that "pleasure," "resistance," and "struggle" refer to complex sets of different effects that have to be specified concretely, but also that the relations among them are themselves complex and never guaranteed in advance. Only in this rather messy terrain can we begin to sort out how people recognize and transform themselves and their world within existing popular cultural practices.

The Historical Hijacking of Cultural Studies. The current roadblock confronting cultural studies—its inability to address the specificity of the relations between popular culture and systemic politics in the context of a hegemonic struggle—has been determined to some extent by the history of its theoretical responses to the specific political conditions it has engaged. If we are to begin interrogating the relations between American popular culture and the rise of the New Right, it is useful to try to disarticulate the project of cultural studies from the strategic assumptions that have constructed its identity in response to those conditions.

We can begin by recognizing that cultural studies emerged at a particular historical conjuncture, a moment in which Williams (1965) could not only reconstruct the history of modernization and of radical left struggles as "the long revolution" but also locate its most powerful motor force in the cultural domain. This historical moment has shaped our understanding of the politics of culture and of the analytics of culture. This conjuncture is often described as the fullest realization and institutionalization of the "corporatist" or "social democratic" compromise. That is, the years surrounding the Second World War were characterized by the construction of a powerfully effective social consensus committed to (1) a high-consumption domestic economy within a culture of expanded personal freedom, and (2) the active interventionist role of the state in reconciling the interests of the major economic blocs and in managing social problems. The establishment of this "consensual politics" created the conditions for the erasure of political ideology, for within the corporatist compromise the ideological differences between classes or parties seemed, at best, secondary to the apparently unified interests of the society. Not surprisingly, the liberal celebration of this consensus as both real and permanent announced "the end of ideology," and it has to be admitted that, within the terms of the consensus, this was at least a reasonable discourse. In fact, the Left was complicitous in this insofar as its search for more sophisticated models of ideology helped erase the more immediate and specific struggles of ideological politics and increasingly emphasized the place of ideology in everyday life, as "common sense," as a lived system of shared beliefs. But this compromise—and its implicit consensus—is precisely the object of a concerted attack. The New Right is effectively challenging, and to some extent has successfully dismantled, the conditions of the postwar conjuncture.

A second condition of the specific shape of cultural studies can be seen in the extremely personal form within which the question was raised. Unlike the vast majority of the writers whom Williams (1958) gathers together into the "culture and society tradition," the position of the various founding authors of cultural studies was such that the problem of culture was defined in terms of the problematic of participation. As Williams's novels make clear, there was a real problem for what Hoggart (1957) called "the scholarship boys." Caught between two worlds, two incommensurable languages, systems of social relations and values, they struggled to make sense of their experience of belonging to neither fully. The question of social mobility and change was translated into a cultural vocabulary that attempted to understand the creation of community, and of a livable place within the community for an individual, through the communicative creation of a shared system of meanings (what Williams called a knowable community). The problematic of cultural studies was defined by the mediating role of culture between social position and cultural identity, a role that was understood—because it had already been located within the uncertainty of their own experience of participation—in terms of the relation between community and communication, and the production of consensus.[4] This model of the relationship between the critic and culture as one of participation continued into the subcultural work of the Centre in the mid-seventies, however vicarious that participation may have been at times.

Three things happened when cultural studies was institutionalized at the Birmingham center: First, a cultural theory of communication was transformed into a communicational theory of culture; second, the terms of the problematic—culture and society—were bifurcated and disciplinized into literary-textual studies and sociology; and third, these two theoretical structures were mapped onto each other so that the focus of cultural studies became the ideological relationship between the production of meaning and experience. The precarious relationship between cultural studies and contemporary theories of communication was perceived quite early: "*The Uses of Literacy* was read—such were the imperatives of the moment—essentially as a text about the mass media. Its graphic portrayal of the extremely complex ways in which the 'springs of action' of a subordinate class might be 'unbent' by a dominant culture intent, with the new means of communication at its disposal, on winning consent precisely in that class . . . was, on the whole, neglected. The notion that the Centre, in directing its attention to the critical study of 'contemporary culture' was, essentially, to be a Centre for the study of television, the mass media and popular arts . . . though never meeting our own sense of the situation, and always resisted as an inadequate account of our project—nevertheless came, by default, to define us and our work" (Centre 1969–71).

The conception of cultural studies as a paradigm for the study of mass communication (a paradigm that could be retrospectively returned to the field of its origin as an alternative model for literary studies), as an alternative to liberal effects theory, as well as to both the right and left versions of mass culture theory, was not merely constructed by default. Rather it has a specific history. It was made possible, first, by the assignment of each of the terms— culture and society—to its appropriate disciplinary body of theory. Cultural studies involved the bringing together, first, specialists but later the specialized knowledge and skills of the textual critic and the social theorist. If literary criticism seemed too intuitive, semiotic methods could be appropriated to investigate the relationships between textual practices and structures, and the production of systems of meaning and value. If sociology seemed too positivist, this could be ameliorated by turning to the phenomenologically oriented work of the interactionists (hence the interest in deviancy theory, from which subcultural resistance theory emerges) to investigate the relationship between social structures and practices and the production of subjective meaning. (And the fact that both literary and sociological studies tended to be politically unreflective and ungrounded provided the welcome occasion for a return to the explicit marxist problematic in such authors as Sartre, Gramsci, Lukacs, and eventually Althusser.) Between these two disciplines, the common ground was defined by the ideological question of the production of meaning, by the relationship between public expression and private meanings, and by the domain of experience that brought together the subjective and the social. Once the question of experience had been constructed as the mediating term between textual practices and subjective interpretations, it was a short distance to the communicative model of a relationship between subjects and texts, each existing independently of their specific encounter, but each located within a larger social context of codes and intentions. Nor was this communicative model substantively challenged by later work in discourse theory, which, while refusing to locate the subject outside of the text (by reducing the subject to a textual product), continues to define the problematic of culture as the relationship between text and subject. It is this fundamental dichotomy (and its refusal of other sites and sorts of effects) that has, as well, dictated the contemporary voice of cultural studies and its appropriate forms of reflexivity: the cultural critic must refuse participation in order to reaffirm a reflective distanciation.

This transformation of cultural studies according to the terms of a communication model was further stitched into place by a particular response to the growing complexity of the mass media and the media audiences: namely, the sociological appropriation of the encoding-decoding model. Hall's (1973) explicitly semiotic analysis of the displaced relations between the structurally unequal moments of production and consumption was reinscribed in the *Nationwide* studies (Brunsdon and Morley 1978, Morley 1980) into a communication model that assumed the factual existence of specific texts received by identifiable sets of individuals. Moreover it was assumed that cultural studies had to address the question of the actual interpretations made (or at least offered) by various audience fractions, and that these differences were to be explained by the determining effects of already constituted social differences that constructed the experiential context into which individuals appropriated the text, and from which they constructed their own meanings.

Let me summarize, for a moment, the results of the history I have attempted to construct: Culture is bifurcated into the relationship between texts and lived reality; lived reality is reduced to the social determination of experience. The result is that cultural studies is always caught in the twin pulls of textual and sociological research. Thus it is not surprising that most of the work in cultural studies can be displayed in one of these two tendencies: the effort to read experience off texts (producing a kind of literary cultural studies) or the effort to read texts through experience (producing an ethnographic cultural studies). In either tradition, the ultimate object of research is ideology, located in the relationship between social position, meaning, and experience. This tripartite view of ideology demands further elaboration, for it will enable me to describe the final historically determined direction of cultural studies I want to consider: a populist politics based upon the identification of the popular with social position.

It may be useful here to return to Williams and to offer an alternative reading of his theory of culture. Williams argued that cultural discourses could only be understood within the context of culture as the relations among all the elements in a whole way of life. Culture is not reduced to either the textual production of meaning or the structures of experience. Williams's assumption, perhaps mistaken, was that there existed structural homologies between the different formations within a culture (textual, experiential, technological, etc.). There are two points here that significantly differ from the Birmingham reading: First, texts can only be understood insofar as they are inserted into the cultural context formed at the intersection of everyday life and the social formation, and second, that context cannot be described merely as a structure of meaning or experience, but rather it is something more complex and multidimensional: a structure of feeling. Consequently the relationship between discourse and politics was always indirect, articulated through and by its place in the complex relations of the cultural totality. In a sense cultural studies at the Centre was built upon E. P. Thompson's critique (1961), which, in the end, identified ways of life with ways of struggle, that is, identified cultural and political positions. This gave rise to a particular form of populism predicated on the direct inscription of the voices of the people. For Williams, the politics of the people's voices was not guaranteed outside of their inscription into the contradictory relations between the cultural landscape of everyday life and the political struggles of the social formation, mediated through competing structures of feeling.

Let me take another route to explain this distinction. In his classic essay, "Base and Superstructure in Marxist Cultural Theory," Williams (1973) offers two descriptions of cultural differences. The first describes what we might call a cultural topography: the social and temporal relations between different cultural formations—dominant, emergent, and residual. The second describes a political topography: dominant, incorporated, and oppositional.

Cultural studies first located the popular on the cultural map as other than the dominant (thereby rendering the mainstream commercial culture as something other than popular) and then equated the two maps. The result was that cultural marginality guaranteed political resistance, even if only at the level of culture (hence the notion of "magical" solutions in subcultural theory). But there was, implicit in the construction of this theory, another assumption: namely, that the cultural topography corresponds to a social topography. This ensures that the culturally marginal is always produced by the socially marginal, that is, the politically subordinate. The resulting theory constructs a cultural map in which the popular is defined, in the first instance, by its social difference and, in the second instance, by its guaranteed political difference. This is, I would argue, the basis of subcultural "resistance theory," which offered the clearest statement of the populist model of political struggle for cultural studies: the voice (experience) of the socially subordinate is directly inscribed in the culturally marginal, which serves, at the very least, to offer a cultural articulation of political resistance. The fact that some current work in cultural studies has abandoned the celebration of marginality (against the mainstream) and now finds the voice of resistance everywhere does little to challenge this populist model, since it assumes that social and political subordination guarantees political resistance.

Recognizing that cultural studies, even in its institutionalized form, is not as unified, homogeneous, and consistent as the above construction suggests, nevertheless I think that this idealized history of the formation of cultural studies helps us to understand its contemporary inability to address the hegemonic challenge of the New Right, and the close relationship between that challenge and the terrain of the popular. Specifically, if we are to approach these questions, I think we have to challenge the communicational model of culture and the related reduction of culture to ideology, the disciplinary bifurcation of everyday life, and the subsequent reduction of the popular to a set of discursive products; the communitarian (participatory) model of the social formation and the related reduction of systemic politics to consensus formation; and the populist model of the relationship between social position, cultural practices, and political relations.

The Impossibility of Cultural Analysis.[5] Rereading Hoggart's *Uses of Literacy* (1957), I am struck by the confidence with which he could describe the terrain of the emergent mass culture. And Williams's *The Long Revolution*

(1965, originally published in 1961), operating on an even grander scale, casting his glance over the centuries of modernization and modernity, confidently isolated and often meticulously chronicled the tendential cultural forces that had reshaped and would continue to reshape the social formation. I have said nothing about the validity of their interpretations: Hoggart's overly pessimistic projections of the power of the mass media, Williams's overly optimistic narratives of the possibilities of culture as the leading force in revolutionary history. I have spoken only of their voice—their confidence—which is perhaps inseparable from the source of the passion of their labor, a labor that attempted to translate an immediate and powerfully personal experience of social dislocation into a historical understanding of the relations between culture and society. But it is also inseparable from the structure of the cultural terrain at the moment they were writing.

The conditions that enable cultural analysis have changed. Apart from the more explicitly theoretically and politically driven questions of what sense one makes of contemporary popular culture and how, it is difficult to know where to begin to describe the terrain itself, to locate its significant exemplars and to identify its most powerful vectors. This is not only a matter of our theoretical assumptions: not only can we no longer confidently read the meaning or ideology of a text off its surfaces, but even the notion of a single identifiable fixed text is problematic. It is also a matter of historically different conditions, of the changing spatial and temporal complexity of the cultural terrain itself. How does one talk about even something as apparently limited as television in the contemporary United States? New technologies and changing economic conditions have rapidly expanded the range of leisure activities and popular culture: cable has expanded the number of television stations; video recorders have given consumers the power to control the screen in multiple ways, even to the point of producing their own rap videos; the number of video rental stores expands weekly, to the point where this service is increasingly incorporated into apparently unrelated sites (e.g., truck rental stores, supermarkets); bars, discos, and even record stores have appropriated the television screen into their own rhythms and commercial imperatives. How do we possibly construct the appropriate intertextual "reading formations"? How do we stabilize the mobile and shifting alliances of audiences and subjectivities, of relations to and investments in various televisual sites, events, and activities? The television screen provides little assistance, even apart from the practical difficulties of knowing ahead of time what to watch and what to videotape for further analysis. It is difficult to know the appeal of specific events—ranging from those presumably targeted to particular audiences to those apparently addressing the broad mythic American viewer.

American television is, to say the least, strange. And that strangeness is marked not only by particular programs and styles (e.g., *Pee Wee's Playhouse, Crime Stories, Moonlighting, The New Adventures of Mighty Mouse, America's Most Wanted,* etc.) and not only by television's increasingly problematic relationship to whatever it constructs as being off the screen (e.g., news, talk shows, docudramas, live documentaries, etc.). Television's strangeness is most powerfully marked by the disturbing heterogeneity of its appeals, and by the rapidity with which it moves—presumably reconstituting its viewers— through that diversity. One need not watch MTV; one can watch network prime-time programming or look at the seasonal ratings. Or, perhaps most mysteriously, one can consider any sequence of commercials, which are likely to range from traditional sentimental or star appeals, to informative discussions of health, to absurdist fragmented scenarios, to postmodern cynical narratives (e.g., a woman sitting in a bar imagines a relationship with a handsome stranger, tracing it through a romantic courtship and a yuppie version of family life to its inevitable bitter collapse. She turns to the stranger and proclaims, "I can buy my own, Mr. Fancy Perfect").

Of course, in the end, one cannot isolate television any longer. No one's relation to popular culture is defined simply by their relation to television; everyone is constantly exposed to a variety of media and forms, and participates in a range of events and activities. Even if we could construct the intertextuality of television, and even if we could then relate it to other forms of textual choices and exposures (music, film, books, fashion, magazines, comics, etc.), we cannot separate it from the range of leisure activities that fill the interstices of our everyday lives: jogging, shopping, mall walking, games, exercise, dancing, and so forth. We cannot separate it from the contrary and often boring demands of work (both paid and unpaid, both domestic and nondomestic), education, politics, taxes, illness, and so on. We cannot ignore the relations between the changing cultural terrain and the changing forms, practices, discourses, and sites of labor. Beyond the important feminist arguments about the gendered construction of the places and meanings of leisure and work, we need to take account of the growing importance of service and leisure employment in the current economy (and its limited success), of the acceptance and exploitation of more flexible arrangements of productive time and space, and of the increasing reality of an enforced leisure time (through unemployment, cutbacks in school hours and daycare facilities, and so on).

Similarly the very possibility or reasonableness of trying to identify and isolate audience fractions, communities, or taste cultures seems increasingly problematic. Our theories haunt our efforts to construct a theory of popular culture through audiences rather than texts (since our theory seems to have largely dismantled the latter possibility already). The cultural analyst must confront the problematic status not only of audience interpretations and reports, but of his or her own interpretations. The question of what one knows when one knows how an audience (thinks it) experiences a specific program can only be answered by locating that experience itself within the broader context of the social formation, of historical struggles, and everyday life. But there are also apparently historical conditions that have made this project problematic. I live in a small midwestern town whose population is evenly divided between local residents and a university population, each exhibiting its own heterogeneity. Life is organized around economies of farming, leisure/service, and education/sports. Yet even here there are no homogeneous communities (which is not to deny overlapping interests, both economic and cultural). There are no "taste cultures"; I doubt that there are two people who watch exactly the same constellation of programs. There are only multiple, mobile, and contradictory subjects constantly moving through, proliferating, and transforming temporary alliances and formations. Moreover we cannot know ahead of time what are the pertinent social differences that construct cultural audiences, or when we have arrived at an appropriate level of concreteness that would enable us to define either a community's identity or its determined relations to popular culture.

Historical conditions, then, have forced us to recognize that the traditional assumptions that enabled us to confidently divide up the terrain of culture into texts, forms, and media and of cultural subjects into audiences and communities are no longer viable. This should come as no great surprise; in fact, the same conclusion could be reached, and should have been, through our commitment to interdisciplinarity, except that too often we accepted the need to transcend disciplinary boundaries only in our theoretical perspective. But the disciplines were quickly reinscribed in the ways we divided up the field of cultural objects—and hence divisions that often preserved our own critical identities. But of course one cannot so easily separate the effort to describe the cultural landscape from the project of understanding its place in the historical production and reproduction of the structures and relations of the social formation, the project of cultural studies. Cultural studies is concerned with describing and intervening in the ways discourses are produced within, inserted into, and operate in the relations between people's everyday lives and the structures of the social formation so as to reproduce, resist, and transform the existing structures of power. That is, if people make history but in conditions not of their own making, cultural studies explores the ways this is enacted within cultural practices and the place of these practices within specific historical formations.

THE SPECIFICITY OF AMERICAN HEGEMONY

Hegemony by Any Other Name . . . . [6] We can only begin to redefine the problematic of the politics of popular culture in relationship to a reconsideration of the politics of the contemporary social formation. The concept of hegemony is useful in this task, but unfortunately it has proven useful to almost every position on the Left. We need, then, to undertake the arduous and, at this stage, speculative task of bringing the concept to bear upon the particular context of the United States. Hegemony is a specific, historically emergent project of restructuration, with its own conditions of possibility and its own strategies of struggle. Moreover hegemonic politics can take on radically different forms in different social formations and national contexts.

There are certain rather unsettling features of the contemporary political situation, marked by the rise, in a variety of national contexts, of a new conservative formation. This is, by itself, not sufficient to suggest a radical restructuring of political struggles. Rather what is most perplexing is the combination of the broadly based populist appeal of this formation, the contradiction between its explicitly stated project of deconstructing the social democratic compromise of the postwar years (i.e., its antistatism) and its public reconstruction of a powerful, politically aligned state apparatus, and, perhaps most threatening, its ability to win the electoral support of class fractions that would seem to have strong reasons to oppose the interests and policies of the new conservatives. Stuart Hall (1987, 1988) has turned to Gramsci's notion of hegemony in order to make sense of this political arena by distinguishing hegemonic organizations of national power from other historical efforts to establish power through (cultural) domination. The difference is not merely between two different theoretical models of power but between two alternative, historically specific modes of national political struggle. While both of these are responses to the increasing complexity and importance of civil society as a site of political struggle, their structures and strategies are significantly different. Struggles for domination are enacted when the social formation can be effectively divided into two mutually exclusive worlds corresponding to two social groups, each with its own realities, experiences, and cultures. The relations between the two social groups are defined hierarchically and maintained through processes of incorporation. That is, the dominant group organizes the subordinate population and culture from above, as it were, struggling to win a consensus that disarms any resistance by making over the subordinate population in the mirror image of the dominant group. A hegemonic struggle, on the other hand, responding to a situation in which the masses define the appropriate subjects of the social formation, cannot divide the social arena into two competing groups, each with its own corresponding worlds, cultures, and politics. The masses confound any such simple divisions; within the masses, social differences proliferate. The difference between the subordinate and the dominant cannot be understood on a single dimension. Power in such a formation is always organized along many different, analytically equal axes: class, gender, ethnicity, race, age, and so on, each of which produces disturbances in the others.

Consequently hegemonic struggles do not seek to dominate the masses through the production of an unequal consensus or through practices of incorporation; instead a specific alliance of class fractions, the "ruling bloc," attempts to win a position of leadership by rearticulating a shared social and cultural landscape and its own position within it. But this rearticulation is never a single battle; it is a continuous "war of positions" dispersed across the entire terrain of social and cultural life. At each site, in each battle, the ruling bloc must rearticulate the possibilities so as to establish itself in and as the leading position. The hegemonic struggle for power takes place on and across an already constituted field, within which the identities and positions of the contesting groups are already being defined but are never fixed once and for all. If it is to win hegemonic leadership, then, the ruling bloc cannot ignore resistances to its specific struggle nor to its longer-term projects; it has to recognize and negotiate with at least some of the resistant fractions. It need not incorporate them into its own position, nor entirely disarm the differences. These fractions can remain outside the hegemony, apart from the ruling bloc, retaining their subordinate position. But their subordinate relationship to the ruling bloc is an active, empowered one. They have real power because they have to be taken into account, and their resistances have to be constantly negotiated with, even to the extent of redefining and restructuring the hegemonic project itself. Thus a hegemonic politics always involves the ongoing rearticulation of the relations between, and the identity and positions of, both the ruling bloc and the subordinate fractions within the larger social formation. A hegemonic politics does not incorporate resistance but constructs positions of subordination that enable active, real, and effective resistance. (Hegemony also defines the position of the excluded: those resistant fractions with whom it cannot or will not negotiate, whom it therefore seeks to place outside the hegemonically restructured social formation.) This is not, then, the construction of a consensus in which all resistance is incorporated into the dominant ideological positions; rather it is the ruling bloc securing for itself a position of leadership.

Hegemonic leadership, through which the ruling bloc attempts to rearticulate the structure of the social formation, has to operate where the masses live their lives. It has to take account of and even allow itself to be modified by its engagement with the fragmentary and contradictory terrain of common sense, of popular culture, and of the "national popular." It is here where the social imaginary is defined and changed; where people construct personal identities, identifications, priorities, and possibilities; where people form and formulate moral agendas for themselves and their societies; where people constantly reconstruct their future in light of their sense of the present; where people decide what matters, what is worth investing in, what one is, can be, or should be committed to. It is in this sense that the hegemonic struggle must touch ground upon or pass through the popular: not the popular as a fixed set of texts or practices, not as a coherent ideology, nor even as some necessarily celebratory and subversive structure (the carnivalesque). It is the complex and contradictory terrain, the multidimensional context, within which people live out their everyday lives. Although it always has a political registration, it is never guaranteed in advance. Entering onto the popular, struggling over its articulation: that is what hegemonic struggles are about. There can be no assurance ahead of time what the results will be, for it depends upon the concrete contexts and practices of struggle and resistance. Speaking in the vocabulary of popular ideologies, using the logics by which people attempt to calculate their most advantageous position, celebrating the pleasures of popular culture, appropriating the practices of everyday life—this is where hegemony is fought over.

But there is more to hegemony. Specifically, Hall (1988) argues that there are three additional requirements, for it is not the case that the political and economic construction of hegemony can be equated with either the ideological reconstruction of common sense or the cultural reconstruction of a "national popular." While these are necessary for the establishment, however precarious, of the hegemonic position of leadership of a ruling bloc, that bloc is always composed of an alliance of class fractions that (1) has or is attempting to win the control of first the economic and subsequently the state apparatuses; (2) that is itself consensually organized (3) around an explicitly defined national project of radically restructuring the social formation. Hall's analysis of Thatcherism is, of course, an exemplary if not paradigmatic analysis of a hegemonic formation. But I want to argue that, in significant ways, it is inapplicable to the context of contemporary struggles in the United States. This is not just a matter of the differential success of the Thatcherite and the Reaganite projects; rather their differential success is a result of their different contexts and projects, despite the very real similarities that exist between them. Both, after all, are the product of real historical work, within their respective parties (in the United States, this began immediately after the defeat of Goldwater in 1964) and in the intellectual sphere (through various privately endowed think tanks). Both can be seen as responding, in the first instance, to changing economic conditions; both are fundamentally committed to the centrality and primacy of capitalism (and to the power of finance capital and a service economy rather than manufacturing); both have attacked the corporatist state and the social democratic compromise of the postwar era (constructing a contradictory position in which the state intervenes into private life but not into public economic relations); both have sought to install economic definitions of freedom over individual rights and civil liberties (i.e., the right to compete and fail); and both are embodied in the figure of a single person—a national leader.

While these shared conditions define the general rise of a contemporary conservatism within the world of late capitalism, they tell us little about the ways in which these conditions have been articulated into specific national struggles. Here we must begin to look at the conditions and characteristics that define and enable their differences. Let me begin by briefly describing some of the major features of Thatcherism and the hegemonic struggle in

England. First, Thatcherism arose and gained ascendancy in response to a very real, very particular, and powerfully experienced sense of national economic crisis. Thatcher's project—despite its ideological, cultural, and moral dimensions—was primarily directed to that crisis. What emerged was a fairly specific national project that demanded sacrifice in return for the imaginary construction of a promised community of prosperity. Second, the alliance Thatcher put together and that has been installed in a position of leadership is particularly (at least by comparison with other nations) consistent; to the extent that contradictions arise within the ruling bloc, Thatcherism seems quite willing and capable of purging specific fractions. Third, Thatcherism operates within a political system in which the political, legislative, and executive functions are condensed into the same organizations. This has not only enabled the enormous success of Thatcher's program as well as specific proposals, it has also guaranteed an ongoing public debate around her legislative agenda. Finally, there is the figure of Thatcher herself. She is, it must be admitted, extremely powerful. She is positioned as both the originator and representative of the ruling bloc and its project; consequently, she is identified with every specific proposal and with each victory (and defeat) as well. Moreover her success rests not only on legislative control nor on a taken-for-granted popular constituency, but upon her ability to forge a different temporary popular political alliance around any particular issue. While her power is quite personalized, depending in part on her female positioning, Thatcher is not merely the "iron lady": she is the lower-middle-class housewife, but with authority; she is the English "schoolmarm." This last image, perhaps the most evocative, largely defines the homology that exists between Thatcher's personal authority, the hegemonic project of Thatcherism, and its struggle over the popular.

Hall has described the project as "authoritarian populism": "a movement towards a dominative and 'authoritarian' form of democratic class politics—paradoxically, apparently rooted in the 'transformism' . . . of populist discontents" (1988). Thatcher's populism is defined not only by its organization and rearticulation of popular discontents, experiences, languages, and modes of calculation; it is defined as well by an explicit attempt to reorganize the boundaries between the popular and the elite. For example, Thatcher's attack on education condenses a conservative articulation of parent power, an anti-elitist or popular economy of education, and an elitist view of the curriculum. That is, on the cultural terrain Thatcher does not so much attack popular culture as ignore it in an attempt to reinstall an imaginary vision of British culture. This is, of course, an instance of her broader ideological struggle, carried out across the range of social positions, practices, and identities, to reshape common sense by constructing a limit within the terrain of the social formation beyond which one cannot go: on the one side a reconstructed "England" organized around an imaginary past, an imaginary definition of "Englishness," and on the other side the enemy within, "the alien wedge." The form of this project has two significant consequences. First, because "politics leads culture" and because the cultural position of Thatcherism is an elitism that largely renounces any relation to popular culture, Thatcherism has had much less success in or even impact on the reconstruction of popular cultural production and taste. And second, it has meant that there is a clear sense of opposition, quite public and explicit, often located within popular culture, not only to individual programs and changes but to the broad project itself.

The conditions of the hegemonic struggle in the United States, and the form it has taken, are significantly different. There were very real economic problems that, for American-based multinational corporate interests, presented a significant challenge. Economically it was the result of what has been called the "disorganization" and reorganization of late capitalism, involving changing relations between national and world economies, the changing social organization and distribution of the working population (including the emergence of new forms, locations, and organizations of labor, the rise of the service class, and the changing ethnic and gender composition of the labor force), and the subsequent declining rate of profit. The challenge was met by the increasing direct involvement of corporate capital in political activities and capitalists' publicly expressed dissatisfaction with the corporatist state. This new involvement took a variety of forms (especially funding PACs and various think tanks, but also entering directly into national advertising campaigns on a variety of issues) and was itself a crucial element in the construction of an American hegemony. But the economic crisis facing the United States was not as immediately and powerfully experienced as a radical collapse of the American economy. It was, in fact, not particularly obvious for the majority of the middle class until the beginning of the eighties, and even then it was often perceived in terms of the recurrent problems of recession, unemployment, and inflation. For the general American public, the problem was often constructed and understood in terms of the changing position of the United States in international relations. The crisis was a matter of our having lost our economic, political, and military leadership in the world. It was a problem of national ego rather than survival. Consequently it was most powerfully marked by specific events (e.g., the oil embargo, the hostage crisis) within a decidedly nationalistic rhetoric.

A second major difference can be seen in the struggle to win control of the Republican Party and the alliance that was constructed. The party does not have a significant history of aristocratic, paternalistic conservatives (the so-called wets); rather those within the party who were cast in the role of enemy were the predominantly East Coast, wealthy, elite-educated liberals. Their wealth, which was largely rooted in manufacturing, had been extended into finance capital. Consequently the struggle within the party was partly constructed geographically—everyone against the northeast—bringing together southern and midwest moral conservatives, western libertarian capitalists, and southwestern mineral money (invested in mining, oil, etc.). The New Right in the United States is a fragile and necessarily temporary political bloc. As Clarke (1991) has suggested, the formation of this "ruling bloc" has involved enormous work not only of consensus building within the alliance, but of the active suppression of the differences between the fractions. This can be seen most clearly if we consider the ideological contradictions covered over in the notion of an American New Right, for it involves at least three different groups that in many ways are antagonistic to one another. First, the economic neoliberals, who are absolutely committed to the free play of market forces: Anything is permissible if, under free-market conditions, it makes a profit. (Within this group, there is a subfraction of the supply-side economists, but that need not concern us here.) Second, the moral traditionalists, whose major project involves redirecting the nation's cultural agenda according to their own religious fundamentalism: they are perhaps the most successfully populist group, having combined the techniques of televangelism and direct mail appeals (for letter writing campaigns and fundraising) in single-issue antiliberal campaigns. And third, the neoconservatives (many of whom were New Left liberals in the sixties), whose rhetoric focuses on the "world mission" of the United States and the need to reinscribe powerfully nationalistic feelings in order to recapture the "traditional" American values (usually defined only by their assumed difference from an imaginary communism), which were undermined by internal forces in the fifties and sixties. Three projects, three enemies: state regulation, the Antichrist, and communism. The construction of the "unity" of the New Right depends largely on the precarious but decidedly American condensation of these three enemies into the single figure of communism, and on the active work of overlooking the contradictions between the projects.

A third difference stems from the American political system, especially the separation of political, executive, and legislative functions. Political popularity, executive power, and legislative success are radically distinct. The result is that the New Right alliance has been much less successful in its legislative program, in institutionalizing its policies. Ironically its major effects in dismantling the corporatist state have come through the executive's control over the state apparatus: through a refusal to allocate budgeted funds and through appointments to various state agencies (including, most frighteningly, the Supreme Court), thereby selectively strengthening or weakening, regulating or deregulating various aspects of social life, and through secret, if not illegal, executive orders and actions. One immediate consequence of this unique form of influence has been the decided absence of public debates about many policies and proposals, except in the context of already enacted decisions (which have already had their effects) or scandals.

Finally, we can consider the figure of Ronald Reagan himself. Obviously a great deal of the popular support for this conservative alliance is organized around the personal popularity, power, and image of the president. And so it is often assumed that whatever hegemonic ground may have been gained under Reagan cannot be held by the Right, even if the Republican candidate wins (since Reagan cannot stand for a third term, one of those instances when we can be grateful for the Constitution). There is no doubt that a larger part of the work of holding the various fractions of the ruling bloc together was accomplished through the figure of Reagan. However significantly threatening another Republican victory might be, it is unlikely that Bush will be able to hold the alliance together. He is, in the worst sense of the term, a cold war bureaucrat, with little direct and immediate appeal to any of the major fractions.

But this assumption, albeit of limited optimistic value, needs to be challenged, because it rests on too simple a reading of both Reagan and the form of hegemonic politics in the United States. For the question that remains unanswered is What is the source of Reagan's popularity and political success? And what is his relationship to the hegemony of the ruling bloc? After all, Reagan is neither the founder of nor the most articulate spokesperson for nor even always a representative of the policies and ideologies of the ruling bloc.

His power and popularity clearly do not rest on any popular agreement with his specific positions; nor do they depend upon the success of any policy or the instantiation of any ideological position. If he loses a battle, it does not diminish his position. If he acts in ways that seem to contradict his image or his public posture, his power remains intact. In fact, it is not clear what his image is or where it is constructed. Insofar as he has an identifiable image, it is full of ideological and personal contradictions. Reagan is an anticommunist who has helped construct a second detente; a militarist who has negotiated a disarmament treaty; a free enterprise capitalist whose administration has often intervened directly into the market; a moralist whose administration is riddled with scandal and dishonesty; a strongly pro-family father whose own family is, well, to put it mildly, an abomination; a strong leader who is often seen, by the general public, to be incompetent and ill-prepared; a sincere man who is generally recognized to regularly lie to his public.

Perhaps the source of his position lies in the hegemonic national project that he embodies for the ruling bloc. But unfortunately, unlike Thatcherism, the American New Right has never offered an explicit project except insofar as it claims to want to return America to its former glory and strength, without ever specifying when that "former" moment might have been or even, in imaginary terms, of what it might consist. Unlike Thatcherism, it does not have even an imaginary history of America to which it can turn and which it can put in place as America's future. Moreover, unlike Thatcherism, the American New Right is, with few exceptions, not elitist. It does not oppose or ignore or even stand outside the formations of popular taste and popular culture. It is as much imbricated within the distribution of popular taste as the audiences to which it speaks. Its spokespersons (even the most elite, like William Bennett) are more comfortable quoting Bob Dylan, the Beach Boys, or Bruce Springsteen than they are any representative of the elitist canon. In fact, it is here, in the popular, that the New Right struggles in order to constitute not a popular elitism, but an elitism of and within the popular—a populist elitism. It is less a matter of the ideological meanings of the popular than of their material distribution, of the ways in which they are presented to us, of the ways we take them up, and of the forms of our commitments to and within the popular.

The crisis of America, according to the New Right, is neither economic nor ideological but rather affective. It is a crisis of our lack of passion, of our not caring enough about the values we hold. It is a crisis of nihilism, which, while

not restructuring our ideological beliefs, has undermined our ability to organize effective action on their behalf. Americans were not working hard
enough—at their jobs, in their families, for their nation, or in the service of
their religion. But if this is the case, then perhaps it is also the case that
the American New Right does not have a political agenda, or rather that its
agenda operates in the conjuncture of economics and popular culture rather
than that of economics and the state. The latter demands an ideological struggle by which politics can lead culture. The former demands a popular struggle by which culture can lead politics. What I am proposing is the disjunction
between two hegemonic sites: the rearticulation of common sense and the
reconstruction of a national popular. Reaganism, insofar as it represents a
partially successful hegemonic moment, does not attempt to restructure our
commonsense assumptions about the world. As I will argue shortly, Reaganism seems to have been built upon the increasingly general shared mis-
trust of common sense that renders ideological differences less important
than the passion of one's commitment. Instead it attempts to inaugurate a new
national popular through affective work, through restructuring our investments in the sites of the popular. Thus for example Reaganism did not reconstruct an ideology of anticommunism; if anything, it parodies an already
taken-for-granted ideological site. But it was a site that had lost its powerful
affective resonance. Precisely by rendering the explicit ideology irrelevant—
no one could take it too seriously—Reaganism made it possible again to affectively invest oneself within it. This is neither anticommunism as a political
platform nor as an ideological interpretation but as an emotionally empowering state.

If this description is at all accurate, it has two important consequences:
First, it explains why it is so extraordinarily difficult to articulate and organize any resistance, either issue-specific or broad-based, to this mode of hegemonic struggle. And second, it suggests that it is almost accidental that the
New Right captured the control of the state at this point, or at least that the
control of the state is not a necessary condition for its hegemonic leadership. I
am aware that this must sound rather strange (but is it any stranger than life or
television in America?). I do not mean that the New Right alliance does not
want state power, nor am I denying that there are and will continue to be
devastating consequences of this control of the state apparatuses. But the
question of how they have achieved this control, and how it is maintained,
must be considered if we are to struggle against it. I am claiming that there is

another hegemonic strategy that operates directly within the popular and remains there; if it can accomplish its victory there, it will have already won the terrain within which any democratic state, no matter who controls it and with what ideology, must operate. Although I will argue that this hegemonic struggle is not ideological, or rather that it is taking place on the edges of the ideological, again I do not mean to deny that there are real ideological battles being fought, battles around both conscious political positions and taken-for-granted structures of common sense. In fact, what has become clearer in the past decade is that, in this domain, we need to reintroduce a good dose of conspiracy and manipulation theory. The American public is being lied to and events are apparently quite consciously selectively described and reported. One need not assume any intentionality on the part of the news media in this process—it is rationalized in the terms of state bureaucracy and objective reporting. But we can no longer explain the apparent success of such processes of domination by falling back on images of the masses as somehow intrinsically manipulatable, as cultural and ideological dupes. In fact, vast numbers know or assume that they are being lied to. The question that remains unanswered is always What is the work, the grounds, on which these ideological manipulations and state struggles are made possible? Laclau and Mouffe (1985) offer a useful theoretical view when they argue that hegemony involves the construction of an internal frontier within the social formation. That is, a hegemonic struggle involves competing attempts to divide the social terrain, to organize the different and often antagonistic social groups into two opposing camps, each defined by an "imaginary" equivalence between its own fractions. Hegemony, then, involves the construction of a fundamental boundary, an organizing difference, within a society through the distribution of social fractions and cultural articulations. The New Right has constructed its own DMZ within the national popular.

My claim is that the hegemonic struggle in America is being organized around the articulation of a frontier that has been constructed elsewhere, through a redistribution of the cultural sites of our affective investment, to a reconstruction of the political investment in and of the nation. Thus my fear is that the hegemony of the New Right has been more successfully established than we often optimistically assume, but it has been established elsewhere than where we often pessimistically assume. That is, we are not losing some grand hegemonic war to the nihilism of postmodernity, nor to the commodification of late capitalism, nor to the ideological conservatism of political ideologies. But we are losing a specific set of battles, and we do not know the consequences or how to struggle against it because we have not yet grasped its specificity. Unlike the hegemonic struggle for control of the state or for ideological leadership, this cultural hegemony is largely the product of an anonymous history; whatever the intentions and interests that propel various cultural discourses into these struggles, the frontier is being constructed through antagonistic resources and unintended effects. The identity and effects of any event have to be produced, articulated, not merely by the appropriations of subjects or the interventions of critics, but by active historical practices and structures, tendential forces and struggles, relations of domination and subordination. A theory of articulation does not claim that people make history according to their own intentions, but that history is being made by people struggling in conditions not of their own making. We do not control the effects engendered by any event any more than we controlled the effects that engendered it. We are not in control of the multiple and unforeseeable consequences of our actions; events can always be reinflected, detoured, rerouted, and even hijacked by other forces and practices. It is always in this context that people are empowered and disempowered, and that their agency is itself constituted. Thus the production of a hegemonic frontier cannot be separated from the historical, economic, social, and cultural conditions that define the broader context within which everyone, including the New Right, struggles to rearticulate history. But it is apparently the New Right that is claiming this frontier as its own and, increasingly, taking advantage—sometimes strategically entering into its construction—of this history, rearticulating what is already determined elsewhere.

PATROLLING FRONTIERS:

THE ARTICULATION OF THE POPULAR

Reading the Landscape.[7] How then do we survey the cultural terrain so as to make visible the sites where and practices by which this frontier is being constructed and rearticulated? What critical practice is appropriate to describing a hegemonic project aimed at the national popular? It will come as no surprise, given my critique of cultural studies, that I refuse to limit the effects of cultural events to the planes of meaning—signification and representation. Discourse may produce something other than meaning (capital, desire, materialities, etc.); sometimes it produces meaning-effects merely on the way to producing other effects; sometimes these other effects are only possible through the mediation of meaning; sometimes the production of meaning may be little more than a distraction, a by-product. The difference is not a matter of intentionality or teleology but of the fact that not all effects are "qualitatively" equal. Different events have different force within, purchase on, or reach into everyday life and the social formation. After all, human life is multidimensional. It is organized by more than material, signifying, and ideological structures; it is also organized by complexly produced affective structures—structures of desire, emotion, pleasure, mood, and so on. For example, the effects of video games may be less determined by their ideological maps of meaning than by the complex movements and abilities through which the player produces the sequence of lights and sounds that engulfs and produces him or her as a rhythmic body. The different structured planes of affects, while always implicated and imbricated in ideological maps of meaning, cannot be reduced to them. But ideological maps—maps of meaning—are flat and lifeless descriptions of human existence. For ideological positions are never merely passively occupied; they are taken up, lived in different ways, to different degrees, with differing investments and intensities. Our agency, our active relation to the world, is always more than that of a knowing (ideological) subject.

Our critical practice will be inappropriate, not only to the terrain of this hegemonic project, but to its rhythms and force as well, if we assume that all cultural events are taken up, lived, practiced, effective in just the same ways. That is, we simply cannot assume that we know in advance that our task involves seeking the "proper" meaning (whatever the measure of its propriety) of the various sites of contemporary popular culture. Nor is it merely a matter of locating the intertextual relations that can be traced out upon the surface, as if articulation involved merely the insertion of a text into passive structural links or grids. Texts are the sites of many different activities and effects; they can be enacted or practiced in many different ways, at different tempos. There are in fact many different practices and effects gathered together within the concept of articulation. I propose to describe one form of articulation as the construction of a "disciplined mobilization" which produces, that is, locates any text within, simultaneously, a spatial organization of events and a temporal organization of vectors. The former describes a system of dispersal that can be measured by the distances and densities between events. It constitutes practices as temporary moments of stability, sites at which we may stop and "install" our "selves" into practices. The latter describes a system of organization that can be measured by the directions and velocities with which the distances between events can be traversed. It constitutes practices as techniques of mobility, enabling us to move between and through the sites of stability. These techniques of mobility produce and organize the spaces between events, just as the system of dispersion produces and organizes the places marked as events and the ways they can be taken up. Together they constitute a spatiotemporal topography of practices, of enabled and enabling activities, which define the mobilities and stabilities of everyday life. A disciplined mobilization, then, defines the possibilities for enacting and connecting cultural practices; it defines the contours and rhythms, if not the substance, of our everyday lives.

A disciplined mobilization describes the ways we travel across the surfaces of culture and the ways we anchor ourselves into their imaginary depths. It is a historical organization, both spatial and temporal, which enables and constrains the ways space and place, mobility and stability are practiced or lived. Consequently it is more than a map (which defines a rigid system of places) and more than an itinerary (which defines an enacted mobility). It is precisely the conditions that make both the map and the itinerary possible. It defines the very possibilities of where and how we move and stop, of where and how we place and displace ourselves, of where and how we are installed into cultural texts and extended beyond them. While it can never guarantee how a text will be enacted at any particular instance—it does not totally determine what one does at a particular site—or how one moves on, it does construct the highways that structure and constrain our possibilities at any moment, the intersections that define the ambiguous possibilities of changing directions and speeds, and the addresses at which we can choose to take temporary lodging for various activities. A disciplined mobilization is a constant transformation of places into spaces and spaces into places, the constant shuttling between the dispersed system of stabilities within which we live out our everyday lives. A disciplined mobilization is an apparatus organizing a topography of cultural practices—defining the sites we can occupy, the investments we can make in them, and the planes along which we can connect and transform them so as to construct a consistent, livable space for ourselves.

I am concerned here with a particular disciplined mobilization, one that works as an exclusionary machine. That is, it is organized around the construction of a frontier as an unbridgeable gap between the livable and the unlivable, the possible and the impossible, the real and the unreal. It dis-

tributes both practices and social subjects by reconstituting the space of social differences according to its own structures and rhythms of stability and
mobility. By creating its own plane of consistency, it excludes any alternative
as inconsistent and unlivable. Thus it is not so much a question of what the
specific sites and vectors of the frontier mean but of the context of possibility
they construct, the parameters of mobility and stability they enable, the limits
of consistency that their existence, proliferation, and popularity establish.
But it is, furthermore, a question of the way in which this particular disciplined mobilization is being established as a frontier within the American
"national popular," rearticulating the limits and significance of the American
popular into a hegemonic project of the New Right. Taken by itself, the frontier may have many effects and many political possibilities; it need not become a marker for a hegemony of the Right, but unless this "secondary"
articulation of the frontier is challenged, it seems powerfully capable not
only of "winning the popular" to a specific and fairly narrow range of political positions, but also of "stitching up" many of the contradictions within
the conservative alliance, allowing it to continue operating as a contradictory unity.

In fact, many of the sites of struggle at which this secondary articulation
is accomplished are quite obvious—the family, nationalism, consumerism,
youth, pleasure, heroes—for it is not the case that the Right has produced
them in the first instance. They are determined elsewhere (e.g., by the life
histories of the baby boom generations, by the demands of contemporary
capitalism, by the possibilities of new technologies, by the proliferating popular sensibilities of postwar culture). What is not clear is how the relations
and spaces between them are being organized into a disciplined mobilization, a frontier that is then articulated to a project of reconstructing the national popular. There are many ways of entering this topography and mine is
determined as much by my own biography as by my intellectual and political
positions. I will suggest that this frontier is being constructed and articulated
by the contradiction between two interrelated organizations of the postwar
cultural space: on the one hand an emergent popular sensibility (postmodernity) and on the other an identification between the national identity of
America and a specific generation and culture of youth. Each of these formations partially determined and incorporated the other and, at the same time,
maintained their distance and even antagonistic difference. Postmodernity
negates any possibility of an ideological significance to cultural investment.

It is their frontier, a gap between affect and ideology, between fans and fanatics, that is rearticulated into the national popular as an increasingly unbridgeable chasm that leaves us standing on the border of our affective relations, unable to anchor ourselves ideologically. By disarticulating youth and cultural fandom from America and fanaticism, the New Right is constructing America as a powerful affectively charged but ideologically empty identity. It is articulating the postwar national popular against itself, using the very sites of everyday empowerment to undermine the possibility of any resistance.

A Postmodern Frontier. Let me suggest that there is something "postmodern" about the context of both everyday life and popular culture in contemporary America. However, "postmodernity," like hegemony, has already been given widely disparate meanings by various authors, and it has rapidly entered into the public and popular languages, from media criticism, social descriptions, and political agendas to advertisements of luxury ("postmodern") apartments. It is necessary, then, to dissociate myself from all the things I do not mean by describing these contexts as postmodern. I do not think that some texts are intrinsically and essentially postmodern, that their postmodernity can be read off their surfaces. In fact, I do not think postmodernity is primarily a question of textual practices or aesthetic form. I do not conceive of postmodernity as the ideological representation of late capitalism, rampant commodification, or our own radically fractured and incoherent subjectivity. I do not think postmodernity entails the absolute fragmentation and dispersion of meaning and/or power. And I do not think it refers to a total historical rupture, whether this is understood as the implosion of all difference (including the difference between the image and the real), the replacement of productivity by simulation, the collapse of all metanarratives, or the media as the screen of the new historical subject/object—the silent masses. Nor, by speaking about postmodernity, do I mean to claim that this formation is without historical roots, nor that it has entirely left modernity behind, nor that it has become hegemonic in the contemporary world. I want to use the notion of postmodernity in two related but restricted senses: first, to refer to an emergent and problematic aspect of the contemporary context, one that has powerful implications for the determination of our experience; and second, to refer to a particular sensibility (in Bourdieu's [1984] sense), a logic by which we appropriate cultural practices into our own lives. Neither of these describes the totality—or even, I am convinced, the dominant moment—of our historical and cultural lives. But they are increasingly powerful determining moments in culture and everyday life, and they are spreading with increasing rapidity.

For those generations that have grown up after the war (as a result of a number of specific conditions, events, and contradictions), the relations between affect and ideology (and later, between affect and libido) have become increasingly precarious. There has been a growing distance, an expanding series of ruptures or gaps between these various aspects of everyday life: between the available meanings, values, and objects of desire that socially organize our existence and identity, and the possibilities for investing in or caring about them that are enabled by our moods and emotions. In other words, it has become increasingly difficult, if not impossible at certain moments, to make sense of our affective experiences and to put any faith in our ideological constructions, even though they still may operate as "common sense." It is not the content of common sense that is challenged, merely its place in our everyday lives. We do not trust our common sense even as we are compelled to live it. It is increasingly difficult to locate places where it is possible to care about something enough, to have enough faith that it matters, so that one can actually make a commitment to it and invest oneself in it. Whatever the reality of such perceptions, the future has become increasingly uncertain (and its images bear a striking resemblance to contemporary Beirut!). It has become increasingly difficult, or perhaps irrelevant, to differentiate between reality and its images, and most of the traditional values and pleasures (love, family, sex) which may have given our lives some meaning or purpose have become treacherous traps that never seem to deliver on their promise.

Postmodernity, then, points to a crisis in our ability to locate any meaning as a possible and appropriate source for an impassioned commitment. It is a crisis not of faith, but of the relationship between faith and common sense, a dissolution of what we might call the "anchoring effect" that articulates meaning and affect. It is not that nothing matters—for something has to matter—but that we can find no way of choosing or of finding something to warrant our investment. It is as if we had to live two lives, one defined by the meanings and values available to us to make sense of our lives, and the other defined by the affective sense that life can no longer be made sense of. It is the new status given to the affective as the unrepresentable that defines the postmodern rupture. It is not that the postwar generations do not live the ideological values of their society and their parents; rather they find it increasingly impossible to represent their moods and emotional contradictions, their affective relationships to the world, in those terms and at the same time to seriously invest themselves in such values. Postmodernity demands that one live schizophrenically, trying on the one hand to live the inherited meanings and, on the other hand, recognizing that such meanings cannot enable one to respond to one's affective situation. Their "mattering maps" no longer correspond to the available maps of meanings. Meaning and affect—historically so closely intertwined—have broken apart, each going off in its own direction. Each takes on its own autonomy, even as sanity demands that they be reintegrated. Of course, the gap is never complete and stable, but always multiple, mobile, and temporary. As it has, more recently, extended into and disrupted the relations between affect and libidinal desire and pleasures, we have become increasingly suspicious of any object of desire as well, and even of desire itself. The result is that it is ever more difficult to make sense of our affective experiences ("Life is hard and then you die") and to put any faith in the taken-for-granted interpretations of the values of our lives and actions. Even the promise of "sex and drugs and rock 'n' roll" has given way to "romance, rejections, and rock 'n' roll." We are condemned to constantly try to make sense of our lives in structures that clearly contradict our experiences, and to invest in structures without any clear faith or even ability to distinguish their merit.

This condition has often been described as cynicism or nihilism, but neither term seems quite adequate. Yet there is something "cynical" about our contemporary relationship to ideology. In the rush to appropriate Gramsci's notion of ideology as common sense, we have too often too quickly forgotten that, somehow, the notion of mystification is central to Marx's description: "They don't know it but they are doing it anyway." That is, ideology entails a gap between one's beliefs and one's actions. People know how things really are, but they act, for example, as if they had mystical beliefs (e.g., in capital as universal value). But increasingly there is a cynical logic operating in the realm of contemporary ideology because the gap has disappeared. People know what they are doing but they continue doing it anyway. They are aware of ideological mystification, but since they have no grounds to question their investment, they feel free to enter into it. This collapse of the distance, which is made possible by the gap between affect and ideology, operates by refusing to take its own ideological positions—or anything, for that matter—too seriously. In fact, the only real evil is taking any ideological belief too seriously, whatever its politics. For example, it makes perfect sense for people to admit that they "believe in the truth though [they] lie a lot," or to love the music of a group like Midnight Oil except for their "biased" politics.

But this relationship to explicit ideological and political positions is merely one instance of a much broader cultural sensibility or logic, which I have described as "ironic nihilism" or "authentic inauthenticity" (not to be confused with inauthentic authenticity). Within this logic, a cultural practice has not only renounced its claim to represent reality, it has renounced its place in any representational economy; it's not quite even a fantasy. Its meaningfulness is only the means of producing something else. Its value is no longer that of the imaginable real—whether fantasy or utopia. It does not provide rules for learning because the question of its credibility (or incredibility) becomes irrelevant; narratives, when they are present, go nowhere. For whatever reasons, these are no longer situations we can even imagine ourselves into, despite the fact that all situations are personalized and presented as if they were ideologically related to our own lives (i.e., the characters are often "just like us" yet fantastically different). Within this logic, cultural practices refuse to make judgments or even to involve themselves in the world. This is perhaps too strong; let me say rather that if authentic inauthenticity does not hermeticize the world, it does anesthetize it. It starts by assuming a distance from the other that allows it to refuse any claim or demand that might be made on it. This "hip" attitude is a kind of ironic nihilism in which distance is offered as the only reasonable relation to a reality that is no longer reasonable. Popular culture, however unreasonable (and it certainly is strange these days), is as reasonable as reality. In fact reality is already stranger than any fantasy we could construct. And consequently the strange is always disturbingly familiar. This estrangement from the familiar and familiarization of the estranged means that the lines separating the comic and the terrifying, the mundane and the exotic, the boring and the exciting, the ordinary and the extraordinary disappear. If reality is already clichéd, the clichés can be taken as reality. If we are in fact totally alienated, then alienation is the taken-for-granted ground upon which we build our lives.

The fact that all images become equal, that all styles are temporary and likely to be deconstructed even as they are celebrated, and that perhaps everything is an image does not necessarily negate the necessity and importance of images. But it does deconstruct the inherent possibility of investing in any single image. Authentic inauthenticity is indifferent to difference. It does not deny differences; it merely assumes that since there are no grounds for distinguishing between the relative claims of alternatives, one cannot read beyond the fact of investment. For example, the day after the INF treaty was signed, one of the network news teams went to the town in which *The Day After* was filmed to ask the residents whether they really felt safer. On what grounds are these people taken to have privileged experience, except that they have already come to be identified with the image of nuclear terror? To appropriate, enjoy, or invest in a particular style, image, or set of images no longer necessarily implies any faith that such investments make a significant (even affective) difference. Instead we celebrate the affective ambiguity of images, images that are "well developed in their shallowness, fascinating in their emptiness." After all, reality can be so constraining on our lifestyle choices.

Within this logic one celebrates a difference knowing that its status depends on nothing but its being celebrated. In the end only one's affective commitment, however temporary or superficial, matters. Authentic inauthenticity, as a popular sensibility, is a specific logic that cannot locate differences outside the fact of its own temporary affective investment. If every identity is equally fake, a pose that one takes on, then authentic inauthenticity celebrates the possibilities of poses without denying that that is all they are. It is a logic that allows one to seek satisfactions knowing that one can never be satisfied, and that any particular pleasure is likely, in the end, to be disappointing. For even if all images are equally artificial and all satisfactions equally unsatisfying, one still needs some images, one still seeks some satisfactions. Although no particular pose can make a claim to some intrinsic status, any pose can gain a status by virtue of one's commitment to it.

Difference is relocated so that only the affective matters. And all images, all realities, are affectively equal—equally serious, equally deserving and undeserving of being allowed to matter, of being made into sites of investment on one's mattering maps. If the equality of all images assures a perpetual search for difference, the irony of this sensibility ensures not merely the impossibility but the absurdity of such difference. That nothing matters itself does not matter! But this "nihilism" is always inflected by its affective knowledge that the only possibility for difference is in the fact that something—it does not matter what—matters. Or, more accurately, the only difference that the specific content makes is that, because it matters, it makes a difference.

There are no hidden truths within authentic inauthenticity. Any secret is instantly available and constantly repeated for any viewer. The only secret is the irony that there are no secrets because there is nothing behind the screen, nothing written upon its surfaces. While this doesn't guarantee that everyone will "get it," its elitism does not depend upon constructing a privileged audience, for it is not a question of its limited availability but rather of the irony and fragility of the appropriation itself. Its "hipness" is democratic and, in a sense, unimportant. Secret knowledge is dissolved into the distinctions within public taste. But these distinctions are themselves as tenuous and undeserving as any other image. Authentic inauthenticity, then, undermines the very possibility of a privileged marginality that can separate itself from and measure itself (favorably) against an apparently homogeneous mainstream. It marks the collapse, or the irrelevance, of the difference.

But there are still significant differences within the possibilities of authentic inauthenticity, different strategic relationships to any particular affective investment, different ways in which difference can be marked affectively. I want to distinguish, then, between ironic inauthenticity, sentimental inauthenticity, hyperreal inauthenticity, and grotesque inauthenticity. Ironic inauthenticity is perhaps the most pervasive strategy in what is often thought of as "postmodern" culture. It is the most purely ironic, inflecting sentimentality into the fleeting moments of its temporary investments. It refuses to make any distinctions between investments on any basis, either qualitative or quantitative. Although it seems to celebrate the absence of any center or identity, it actually locates that absence as a new center. That is, it celebrates the fragmentary, the contradictory, the temporary. And it celebrates them with all the seriousness (or lack of seriousness) that is necessary. It can take everything equally seriously or equally humorously because the difference is less important than the temporary construction of an image of the center. David Letterman, Pee Wee Herman, Madonna, Robocop: all invest themselves in the image, but the image itself is unimportant. What is important is the fact of the investment itself, with no claim beyond that. It doesn't matter what image one takes; take any image and live it for as long as you want or like. It is the construction of any identity as absolutely real and totally ironic. One can deconstruct gender at the moment of celebrating it (and celebrate it precisely because one can deconstruct it). One can take on an identity predicated on the deconstruction of identity itself (cyborgs such as Max Headroom). The issue is not investing in the ideological consequences of particular images but the fact that one must inevitably invest in some images, regardless of what they are. HBO can construct a presidential candidate who becomes indistinguishable from the real candidates (*Tanner*), while MTV offers us a series of ads promoting Randee (the imaginary leader of an imaginary rock group, Randee and the Redwoods) for president. His entire media campaign is composed of clichéd paradoxes; for example, at a press conference Randee says that he was misunderstood when he said that "First there is a mountain, then there is no mountain, then there is." He points out that he did not mean to say that there is no mountain. "There is one," he says to thunderous applause. "And after I'm elected, there will be one." Feeling something, anything, is better than feeling nothing. Living some identity, however temporary, is better than living none. And the choice may have little relation to the significance of the identity itself but merely to its temporary ability to mark some affective difference and distance. Ironic inauthenticity celebrates its own investment in the image precisely because it is self-consciously taken as an image, no more and no less. In the end, crocodile tears are as good as real ones, perhaps even better because they require no anchor in the real in order to be effective. Of course, if one fails to see the irony, one is left only with the despair of illusions and lies, a depoliticized nihilism.

The second strategy, sentimental inauthenticity, begins with the inability to distinguish the relative merit of any site of investment. One does not, and cannot, trust the content image, identity, or activity, even the most temporary and ironic one. Certainly this cannot mark any difference; certainly it does not mark any difference in a world that has increasingly appropriated ironic inauthenticity. Yet sentimental inauthenticity celebrates the magical possibility of making a difference against impossible odds. And what enables that possibility is not any specific affective investment but rather the intensity, the quantitative measure, of the investment itself. Cultural practices become merely the occasion for a temporary and intense affective investment, for a constant movement between emotional highs and lows; such investments need not be located in the possibilities of our own lives, nor even in the believability of someone else's. Heroes can accomplish the fantastic within the conventions of realism; for example, it is becoming increasingly common on TV and in films (*Crime Story, The Predator*) for individuals— whether good or bad—to survive atomic blasts, without any suggestion that this is a real possibility. Such practices become the occasion of an overindulgence of affect as the celebration of the very possibility of any affective investment. The particular investment is liberated from any significant anchoring in reality or intelligibility. They are the site of emotions more real because more extreme, more excessive, and the fact that the excess is constructed precisely through the unbelievability and unintelligibility of the message makes it all the more powerful. In such practices, we get to live out affective relations that exceed our lives and always will (perhaps because we will have already experienced them on TV). It is as if it were only necessary to feel something more intensely than is available to us. While it is necessary to feel something—anything—that strongly, it is irrelevant what one feels, because no particular feeling matters in itself. What matters is affective excess; Faulkner's poetic choice of grief over nothing has become culture's unquenchable need not only to never feel nothing, but to constantly raise the stakes by which feeling something—anything—is measured. The result is a democracy of affect that can be traversed only by an ever-spiraling search for an excessive affect necessarily divorced from the contingencies of daily life.

Such a strategy requires the absolute ordinariness of the subjects: their only difference is that they care about something, that something matters to them so much that they are reidentified with and empowered by it regardless of what it is. This is a strategy that constructs images of victory, but the site and stake of the battle—or even whether one recognizes the moral rectitude of the subject—is irrelevant. Rather the subjects are just like us except that they care about the struggle, they believe in something, to a degree beyond our sense of our own realities. One wears one's affect, one's passion, on one's sleeve, and it is this that converts ordinary skills into magical victories. Such "ordinary heroes" abound in contemporary culture: Springsteen, Rocky, and Rambo come to mind. Sentimental inauthenticity is often the dominant strategy in many contemporary youth movies (*Top Gun, The Secret of My Success, Quicksilver,* etc.), so that whatever the ideology of the hero, his or her heroism is not tainted by the reality of his or her position. One need never agree with, or identify with, the particular content of a commitment; it can seem to be entirely trivial. One need only recognize that something matters so much that one is transformed from an ordinary individual into something heroic, if not superhuman. The current popularity of the talk show host Mort Downey makes little sense apart from the sheer passion of his diatribes and attacks; he has no ideologically consistent position of his own. Of course the danger of such statements is that one can confuse the celebration of the intense commitment with an identification with the content of the commitment. Because of the often traditional activities and values represented, this strategy is easily appropriated by a conservative politics.

The third strategy, hyperreal inauthenticity, distrusts, and often rejects, not only the specific form of any affective investment but the very fact of affect itself. Its articulation to sentimentality is purely neutral, refusing affect itself. Its tone is bleak; its practice is superobjective. Portraying the grim reality—in all its dismal, gritty, and meaningless detail, with no affective difference inscribed upon it—is the only statement left available, and it matters little whether that reality is contemporary or futuristic: all images have become post-holocaust because the true holocaust is the very destruction of any possibility of caring, of making a difference. In fact, affect has become impossible because the last site of potential investment—desire and pleasure—has become the enemy. Caring too much is dangerous and often destructive (*The Name of the Rose*) and desire kills (AIDS). There is no transcendence, no possibility of moving to a position outside of the grainy detail of reality. No narrative voice is capable of any judgment or discrimination because, in the end, no matter how apparently special, they are just like us. Thus we are even denied the grandeur of existential meaninglessness and given only the sheer facticity of existence. Making a difference is no longer a matter of inserting oneself into even a temporarily privileged position; nor is it a matter of controlling a chaotic world. For there are no longer any guarantees that chaos is not more deserving of our affective commitment than order. There is only individual survival and normality (however abnormal). One sees this in movies such as *Star 80* (perhaps the precursor), *River's Edge, Full Metal Jacket, The Boys Next Door,* and *Blue Velvet* (although this last is perhaps also surreal) and television programs like *The Max Headroom Show, The Life and Times of Molly Dodd* (at least as it has attempted to frame itself), and *Miami Vice* (especially in those episodes in which the cops confront the impenetrable machinations of the multinational/government apparatuses, or in which romantic involvements always end in Peckinpah-type killings). But it is perhaps most visible in a new generation of ads and promotions (e.g., Jordache's film-noir ads, Converse's scene of a young couple breaking up, and MTV's promo in which a young yuppie woman in front of a computer contemplates all those people younger than she who have accomplished something and asks, "What do you do when you realize you aren't going to rule the world?"). Without the ironic inflection, such statements merely reproduce a structure of cynicism and pessimism that, in the end, offers egoism as the only viable political strategy.

The final strategy I want to mention (I do not mean to deny that there may be still other strategies) is grotesque inauthenticity. In such practices, the only allowable affective investment is a negative one. That is, one celebrates the terrifying, the destructive, the horrific. Reality becomes a meaningless and dangerous place in which the only possible response is to further attack the last vestiges of meaning and pleasure so that nothing but the sheer spectacle of a negative affect remains. As Crane suggests, "The horrific constructs available do not offer any possibilities beyond that of being able to confront terror. The engagement with such images is neither cathartic nor reassuring . . . Watching a horror film is a reality check . . . For the horror film, and everyday life, today is the last day of the rest of your life . . . The truly repellent creatures do not come from outside our nebulous social networks . . . They are us, and we never know when we will act as monsters . . . The central operation of contemporary horror films, the inexorable splintering of meaning" (of the body and any site which purports to remain "good" as the last remaining sites of meaning), depends upon a number of assumptions about the world: "All collective action will fail; knowledge and experience have no value when one is engaged with the horrible; the destruction of menace, should it occur, carries no guarantee that the future will be safe: the menace will return" (1988, 372, 374). Horror films are only the most obvious site of this celebration of negative affect. Grotesque inauthenticity makes the very site of "gore"—the more realistic the better, even if we know it is produced by special effects—the most important moment of many texts, even rendering the narrative and the characters irrelevant. It has recently entered television through such programs as *America's Most Wanted,* which, despite its supposed intentions of aiding the police, seems to end up celebrating the threatening possibilities of everyday life: your neighbor could be a wanted criminal. It also plays an important part in the new generation of comic superheroes in which the hero is simply a destructive, often paranoid killing machine (e.g., *The Dark Knight Returns, Elektra Assassin*), reducing all issues of justice and value to a question of who remains alive at the end.

Each of these strategies reconstitutes the ability to make a difference when nothing makes a difference, to enable a difference to be defined when there is no center to measure it against, to proffer strategies for being different predicated on the absence of difference. Each creates a series of images of stars who embody not authentic instances of subjectivity and political resistance or even ideological statements, but temporary moods that can be appropriated by fans as temporary places rather than impossible identities, strategies by which individuals can continue to locate themselves within affective maps, and continue to struggle to make a difference, if not in the world, at least in their lives, even though difference has become impossible and possibly irrelevant. Such strategies do not offer us positions as identities from which we can judge ourselves and the world, but as places in which we can temporarily install ourselves so that we can act, so that we can gain some control over our lives, so that we can negotiate the spaces between pain and comfort, between terror and boredom. What distinguishes them from one another is the ways they use affect as a strategy for enacting their own authentic inauthenticity.

These strategies are sites at which we can connect the empowering, "tactical" politics of everyday life to the "strategic" political struggles to reorganize the social formation. While these strategies do not seek to combat the gap between affect and ideology, they offer the possibility of empowering their audiences to survive within it. But for just that reason, they are also strategies of articulation that can be placed in the service of the New Right, providing at least a part of the context and the resources for its project of rearticulating the postmodern frontier into a hegemonic structure of the national popular. Thus the current political work of the Right on this terrain may be less a matter of circumscribing moral possibilities than of rearticulating the place and structure of the national popular.

The New Right and the Postwar National Popular. The meaning of "America" has always been a problem. Except for rare moments, Americans have rarely had a shared sense of identity and unity. Rather the United States has always been a country of differences without a center. The "foreign" has always been centrally implicated in our identity because we were and are a nation of immigrants. (Perhaps that partly explains why Americans took up anticommunism with such intensity; here at least was an "other," a definition of the foreign, which could be constructed as non-American, as a threatening presence that defied integration.) It is a nation without a tradition, for its history depends upon a moment of founding violence that almost entirely eradicated the native population, thereby renouncing any claim to an identity invested in the land. And despite various efforts to define some "proper" ethnic and national origin, it is precisely the image of the melting pot, this perpetual sense of the continuing presence of the other within the national identity, that has defined the uniqueness of the nation. It is a nation predicated upon differences, but always desperately constructing an imaginary unity. The most common and dominant solution to this in its history involved constituting the identity of the United States in the future tense; it was the land of possibility, the "beacon on the hill," the New World, the young nation living out its "manifest destiny." Perhaps the only way in which the diversity of populations and regions could be held together was to imagine the country constantly facing frontiers. It is this perpetual ability to locate and conquer new frontiers, a sense embodied within "the American Dream" as a recurrent theme, that has most powerfully defined a national sense of cultural uniqueness.

After what the nation took to be "its victory" in the Second World War, it anxiously faced a depressing contradiction. On the one hand, the young nation had grown up, taking its "rightful" place as the leader of the "free world." On the other hand, what had defined its victory—its very identity—depended upon its continued sense of difference from the "grown-up" (i.e., corrupt, inflexible, etc.) European nations. It was America's openness to possibility, its commitment to itself as the future, its ability to reforge its differences into a new and self-consciously temporary unity, that had conquered the fascist threat to freedom. The postwar period can be described by the embodiments of this contradiction: it was a time of enormous conservative pressure (we had won the war protecting the American way; it was time to enjoy it and not "rock" the boat) and a time of increasingly rapid change, not only in the structures of the social formation but across the entire surface of everyday life. It was a time as schizophrenic as the baby boom generation onto which it projected its contradictions. Resolving this lived dilemma demanded that America still be located in and defined by a future, by an American Dream, but that the dream be made visible and concrete. If the dream had not yet been realized, it would be shortly. Thus if this dream were to effectively define the nation in its immediate future, if there were to be any reality to this vision, it would have to be invested not just in some abstract future, but in a concrete embodiment of America's future, that is, in a specific generation. Hence the American identity was projected on the children of those who had to confront the paradox of America in the postwar years. But if the dream was to be real for them, and if it were to be immediately realizable, people would have to have children—and have children they did! And they would have to define those children as the center of their lives and of the nation; the children would become the justification for everything they had done, the source of the very meaning of their lives as individuals and as a nation.

The "baby boom" created an enormous population of children by the mid-fifties, a population that became the concretely defined image of the nation's future, a future embodied in a specific generation of youth who would finally realize the American Dream and hence become its living symbol. This was to be "the best-fed, best-dressed, best-educated generation" in history, the living proof of the American Dream, the realization of the future in the present. The American identity slid from a contentless image of the future to a powerful, emotionally invested image of a generation. America found itself by identifying its meaning with a generation whose identity was articulated by the meanings and promises of youth. Youth, as it came to define a generation, also came to define America itself. And this generation took up the identification as its own fantasy. Not only was its own youthfulness identified with the perpetual youthfulness of the nation, but its own generational identity was defined by its necessary and continued youthfulness. But youth in this equation was not measured simply in terms of age; it was an ideological and cultural signifier, connected to utopian images of the future and of this generation's ability to control the forces of change and to make the world over in its own images. But it was also articulated by economic images of the teenager as consumer, and by images of the specific sensibilities, styles, and forms of popular culture that this generation took as its own (hence the necessary myth that rock and roll was made by American youth). Thus what was placed as the new defining center of the nation was a generation, an ideological commitment to youth, and a specific popular cultural formation. Obviously this "consensus" constructed its own powerfully selective frontier: it largely excluded those fractions of the population (e.g., black) that were never significantly traversed by the largely white middle-class youth culture. Nevertheless, for the moment the United States had an identity, however problematic the commitment to youth was and would become, and it had an apparently perpetually renewable "national popular"; it had a culture it thought of as inherently American and that it identified with its own embodied image of itself and its future.

But this was, to say the least, a problematic solution to America's search for an identity, not merely because any generation of youth has to grow up and, one assumes, renounce their youthfulness, but also because "youth" was largely, even in the fifties, an empty signifier. As Steedman says, "children are always episodes in someone else's narratives, not their own people, but rather brought into being for someone else's purpose" (1986, 122). Youth has no meaning except perhaps its lack of meaning, its energy, its commitment to openness and change, its celebratory relation to the present, and its promise of the future. Youth offers no structure of its own with which it can organize and give permanence to a national identity. That is, youth itself, like America, can only be defined apparently in a forever receding future. How could this generation possibly fulfill its own identity and become the American Dream—become a future always as yet unrealized and unrealizable? How could a generation hold on to its own self-identity as youthful and at the same time fulfill the responsibility of its identification with the nation? What does it mean to have constructed a concrete yet entirely mobile center for a centerless nation? Perhaps this rather paradoxical position explains the sense of failure that characterizes the postwar generations, despite the fact that they did succeed in reshaping the cultural and political terrain of the United States.

If the state hegemonic project of the New Right entails deconstructing the postwar social democratic consensus, its cultural hegemonic project entails disarticulating the central relationship between the national identity, a specific set of generational histories, and the equation of the national popular with postwar youth culture. The struggle is then, in part, to deconstruct or dismantle the history that—momentarily and mistakenly—filled the center of a consensual national identity. This is clearest in Allan Bloom's recent attack (1987) on an openness that is always "progressive and forward-looking," an openness powerfully associated with contemporary youth and youth culture, and which, Bloom argues, has been made the measure of America. In fact, one can read Bloom's argument as establishing a series of equivalences between youth as a generation, youth as an ideological construct, youth culture, cultural openness, and relativism. To the extent that the unique promise of America, according to Bloom, depends upon a commitment to "natural rights," there must be a contradiction between America and the logic of youth that was (unfortunately) placed at its center. That is, Bloom's attack on youth culture is a struggle over "what it means to be an American." And it is not coincidental that in his attempt to undermine the meanings and investments that we have made in youth, he reserves his most passionate attacks for pop culture, especially rock and roll. On the other side, one cannot help but notice that advertisers are increasingly attempting to appeal to a certain sense of nationalism and national identity and that this identity is consciously constructed out of the images and styles of postwar youth culture (e.g., "Coors— an American original"). It is here that a new frontier is being constructed by reworking the terrain of the national popular, by articulating the frontier constructed by postmodernity as a disciplined mobilization against the very youth culture within which it has largely been constructed. This hegemonic project operates on the visible sites of cultural struggle that have been determined elsewhere—by the contradictions within the postwar youth culture, the changing demography of the nation, and the emergent demands of capitalist reorganization—in order to restructure the national popular according to the postmodern frontier (i.e., strategies of authentic inauthenticity), freed of any entanglements with postwar youth culture.

I want to try to briefly describe some of these sites, which are, whether intentionally or not, articulated into this hegemonic struggle and reconstructing a new frontier within the national popular. Perhaps the most obvious is the increasing proliferation of, and investment in, images of the family. Wherever one looks on contemporary television, one finds popular discourses of the family, not just in programs explicitly about families (e.g., *The Bill Cosby Show, thirtysomething*) but in the construction of nondomestic groups as explicit, if ersatz, families (e.g., *Who's the Boss?*). It is presumably not coincidental that, while *M.A.S.H.* always registered the family back home, *China Beach* constructed itself from the very beginning as an alternative and more real family for its characters, erasing any mark of the family back home. But there is even a proliferation of programs produced for family viewing, whether their appeal is through double-coding (e.g., *Pee Wee's Playhouse*) or through their activities (e.g., game shows for the whole family, like *Double Dare,* which started out as a kids' show). Nor are these images limited to the screens of mainstream television. Families and relationships have replaced sex as a dominant topic of many songs in so-called indie-pop (Reynolds 1986), and many of the so-called mall-culture writers (e.g., Bobbie Ann Mason) are increasingly fascinated by family narratives.

What is at stake seems to be less an ideological rearticulation of the family than an effort to relocate the individual and the American Dream into a familial context. While we can reasonably conclude from the rapid proliferation and popularity of different programs and images that there is a significant change in whether, how, and how much people invest in the family, we can conclude very little about the ideological valences of these discourses. There is little consistency here in the images and meanings of the family. What is most obvious is the multiplicity, however limited, of images and the complexity of the relations not only between the spouses, but between the generations. These are not nostalgic images of a mythical family of the fifties which was outside of every one's experience. (Did anyone really think they were living it, or even could live it?) Not only are the parents always plagued by all of the doubts and insecurities of their collective history as youth, they are commonly constructed, in some essential respects, as themselves youthful and even young. Even Bill Cosby, the most perfect of all the new fathers, is a far cry from Jim Anderson. And the kids? They are neither innocent nor always immature; they are in fact often smarter than the parents. The icon of the contemporary popular family is not Disneyland but Pee Wee's Playhouse, where age is undecidable and its relation to behavior unpredictable.

Of course, there is a very simple explanation for the presence of these images: a large segment of the baby boom generations has grown up and, if they are not already having families, they are at least thinking about the possibility. But this neither explains the diversity nor the popularity of such images, and it certainly does not address the question of how such discourses are being articulated into larger political struggles. Too often the Left has little to say here, apart from an occasional nod to Oedipal economies. Feminists too often assume that any reinvestment in familial economies signals a victory for neoconservative patriarchy. In fact, I want to partly agree with that, not because the family is inherently conservative nor because the forms of the contemporary family are decidedly patriarchal, but because the family is playing a crucial role in the construction of a conservative cultural hegemony. I am not concerned here with the very real ideological struggles that need to be carried out. After all, it does seem to be the case that as soon as you begin to invest in familial economies, as soon as you enter the terrain, as soon as you begin to invest something in these discourses, you find yourself talking a moral discourse. But it is not the content of the morality that is at issue, since I can quite easily refuse the particular ideological positions it offers. But as soon as you allow yourself to care about the problems of the family, you find yourself pulled into those larger discourses, positions, and projects that already validate the investment and at least address the questions. Insofar as the Left ignores this increasing investment, it has given up the struggle to find another discourse of the family.

But there is even more at stake in the politics of the family's place in hegemonic struggles. The discourse of the family is an important site at which the New Right glosses over its own contradiction between neoliberal definitions of freedom and fundamentalist conceptions of morality: the family as the site of consumption within which a new definition of freedom is offered. And even more, the current investment in the family, which seems on the surface at least to erase much of the history of the struggles and positions of both feminism and the youth culture, is implicated in the larger effort to rearticulate youth and the postwar youth generations. For this new emergent relationship to the family suggests a strikingly different relationship between generations that apparently still see themselves as young, and the various institutions that, since the war, have defined the disciplinary apparatus constructed to produce, shape, and control the population of youth. That is to say, it is not merely coincidental that the family has often been an object of attack and rebellion for members, male and female, of youth cultures, because the family has been the dominant context in which the meanings, behaviors, and possibilities of youth were constructed and constrained. The current counterinvestment in images of the family that are not predicated on strict generational differences seems to suggest a new social position, or at least a changing relationship to the various institutions of power aimed at administering (to) youth.

The confusing generational differences within contemporary images of the family point to an even broader and more amorphous struggle within and around youth culture: namely, struggles over the meaning and representation of youth itself.[8] For despite the powerful investment in, and high status of, youth in America, there has never been a consensual (not to say essential) definition of youth, nor has the proprietary claim of any sociological group to the ownership of youth been institutionalized. Again we can easily trace these struggles to the fragmentation of the postwar generations, all of whom, in different ways, think of themselves as young and think of their youth not only as an essential part of their identity, but as their privileged possession. These inter- and intragenerational struggles are visible in the changing experiences and behaviors of different age groups, in the changing institutional relationships between adults and various generations, and in the multiple and contradictory ways youth is represented in our popular culture: youth as embodying all of the (negative) characteristics of adulthood; youth as radically different from—alien to—adults; youth as the repository of adult fantasies of innocence and irresponsibility; youth as savior; youth as better (and more victorious) inhabitants of the modern world; youth as champions of justice; youth as cynics; youth as victims; youth as criminals. Apart from these different images and evaluations, one can identify increasingly disparate forms of investing in the difference between youth and adulthood. David Leavitt (1985) talks about a youth population that seems to want only to be thirty years old and, having arrived there, to remain. Tiffany, the pop singer, claims that she is no different from her peers except that she has a job and is increasingly trying to manage all aspects of her own life. Polonoff (1988) humorously distinguished three generations of yuppies: "the big chill generation" attempt to convince themselves that they have escaped their youth and avoided the harmful consequences of their excesses by posing as adults while retaining their adolescence; the "big thrill generation" pose as adolescents to prove they are adults; and "the chilled drinks generation" simply enjoy their immaturity. While this may appear, on the surface, rather irrelevant to the hegemonic struggles of the New Right, it is easily appropriated into the project of disarticulating youth culture from the national identity and of relocating the frontier of the national popular.

There is of course one cultural struggle in which the New Right has clearly taken the explicit lead, although it is by no means the only antagonist: the attack on the counterculture of the sixties and seventies. This is most clearly enacted in the somewhat paradoxical campaign ("Just Say No") against sex and drugs and rock and roll. It is paradoxical to the extent that the attack on rock, for example, is taking place at just the moment when rock music seems to have been so totally and successfully integrated into every aspect of everyday life that it poses little opportunity for resistance of any sort. Similarly the attack on sex seems rather unnecessary given the chilling effects of herpes and AIDS. On the other hand, the attack on drugs, while rhetorically defined in terms of hard drugs and contexts of labor, is clearly aimed at the increasing acceptance and incorporation of softer drugs into the everyday lives of the middle classes.

But even more significant as an attack on the counterculture may be the efforts to reconstruct the history of the war in Vietnam. I think that, to a certain extent, the attack on countercultural pleasures and freedoms has more to do with the symbolism of Vietnam than with the actual politics of the contrary moralities. Vietnam was, after all, the affective center of the entire counterculture. And it was, significantly, a war fought by youth: the average age of the combat soldier in Vietnam was nineteen, seven years younger than in the Second World War. Vietnam—and the counterculture—has become the symbol of the moment when the identification of the postwar youth generations with America fell apart and, consequently, the moment when America lost not only its center but its faith in a center. In part Vietnam demonstrated the contradictions and differences within youth and within the youth culture. But more importantly it was in response to the war that a significant fraction of youth explicitly attacked America, questioned their identification with it, and rejected the terms of the American Dream. Vietnam became the symbol of the contradiction: a generation negating its own privileged identity at the center of the nation, not by renouncing their youthfulness, but by proclaiming the contradiction between youth and America. (Not coincidentally, the mid-sixties was also the moment when America discovered that its "national" popular culture could not be restricted to the nation. The moment of the British invasion, and the later worldwide expressions of youth counterculture, demonstrated the impossibility of limiting the youthfulness of the postwar generations to a national context. Youth and youth culture were transnational events!)

One cannot help but be astounded by the sudden and rapid proliferation of popular discourses (fiction and nonfiction, books, movies, video histories, and even television programs) built around Vietnam, nor can one reasonably assume that their appearance after so many years is merely coincidental. Many of these popular narratives attempt to place the war back into the familiar frameworks of traditional war narratives or personal drama. There have been very few successful attempts to represent the specific contradictions and problems of Vietnam. But there are significant and important tendencies in these popular discourses that are worth pointing to. I will briefly discuss the two network prime-time television shows, *Tour of Duty* and *China Beach*. It is interesting that these are perhaps the only TV programs with real, and effectively integrated, pop soundtracks. *Tour of Duty* acknowledges the existence of the counterculture in its music, but it seems always to reduce the music to its sonorial presence and its emotional resonances because it has consistently refused any images of the counterculture. Although its images frequently attempt to register the real violence and insecurity of the war, the war itself is always reinscribed in individual relations of guilt and strength, in the personal experiences and fears of the soldiers. In fact, the agenda of its relation to the "war at home" was set in its first episode. A pacifist draftee tells the sergeant who has just picked him for a combat unit that he will not fight because "the war is wrong." The sergeant replies: "Maybe that's not the point." By the end of the episode, the demands of friendship, comradeship, and even morality integrate the protester into the platoon, when he kills to save another soldier's life. We are never told what the point is.

China Beach locates the war "next door." Its scene is a "rest and recreation" facility just a hundred yards from the fighting. Most interestingly, of course, the program's narrative focuses on four women who are all (except one, a nurse) only peripherally involved in the war. Episodes trace out the war's effects on the social relationships within this imaginary family (and it is quite explicit that we are supposed to take the social group as a family). It also quite consciously and explicitly reinscribes Vietnam into the media clichés not only of the war movie, but of the taken-for-granted images of Vietnam (e.g., explicitly citing narratives, themes, and shots from *Apocalypse Now, Deerhunter,* etc.). In its short but successful run, there has been only one reference to the counterculture (when a pilot donned the costume of a hippie for a party), and the soundtrack, which goes back to the pop music of the early sixties—not only before acid rock but even before the British invasion—seems to deny the existence of any counterculture either at home or in Vietnam. What both of these shows erase is not merely the "war at home" but its effects in Vietnam, from drugs to body counts to various forms of protest. The possibility of politicizing the war is raised, only to be reduced to questions of individual moral doubt and the exigencies of circumstances in the combat area. In fact, the very uniqueness of Vietnam—that it was simultaneously a real war and a television show, and that these two discourses continuously disrupted each other without ever being successfully woven together—has disappeared. What was always in large part—at least insofar as it was a significant event in American history—a television war is being replayed on television in ways that render its televisual existence absent. This is demonstrated no more clearly than in the ad for the video of *Platoon:* A woman sits in her kitchen addressing the camera. She tells us that when her husband came home, he refused to talk about his experience. She could understand neither the war nor his silence. But now that she has seen the film, she understands Vietnam and his silence!

This rearticulation of the war in Vietnam is by no means controlled by the Right. And while the attack on countercultural pleasures is more obviously organized by the Right, I think the two are connected. Whether the impetus comes from within the postwar generations (reconstructing their history and reinterpreting their identities) or the New Right, there is a concerted effort to reconstruct the symbolic moment when the postwar national popular failed. From the Right that failure is seen largely as the moment when youth culture attacked America (and American values). From within the youth culture that failure is the moment when the postwar youth generations lost their faith not only in America, but in the possibility of ever finding a center, an identity, in which they could invest. But neither of these projects captures, I think, the way in which the contemporary rearticulation of the sixties enters into the construction of a new national popular. At this point I want merely to suggest that the sixties was the only moment in the postwar history of youth culture when popular cultural taste was taken to entail a specific set of ideological commitments. An entire generation, whatever their experiences and explicit positions, was caught up in ideological issues, embodied not only in the war but in the creation of what came to be called "lifestyle politics." Thus the popular pleasures that are the object of the various "Just Say No" campaigns were not isolated activities; they were interconnected and held together by a rather vague and personal sense of ideological struggle. It is the possibility of anchoring popular taste in ideology (and ideology in popular taste) that is at stake, that must be deconstructed in the production of a new frontier within the national popular. And it is important to notice that this anchoring is perhaps the only obvious moment (at least in the United State) when postwar youth culture violated its own postmodernity.

Two other developments seem to be related to the project of deconstructing the counterculture, both of which involve displacing any ideological content from youth culture and transforming it into purely affective relations. The first is the increasingly felt "affective nostalgia" for images of precountercultural youth cultures (and of precountercultural anticommunism as well). This nostalgia, which takes very specific—often surreal, always self-consciously ironic—forms, is built on particular iconic details with little regard for context, history, or even intertextuality (e.g., Nick at Night, *The Smothers Broth-*

ers *Show*). It seeks to reclaim a mood that it imagines existed before the articulation of youth at the center of American identity was both accomplished and then collapsed. The second involves the rapid expansion of a consumerism built at the intersection of "lifestyles" and "design." There is a continuity here with the counterculture, but it is displaced and difficult to trace out. The American Dream is relocated in a future that can be brought into—if not bought in—the present, as an iconic and affective reality, even if its economic reality is not readily available to us. The American Dream, since the fifties, has been built upon cultural images of prosperity and consumption, but the resonance of these images is changing. This rearticulation of consumption—visible in such infotainment programs as *Lifestyles of the Rich and Famous,* in such image programs as *L.A. Law* and *Miami Vice,* and in the wide diversity of appeals used in contemporary advertising—takes consumption out of the realm of mere comfort and competition (i.e., keeping up with the Joneses) and into the arena of the impossible construction of one's own difference. One consumes, in this new reality, as a way of designing one's self within a lifestyle defined by *affective* appeals and investments. A lifestyle, in its contemporary consumerist forms, is defined less by the specific products than by one's relations to them. As Mort and Green have suggested, the current marketing strategy of "hyping the appeal of the unique you" has to be located not only in the context of "the proliferation of individualities, of the number of 'yous' on offer" but also as a response to the contemporary "social agenda"— "the changing shape of working class culture, the impact of feminism, ethnic spending power, the 'new man'" (1988, 32–33). The contemporary rearticulation of lifestyle as multiple and fragmented, as the displaced arena of social differences, and as the site of production, through consumption, of *affective* identities further dissociates any possible relationship between taste and politics.

Conclusion. It is time to bring the pieces together and attempt to define the hegemonic project of the New Right. I will approach this task by considering Reagan as a contemporary postmodern Hero. In fact, figures as diverse as Rambo, Oliver North, Sonny Crockett, Han Solo, and the new Batman share a number of peculiar characteristics with the president. They are often so simply constructed as to function as little more than parodies. They are often ambiguously positioned in relation to state apparatuses; that is, they are vigilantes who refuse to permanently place themselves in the service of any ideologically marked or even markable institution. (Thus it is always the state that is ultimately the "bad guy" in Rambo movies. And Reagan remains oddly unencumbered by any restrictive relations to ideological or moral content: he remains untouched by scandals within his administration as well as in his life.) And they almost always are taken up as exemplars of sentimental authenticity. They are ordinary people who have made an absolute commitment to something. (The commitment must be absolute, leaving no room for deviation, although lots of room for doubt—for example, the current "0 tolerance" campaign.) Apart from the absoluteness of their commitment, they appear to be not very different from the rest of us and, more importantly, they are no different from the bad guys. In a classic scene from *Miami Vice,* Tubbs is questioning the morality of the police's behavior since it is often indistinguishable from that of the criminals. Crockett responds that it is justified because "We are better." Tubbs looks at him incredulously and Crockett adds, "better shots." Consider Rambo, the hero most easily appropriated by the Right. On a recent *Oprah Winfrey* program, audience members described his films as—are you ready for this?—antiviolent (since he only uses violence in response to oppressors) and even humanitarian. And because he is always better than the oppressors, he enables people to once again know who the good guys are in a world in which the difference seems to have disappeared. How can one possibly make sense of this? It cannot be simply that Rambo is a better soldier, although that is part of it, because we are too familiar with narratives (mainly from the seventies) in which in fact the better soldier is not necessarily the good guy. What makes Rambo the good guy, what makes him better is, in the end, precisely that he is American. In this articulation of the hero, Rambo is a hero precisely because his commitment is absolute *and it is to America.* This enables us to understand the power of Reagan as a political and cultural figure: He is more than a celebrity or star, he is a figurehead whose contradictory positioning constantly undermines any definition other than his absolute affective commitment to America. He becomes the living icon of the nation he leads, at least according to the New Right.

An icon of America because the New Right is (perhaps unknowingly, certainly unintentionally) appropriating the frontier constructed by the disciplined mobilization of postmodernity in order to reconstitute a new center for the American national popular and hence a new national identity we can safely invest in, that is, one that cannot end up working against us. But the frontier of authentic inauthenticity is precisely the impossibility of articulating affect and ideology, or taste and politics. Thus rather than constructing a national identity by retrieving an imaginary past, the Right continues the project of radically dissociating the possibility of establishing any content in an affective center. It constructs America as a purely affective investment and refuses any definition. It plays on the paradox at the intersection of postmodernity and youth culture: that one can invest totally in one's tastes without taking up anything ideologically. America must have a center to which we are absolutely committed, but that center must remain empty. This is a nationalism with no content. America as an affective object has no entailments, although it has powerful consequences. If America does not stand for anything except the appropriate and even necessary site of our affective nationalism, it is in fact impossible to argue against any action taken in the name of America. This is not the same as "My country, right or wrong," for that still allows the possibility of moral judgments that transcend nationalism, even if they are always to be refused. Reagan and Rambo rather represent a nationalism that is indifferent to any moral difference. Thus even while there may always be a moral discourse in New Right nationalism (e.g., Rambo is defending freedom; Arnold Schwarzenegger in *Predator* is a mercenary who only takes on rescue missions and refuses assassinations—so he is tricked into this one), they remain contentless, with no criteria by which any instance can be judged. (Consider the conservative morality that justifies children's turning in their parents for drug possession.) This national popular constructs an "empty fullness" at the center which merely guarantees the existence of the center. By articulating America into the frontier between affect and ideology, it reconstitutes our relationship to the nation in such a way that whatever our affective response (e.g., to specific incidents or to broad agendas), there is no ground on which to even imagine constructing an oppositional or ideological reaction. It is a powerful articulation of the postmodernity of American popular culture to the project of the New Right. It structures a national popular within which only a powerful affective relationship is possible, one that, if it were to succeed, could never be effectively challenged, only overthrown.

POSTSCRIPT: FANS, FANATICS, AND IDEOLOGUES

As soon as I finished writing this conclusion, I began to wonder whether it is overly pessimistic. It seems to leave little room for that "optimism of the will" that Gramsci thought necessary for political struggle. After all, if Americans seem largely unwilling or unable to fight against this empty center, they are also increasingly unwilling to sacrifice much of their lives to it. Yet as I was writing, on the eve of Independence Day, my pessimism was reconfirmed by constraints that seemed to define possible public responses to the news that an American warship in the Persian Gulf had shot down an Iranian commercial passenger flight: it was an unfortunate accident (presumably to be blamed upon some technological failure); it is the sign of the failure of American policy in the Gulf (Jesse Jackson); and America has the right to . . . (implying that the Iranian jet must have been up to something since *we* shot it down). Not only has there been no moral discussion, there seems to be no space within which one can ask if this does not fundamentally contradict everything that America might claim to stand for.

Where then do we find the optimism that will enable us to struggle against this conservative hegemony, or even to think about its possibility? Perhaps it is in America's history. After all, America has always been a society of fanatics; perhaps this is the result of a society whose origins are built upon a rhetoric of salvation, of "the city on the hill," of "god's beacon" leading the true believers out of the corrupt old world and into the new Eden. (The history of religion in America is marked by recurring fundamentalist revivals!) Perhaps it is the result of the enormous disparity between its economic and political promise (and the occasionally real possibilities) and the rather more grim reality of the majority's everyday life. Perhaps it stems from its being a society of immigrants and migrants, fanatically holding on to their marginal identity, for it is all they have, and fanatically struggling to achieve that elusive dream—of freedom but even more of comfort—that will relieve them of the burden of their marginality.

I was introduced to the uncomfortable ambiguities of fanaticism early in my life as I struggled to come to terms with my Chassidic grandparents. I understood that when my grandfather chose to risk my grandmother's life rather than let her travel (i.e., work) on the sabbath, he was acting on the basis of their shared absolute commitment to a center they could only name—Jaweh—but never explain. And I understood that when my mother challenged that commitment to protect her mother's life, she was not only challenging her father's power (which was intimately bound up with that commitment) but the very desirability of fanaticism in their new world. I have never come to terms with their fanaticism; or perhaps it has always been the fan in me who is never comfortable with the somber, self-isolated, and often cruel Chassidic life that had somehow been constructed out of the joyous teachings of the

Baal Shem Tov. (1997: I have since come to appreciate that there were indeed moments and dimensions of great joy in their lives as well.) In any case, fanaticism reentered my life during the counterculture, when my father (and many of my relatives) functionally excommunicated me for what they called my "fanaticism." I knew then, but I could not explain it, that the situations, and the commitments they demanded, were fundamentally different. This difference has perhaps always been fundamental to America, whose history is less a continuous series of fanaticisms than a continuous battle between fans and fanatics, a battle in which ideologies have always had a problematic place.

It is this difference I want to explore, in order to think about its consequences for my own practices as a cultural and political critic. I will begin by distinguishing three forms of commitment, investment, sensibility (Bourdieu), or "taste": fans, fanatics, and ideologues. The differences are not merely quantitative nor entirely self-contained; where the lines are drawn and how the different forms are evaluated is partly the product of discourses of "power/knowledge," of what Bourdieu (1984) refers to as the social production and function of "distinctions." For example, my academic colleagues found it quite reasonable to assume that, as I am a *fan* of popular music, it was not appropriate for me to teach courses on the subject. Implicitly they also assumed that their own relationship to, for example, the literary texts they taught was something other than that of a fan. In fact, I do not want to contest the fact that the forms of our commitment are different; I would and did contest their assumption that their own relationship was privileged and the only proper basis for a pedagogical and academic practice.

There are real differences between these forms of investments, the ways we construct our tastes, although each of them may encompass a number of significantly different relationships, practices, and elitisms (e.g., collectors, specialists). Fans make an affective investment in the objects of their taste and they construct, from those tastes, a consistent but necessarily temporary affective identity. Their preferences are determined by structures of relevance and effectivity; fans are concerned with how particular practices enter into and effect changes within their everyday lives. While in some instances the fans may respond to meanings and narratives, their taste is never limited to these effects. Relevance may be constituted by nothing but the fact that one invests in specific practices. The fan's culture is the site of everyday enjoyment and pleasure, but also of an affective empowerment that, as I have already suggested, provides strategies for survival and for a limited control over one's own identity and life. Ideologues, on the contrary, make an affective investment based upon an exterior judgment of the quality of the specific text. This is not to say that the judgment is always prior to the investment, but rather that the ideologue always justifies taste based upon principles (an ideology) they assume to be valid outside of the demands of their own everyday lives. The criteria may be defined by substantive matters of content (e.g., one refuses to enjoy "godless" texts) or formal (e.g., complexity, origin). In either case, the ideologue's taste is always measured by standards defined outside of and adhered to independently of the pleasures of everyday life. Or, if you prefer, pleasures are generated through the consistency between ideology and taste. Such structures of taste produce a quasi-stable but necessarily contradictory affective identity (since any individual's ideological positions will always be contradictory). Culture is the source of significant social and political differences and the grounds upon which explicit political struggles are waged, for differences in cultural taste are assumed to necessarily represent competing ideological commitments and objectively comparable qualitative differences.

Finally, fanatics invest affectively in ideological sites, but the investment empties the site of any meaning (whether substantial or formal); it becomes merely the necessary occasion for the investment. The objects of the fanatic's taste then can only be named, never given any content, never made sense of apart from the investment. While one can argue and presumably transform the ideologue's criteria, however commonsensical or taken for granted they may be, the fanatic's investment is never challengeable except by some trauma originating from within his or her own investments. Fanatics live their investments as the totality of their identity, which is always consistent and stable because it is defined only by the absoluteness of the commitment. Culture is the space within which an impossible absolute difference is constantly reinscribed. If fans are always relocated by their tastes back into the demands of their own everyday life, and ideologues are enabled to intervene politically, fanatics are compelled to act because the investment demands the continuous affirmation of the specific empty center. Of course, unlike both fans and ideologues, fanatics rarely are able to admit their fanaticism. While this is partly the result of the system of cultural power within which fanaticism is constructed negatively (e.g., the New Right constructs the Iranians, Palestinians, communists, etc. as fanatics but never their own public representatives and only rarely their more marginal or extremist supporters), it is determined by fanatics' inability to confront the ideological emptiness of their invest-ment, the fact that the center is always merely the mirror image of their fanaticism.

Postwar youth culture has had its fanatics (absolutizing their fandom) and its ideologues (assuming a necessary relationship between their fandom and external systems of meaning); there have even been moments when such rela-tions became the dominant public forms of youth culture. Subcultures (in the narrow sense) might be seen as forms of fanaticism in which the absolute commitment to taste was taken as the totality of one's lived identity, a com-mitment within which taste and identity were each other's mirror image. The counterculture, on the other hand, related one's tastes as a fan to ideological commitments that were not necessarily articulated by the objects of their taste. Yet for the most part youth culture has always constructed itself as a domain of fandom. Again, this is not a quantitative difference but a difference in how the effectivity of their tastes was circumscribed. Their fandom, while it often had important implications for other aspects of their life, defined not only the appropriate relation to popular culture, but the appropriate means by which their investments could generate effects extending throughout their lives. Even for those who wanted to live "the rock and roll life," it was less a matter of either an ideological or absolute commitment than a way into the American Dream. In fact, postwar youth culture has always been caught up in the postmodern frontier, and consequently it has always been suspicious of both ideologues and fanatics. Even when it celebrates such images, it only ap-propriates them as fans, as instances of ironic and sentimental inauthenticity.

But I do not intend to rewrite my entire argument here in these new terms. Instead I want to turn my attention to the flip side of the postmodern gap between fans, fanatics, and ideologues. For fans living within this gap, there appear to be no grounds for differentiating and evaluating any specific invest-ment. If postmodernity constructs an impassable frontier between affect and ideology, it has also collapsed the distance between them. But then how is criticism or political struggle possible? How is it possible to do anything but celebrate fandom (as in the politics of everyday life), to be anything other than a fan of fans? Subcultural theory appears to have been the last moment when we could confidently assume another position; discriminating be-tween resistant (marginal) and incorporated (mainstream) popular culture, it constructed cultural studies as a fan of fanaticism.

Many authors have talked about the postmodern collapse of critical distance and the increasing uncertainty about the authority of intellectual and political voices/positions. But they have, too often, treated this as an abstract epistemological problem brought about by the recognition that such positions are implicated within and determined by the political and cultural terrain. This has led them to define the need for reflexivity as a demand for autocritique and self-revelation, as a search for more autobiographical and dialogical writing forms. This response to the challenge to critical author-ity surrenders what little authority may be left to such practices and consequently surrenders the possibility of historically strategic intellectual and political work. Such epistemologically reflexive writing forms continue to assume that the truth of a text or interpretation is measured by the impossible task of "accurately" representing reality rather than by its strategic intervention and empowerment. The limits of this impossible project in any particular case are determined by the conditions of its origin/production. Hence reflexivity demands that the author reveal his or her determining biographical and sociological conditions. But since the author never actually knows which determinations are actually pertinent (and the decision is itself determined), reflexivity becomes the endless production of commentary, of determined interpretations of determined interpretations. Moreover such epistemologically reflexive writing forms assume that any text is ultimately a description of the author's subjective experience of whatever he or she is writing about. Consequently the author must either offer an interpretation of the limitations of that experience or incorporate the voices of other experiences. But this merely reinscribes not only the privileged place of experience, but the privileged place of the author's experience (since it is ultimately the author who interprets the limitations, as well as his or her own voice or the other voices to be included). In the end such demands reduce reflexivity to the demand for an endless and inevitable deconstruction of the communicative relationship between subject and text. But the result is that reflexivity merely serves as an additional catalyst for the undermining of any possibility for critical or political authority; it cannot rearticulate a new structure of authority appropriate to the contemporary context.

But the collapse of critical distance and the crisis of authority is not epistemological but a concrete historical dilemma called into existence by the fact that, as critical intellectuals, we are inextricably linked to the dominant forms of popular culture; we are fans writing about the terrain, if not the objects, of our own fandom. Consequently our critical authority cannot be built on privileged distinctions of taste and distaste. Reflexivity is, then, a possibility for rearticulating the basis of intellectual and political critique; it is a strategic and empowering response to those historical conditions that must take account of the complex ways in which we are already articulated into the politics of cultural tastes, not only as fans but as critics. But if my place as a fan determines my position within the cultural field, it does not constitute the field itself. If my authority is produced through a socially privileged (and historically determined) form of labor, it is not arbitrary and essentially delivered over to the existing structures of power. While it is important to recognize the specific power of intellectual practices, they cannot be separated from our existence as fans in everyday life. Further, it is exactly because we are both fans and intellectual laborers that we can be simultaneously on the terrain but not entirely of it, that we can reconstitute a historically specific form of critical distance, that we can have some idea of the questions that need to be asked, of the connections that need to be made, and of the articulations that need to be challenged. Critical practices are, after all, a form of labor: they transform the world; in this case, they enable us not to deconstruct our affective investments nor to constantly reflect on them (or our experiences), but to move beyond them, through what Marx called "the necessary detour through theory," to a higher level of abstraction in order to transform the empirically taken-for-granted into the concretely determined. My existence as a fan, my experiences, along with whatever other resources are available for describing the field of popular practices and their articulations to social and political positions, are the raw material, the starting point of critical research.

The elitism of our critical labor does not guarantee its politics, nor the politics of our intervention. Its elitism is constituted by its technical practices and resources, by its access to specialized vocabularies, sites of production and distribution, and (actually quite limited) claims of authority. None of this guarantees the stories we tell or their effects; our discourses are after all both constrained and empowered by their conditions and modes of production. As intellectuals we have the resources to articulate social possibilities. Recognizing the limitations of our claims—that every map has its angle of projection—does not necessarily vitiate its value or its strategic truth. We can refuse to narrativize our work in ways that reinscribe the absolute hierarchies of modernist epistemologies (which would violate our fan's sensibility anyway). Recognizing that our task as "critical fans" is not to define the "proper" cultural tastes, we can struggle to make sense of how specific investments are articulated; recognizing that our task as political critics is not to define the "proper" political positions, we can struggle to point to the ways they can be rearticulated. For if we are fans, we are not only fans; nor are we only intellectuals. Like all people, we live in and in between many spaces and places, and our politics is always derived from the ways we can and cannot move within our lives. That is to say, neither politics nor authority can be derived from the discourses we speak as intellectuals. We bring our politics to these discourses from "below," as it were, but as intellectuals we can articulate directions and alliances through which such politics can be effective. And we bring our authority from the labor that some of us are—admittedly—paid to perform. That labor is a part of reality, but it neither constructs reality nor is it directly determined by a simple structure of reality. Our practices may offer us limited possibilities, but if we refuse them, or if we further circumscribe them by our voluntary reflexive self-absorption, we not only exclude ourselves from the everyday world of fans, but we abandon the political possibilities of that world. The problem is not to deconstruct authority, but to rearticulate new forms of authority that allow us to speak as critical fans.

This new model of intellectual and political authority cannot begin with self-assured guarantees that might enable us to confidently measure and judge every investment, every practice, every articulation, and every possibility. It will have to start not from some sense of the radical difference between the critic and the fan, a difference that will always undermine its ability to speak, but from the radical diversity of (and differentiated access to) practices and investments in which we are all implicated. It will have to measure progress, intellectual and political, not by some idealized utopia but by movement within the fragile, contradictory realities of people's lives, desires, fears, and investments. An impure politics, certainly, without the myth of a perfect reflexivity that can guarantee its authority. A contaminated politics, never innocent, rooted in the organization of distances and densities through which all of us move together and apart, hesitatingly sometimes, sometimes recklessly. A politics that attempts to move people, perhaps just a little at first, in a different direction. But a politics nonetheless, one that speaks with a certain authority, though as limited and frail as the lives of those who speak it. A politics for and by people who live in the modern world, people who live in the world of popular tastes. An impure politics for pop people!

Rockin' in Conservative Times

INTRODUCTION

I want in this paper to touch on a wide range of issues. I realize that, at least at one level, they may seem unconnected, but I think that one of the practices of cultural studies is to draw unexpected lines of connection, to construct new contexts. Some of these issues I will touch on because they are, in a direct way, my concern here; others, because I think they have *not* been talked about (enough); and still others, because they *have* been talked about.

In the contemporary world, I think it is important that, whenever we begin to talk about political struggles, we do not ignore the lessons of cultural theory when we talk about the dominant position (e.g., the United States), that we avoid the tendency to describe the formations and sites of dominant power singularly and homogeneously. Let me give two examples of how such oversimplifications have operated. First, the appropriation of a theory of he-gemony as a struggle between the people and the power bloc (as opposed to a struggle between classes, or between the state and civil society) has too often operated without any specification of exactly which class fractions constitute the power bloc. The result is that the notion of hegemony becomes little more than a populist appeal of the powerless against the powerful. But the theory of hegemony argues precisely that such vague descriptions ignore the histor-ical specificity and strategic complexity of the articulations of a war of posi-tions. A second example involves the way we treat media representations in the context of hegemonic struggles; while we would never take the represen-tations in the dominant media of subordinate/minority cultures, identities, and so on as "the real," there is a tendency to assume that the media represen-tations of America[1] by U.S.-based (but no longer only U.S.-controlled) multi-national media corporations can be taken as "the real." I am often amazed at how easily and confidently people talk about the United States, even within the United States, and even including myself at times. The United States is a complexly fractured and conflictual society, with significant class, race, gender, age, generational, and regional differences.[2]

Of course one might reasonably ask, Why, then, is there only one media image of the United States? Obviously the reasons are complex and one needs at the very least to say a few things in response. First, the media lie! They are after all ideological (and representations are never innocent). They are capitalist (and the distribution of images of the United States is itself not innocent). But also there is not only one image, although we don't always see others, and when we do we don't always recognize them. In fact, what I see in the U.S. media and culture is not a single image or voice, but very real and important struggles. I am particularly interested in one: a struggle not only for power or, in cultural studies' terms, for hegemony in the United States, but a struggle over the construction of the United States and its place in the world. This is a struggle not merely over its identity, but over its spaces or territories, a struggle to remap the United States, its population and capital. And this remapping does not stop at its national boundaries. I do not assume, by the way, that the primary players in this struggle can be neatly distributed—left and right—whether we are talking in economic, political, or sociological terms. It is as much a struggle between various fractions of the Right, or of capitalist interests. It is a struggle to remake the map of everyday life in the United States, to simultaneously move the center of American life to the Right via a radical depoliticization of important fractions of the population. It is a struggle for a hegemony of a new conservatism. But, as I hope to explain, it is rather specific forms of hegemony and depoliticization that are being strategically produced.

At this point, before continuing my argument, let me briefly address two questions that will no doubt be raised. First, someone will surely ask, Who is the agent of this hegemony? I do not believe that this can be simply answered, but I will point to three formations, each internally quite complex and contradictory, that are involved: the New Right (which includes everything from born-again anticommunists, to antigovernment and anti-big-business libertarians, to Christian fundamentalists, to free-market capitalists; see Clarke 1991 and Grossberg 1992); the Republican Party; and a rather ineffective opposition, whether one looks to the Democratic Party or to the very active but scattered and largely marginalized Left. In order to understand this struggle for hegemony, I believe we have to acknowledge that the first two formations are in fact actively involved in a large number of conspiracies aimed at gaining power and transforming life. Fortunately, many of these conspiracies compete with others, and most are never fully realized.

But in fact, to begin to answer the question of agency, I think we have to look at the effects of this struggle and ask to whose interests it is articulated. And so, later in this paper, I will turn to a topic too often noticeably absent in discussions of cultural studies, except as the ultimate abstract cause of all our problems—no, not the United States, but capitalism.

Second, having said that you cannot talk about the nation of the United States as a single, homogeneous entity, it may appear that that is exactly what I am doing. And in one sense it is true. That is the level of abstraction at which I am operating. This means, necessarily, that a lot of the concrete determinations and local articulations are missing. But I would justify this on political grounds: I am describing a struggle over the articulation between a heterogeneous population, the state, and culture, a struggle to reconstruct what Gramsci called "the national popular." But at the same time, I want to emphasize that I do not mean to claim that I am speaking about the entire population. Obviously the struggle to depoliticize is aimed only at certain fractions, although I think they are significant in both quantitative and qualitative terms. These fractions are something like the "popular classes"; they cut across class and gender and, to a lesser extent, across race and ethnicity.

My claim is that there is a struggle going on in which culture is not only the site of struggle, and not only even the stake to be won, but also the weapon in that struggle. There is a real struggle taking place over culture and its politics in the broadest sense (touching on "high art," popular culture, education, mass media, and everyday life). And the state is centrally involved in this struggle, which seems to be rather unique in U.S. history. There is a real irony here: those of us in critical and cultural theory have been talking for decades about a war of/over culture. But the first time we are confronted with a real "culture war," we seem to pack up our bags and go home. After developing sophisticated tools and understandings of how cultural struggles are waged, we seem incapable of using them to analyze the particular war, and instead we are reduced to claiming that the other side "is not playing fair," that they are lying or using rather questionable rhetorical strategies. In fact, it seems that the best practitioners of cultural studies today can be found among the legions of the Right and among the new classes of capitalists (e.g., advertising).[3]

Marx supposedly taught us that power always involves both domination and subordination. Cultural studies has done a lot of valuable work looking at the active ways subordination is lived, mobilized, and empowered. It has often sought to find sources of optimism without which resistance and opposition are impossible. But in the contemporary world, and in the United States, we need a good dose of pessimism as well. Or perhaps we already have it and we need to understand why it is very reasonable. I think it is fair to say that at the present moment in the United States, one can only be (and one must be) an optimist against one's better judgment. In other words, we need to understand the specific form in which domination is organized, how it operates, how it too is lived, mobilized, and empowered. We cannot take for granted that domination is always and everywhere the same.

The first question I want to ask is how this new conservatism, this new hegemony, is being produced and put in place. In another context (Grossberg 1993c), I have identified three machines of power, three mechanisms by which power is produced and already structured: an abstract machine which, through stratification, produces and distributes value (e.g., subjectivity, capital, affect, meaning); an ideological or discursive machine which, through coding and decoding, produces identity in/and difference (i.e., subject-positions), which then maps the unequal distribution of value; and a territorializing machine which, through the production of lines of articulation and lines of flight, produces a distribution of places and spaces, a structured mobility.

In my discussion of the new conservatism, I am going to talk only about the third machine. I do not mean to suggest that one can or should ignore the first two. They are crucial, and the three machines are all always working together with and on each other (although they may be resisting or opposing each other as well). It is in fact at the level of the first two machines that the terrifying consequences of this hegemony can be seen—in the alarming rates of poverty and deprivation that characterize not only ethnic and racial minorities but women and children as well; in the horrifying rise of various forms of racism, ethnic hatred, and violence; in the attack on civil liberties and freedoms; and in the increasingly distorted distribution of wealth. I do not mean to underestimate those operations of power. I take them for granted, and instead build upon the work that has already been done here. But I do want to argue that simply describing the role of the first two machines in this struggle is inadequate; something has been and is being left off the agenda. And I think that, as a result, our struggles to oppose the new conservatism often end up fighting the wrong battles, in the wrong places, with the wrong weapons.

I want to describe the emergence of a new territorializing machine. I can give a hint as to what this machine looks like by contrasting it with Foucault's (1977) image of disciplinization as surveillance and normalization. Disciplinization is a territorializing machine in which the individual is placed into a mass space and monitored.[4] To offer an all too frighteningly real metaphor of disciplinization, imagine a car that automatically checks the driver's condition (e.g., for alcohol, drugs) and reports that information back to the state. Now imagine that the car does not report that information back to the state but instead simply limits (or, at the extreme, prohibits) the driver's mobility. This is what I want to call a new territorializing machine, a disciplined mobilization. And it is interesting to note here that both Reagan and Bush have severely curtailed the government's role in data collection, surely not the action of a state operating on principles of discipline.

What I want to do here is present the outlines of my argument from *We Gotta Get Out of This Place* (1992), although I will also modify the argument in places. While this will be necessarily abstract, nevertheless I hope that it will be useful. I will proceed in four steps: First, I will describe the operation or logic of one of the dominant formations in post–World War II popular culture, a formation with youth and rock at its center. Second, I will describe the new conservatism as a rearticulation of this logic; in other words, I will read this formation as an allegory of the new conservatism. Third, I will suggest that this strategic hegemony can only be understood in the context of the changing place of the United States in the global circulation of capital and capitalism. And finally, I will suggest that, as a consequence, we need to rethink the nature of oppositional politics. . . .

A HEGEMONY OF AFFECT

I want to suggest that the affective logic, which I have described in earlier chapters as being at the center of rock culture, as it were, is being reorganized and redeployed in the service of a specific political agenda. What was (and perhaps still is, but that is a different question) an empowering machine is turned (as in *Star War*'s image of "the force" being turned to the dark side) into the service of a disempowering machine.[5] The paradox of the new conservatism is that most people do not seem to agree with its agenda, yet they seem unable to oppose it and consequently they are drawn into its currents. But the real paradox is that, precisely by repoliticizing and re-ideologizing all of the social relations and cultural practices of everyday life, the new conservatism has effectively depoliticized a significant part of the population. It has created an "organization of pessimism," to use Walter Benjamin's phrase, or perhaps more accurately, an impassioned or passionate apathy.

The result is that people seem caught in an inescapable logic: Even if you could organize, you probably wouldn't change anything; even if you did succeed, your success would probably be corrupted; even if it were not, everything is so complicated that you would probably create (or at the very least have to ignore) other significant problems. The result is a kind of disenfranchisement from politics: politics is a guaranteed depressant. Even when people engage in political struggle they are often so locally defined as to preclude any long-term, larger alliances that might challenge the new conservative hegemony. Thus, as you might have guessed, I am suggesting that the new conservatism is an affective structure, an organized and specific form of apathy. People oppose conservative policies but do little or nothing about it. People are outraged, but do little or nothing about it. People know they are lied to, but do little or nothing about it.

First, then, I want to argue that the new conservative strategy operates at the level of affect. Here my task is made easier by some recent research on how the various groups of the Right, including the Republican Party, have actually organized their campaigns (Edwards 1992). Using very diverse focus groups (including people from different political positions) and a technology called Perception Analyzers, they construct "values maps." Such maps do not measure belief or even understanding but something called "average emotional response." They measure the intensity of people's affective response: the higher the score, the better the slogan or appeal. Thus for example "a thousand points of light" was a top scorer although no one in the various focus groups knew what it meant. But that doesn't matter; in fact, it is good, because understanding is "unmanageable" and "uncontrollable." It turns out that speeches, campaign slogans, and larger campaign strategies have been and are being designed this way. (And recently the Democratic Party has begun to use this technique.)

This is not a "feel-good" politics but a mood politics, based on a certain understanding of the "postmodern" attitude that is increasingly colonizing significant spaces of everyday life and significant fractions of the population.

This attitude can best be described as a certain ironic cynicism in which what matters is the fact that something matters, in which what you have to invest in is just the fact that you have to invest in something. This is "pessimism with a happy face," in which "nothing matters and what if it did." It defines a politics that, on the surface, appears selfish but is actually something else: "If you're sailing on the *Titanic,* go first class." What matters is that you care, not what you care about or even how. This may help us understand why the key moments in the Bush-Dukakis race were the two moments that reversed the public's opinion of the relative affect of each candidate: When Bush stood up to a network anchorperson he demonstrated he had passion; when Dukakis answered a question about rape in a bureaucratic tone, he demonstrated that he had none.

After all, less than one-third of all eighteen- to forty-five-year-olds follow news regularly, and the stories most closely followed are often about events that elicit powerful emotional and affective responses (e.g., the *Challenger* disaster) rather than events of political consequence. Lee Atwater, ex-campaign manager for George Bush and ex-chair of the Republican National Party, was quoted as saying: "Everything is bull . . . If you want to look at a solid trend for the last 15 or 20 years, it is that the American people are cynical and turned off about all institutions, and politics is one" (Orestes 1990). That dating of this process (locating it at the end of the 1960s) is significant, for the new conservatism in a way shares the assumption of the rock formation of a break in history. This break represents a crisis, the beginning of the fall of the United States, when certain memories "trapped us" and led us into a crisis of cynicism and/or relativism.

Yet while their rhetoric rejects this fall, their strategy redirects it. If the population is cynical about any and every investment, then emphasize the commitment to commitment itself. Reagan's popularity depended in part on the simple fact that he seemed to care about something (the same can be said about cultural icons like Rambo). What he cared *about* was less important. This suggests a very particular strategy: If the population is suspicious of ideological appeals, market passion. That means that ideally the ideas and values you market should not have any content. Rather they should be like sliding signifiers, affective epidemics, which merely serve to mark the existence of a commitment. And not surprisingly this seems to be precisely how such campaign images as the family or the war on drugs seem to be operating. In fact, "Just Say No" is less a site for passionate investment than a passionate call for disinvestment: Just Say No . . . to drugs, sex, addiction, consumption, politics . . .

Rock itself is a site of powerful affective investments and therefore presents a problem. But the solution is simple: to disarticulate or disconnect rock's territorializing logic from its differentiating logic. That is, one needs to undermine the ability of the investment in rock to mark and make a difference. Partly this is being done already by developments within the rock formation itself. As rock's own ironic cynicism gets turned back upon itself, the very notion of authenticity becomes difficult to sustain. And as the first rock generations enter their middle ages, the notion of youth becomes increasingly unstable and unable to sustain the weight of the rock formation. As a result, rock alliances appear increasingly fluid and tolerant of one another. The pluralism of rock in the 1990s seems to echo the 1950s' image of liberalism: differences that don't make a difference, that don't seem to matter, that don't seem to have any power.

This doesn't mean that fans do not still make judgments about "authenticity," but that such judgments are not invested in the same way. The place of rock, not only in the social formation, but in people's lives, is changing. Rather than being the center and agency of people's mattering maps, rock's power is articulated by its place on other maps, by its relations to other activities. For example, rather than dancing to the music you like, you like the music you dance to.

But the changing power of rock cannot be explained entirely by its internal history, and it would be naïve to ignore the fact that the Right is waging a battle over rock on two fronts. The first front directly addresses rock, but it does so in an intentionally contradictory way. One set of groups, primarily but not only Christian fundamentalists, attacks all rock music as the "devil's work" and anti-American. Another set of groups attacks only some rock, usually everything produced after the "fall" of America into cynicism (which usually means after those attacking it grew up). Such groups (e.g., the Parents' Music Resource Center) argue that parents should control the music children listen to; obviously this violates some fundamental relations of the rock formation. Meanwhile a third group attempts to appropriate and redefine rock, offering a new image of rock success: one can be old, rich, conservative, nice, and a rock and roller. (Here figures like Lee Atwater and Pat Boone have been central.) I think the unity of these contradictory strategies is intentional insofar as representatives of one group are often on the boards of directors of other groups.

I also think the second front in the battle against rock is, at least in part, intentional. It involves a very large and complex struggle over the meaning and status of youth in America. I do not want to go into the details of this struggle here, but it is clearly an attempt to undermine the ability of the rock formation to privilege youth, to identify it with mobility and as a site of investment.

What is left is rock's territorializing logic, its production of lines of flight, its emphasis on mobility within the spaces of everyday life. I would suggest that the new conservatism can be seen as rearticulating this territorializing logic into a different project: a disciplined mobilization. In this project, social reality is itself depoliticized by producing everyday life as a closed circuit. A disciplined mobilization normalizes rock's sense of its homelessness, its sense that its place cannot be fixed, its belief that its production of lines of flight, of mobility, is itself always mobile. But at the same time it disciplines rock's lines of flight. For even while rock's lines of flight remain within everyday life, their vector points beyond it. Rock imagines another space, a space outside of everyday life, a space in which boredom would be transcended forever. But all it can ever accomplish are moments of temporary intensity. Still there is an outside, a space in which, often, authenticity itself is supposed to be located. (Here we can understand rock's propensity to steal from other cultures, especially African American cultures, which it imagines to exist outside of everyday life.)

But the new conservatism disciplines this deterritorializing machine with its imaginary outside. Its lines of flight must be bent back upon themselves, enclosed entirely within the space of everyday life. The result is the construction and celebration of an apparently unconstrained mobility that is nothing but a principle of constraint. This is a strategy by which the very possibility of places (stabilities, sites of investment) is negated through the reification of mobility and space. (Perhaps the best material example of such a disciplined mobilization is Disney World.) Everyday life becomes a space with no places, a system of mobilities with no stabilities, a map of identifications with no belonging, a regime of authority with no legitimacy. Such a space is neither dialogic nor expansive and hence does not fit the normal model of hegemony as propounded by Stuart Hall (1988) or Ernesto Laclau and Chantal Mouffe (1985). It does not seek to construct alliances. It mobilizes ideological positions not to mark differences but to displace investments. It is an organization of social space through the regulation of movement.

Such a disciplined mobilization is not a differentiating machine, even one in which the different is excluded. It is an erasing machine in which the other—that which exists outside its spaces—is simply "disappeared." In fact, it carries out a double erasure. First, those who live outside of its spaces, outside of everyday life, become invisible. This produces a whole new system of local racisms, local systems of sexual, gender, ethnic, and age discrimination. Second, those forces—political and economic—that exist outside of (and shape) its spaces become invisible. Everything, including power and even economics (remember Reagan's attempt to construct the national economic crisis in terms of the family budget), is reduced to, locked into, everyday life.

Hence the disappearance of public political life cannot be understood either in general terms or as an accident. Nor is it merely that politics has been personalized. The disappearance of public political life is being actively produced. Both civil society and private life are collapsed into everyday life. The very possibility of lines of flight into the arena of state and economic apparatuses is disappearing. Politics as the realms of governance and economic policy are increasingly difficult to locate as places that matter. As Lefebvre says, "everyday life has taken the place of economics" (1984, 197). This helps to explain, at least in part, the government's success at home regarding the Iraqi war. The images of the war were articulated and deployed into people's lives so as not to disrupt or break into the closed space of everyday life. The war was absorbed into its rhythms, tempos, and intensities, into its mobile mattering maps.

Ironically, the cultural Left has gone along with this: politics is reduced to lifestyle and commitments in everyday life. Typical of this is Mort and Green, who point to the relation between "rapid changes in time-honored distinctions between something called politics on the one hand and leisure, pleasure and personal life on the other. That is to say that politics in a formal sense is being challenged by a series of 'cultural revolutions' taking place beyond its boundaries" (1988, 33). In this view, racism becomes a matter to be judged by the "discomfort" it produces in its victims and ecology becomes a matter of the microhabits of consumers (rather than structures of the economic and industrial context).

I do not mean to reject the recognition that there is a politics to everyday life. It is often a space of empowerment, a place one can find the energy to go against the grain of social tendencies and against one's own subordination. It is also possible to use the affective investment in everyday struggle precisely to draw people out of everyday life, into larger political and economic struggles.[6] But the empowerment derived from popular culture and everyday life is itself being rearticulated into the disempowering structure of a disciplined mobilization. The result is that often the very activities that empower us, the very forms of empowerment themselves, become politically disenabling, a weapon used against us.

CAPITALISM AND THE NEW HEGEMONY

Before I turn to my final consideration—the implications of this analysis for political strategies—I want to at least point to how I might locate the struggle for this new conservative hegemony in a broader context. Only in such a broader context can we begin to ask questions of agency in the sense of asking To whose interest is this disciplined mobilization articulated? What is its effect? I think the answer lies in the realm of the economic, but not necessarily in the sense of class identity and struggle, nor in the sense of the production of culture. Rather I think that if we are to understand these particular cultural struggles and relations, we must do the work of analyzing the nature and functioning of capitalism today and its relations to the state. And that means that we cannot assume in advance that capitalism is homogeneous or rational. Too often, we act as if we know in advance where the contradictions are (e.g., between classes, or between the forces and relations of production, or between fractions of capital like financial and manufacturing).

We must start instead with the recognition that today capitalism itself is in a state of chaos, if not crisis, and that it has little understanding of its own situation. As the *Financial Times* of London put it:

It is ironic that just as much of Eastern Europe is consigning Communist economic doctrine unlamented to the dustbin of history, Western capitalist economies should be in the throes of their most turbulent upheavals for half a century. One after another, comfortable assumptions about economic and business life which evolved in the industrialized West after the second world war have been exploded or discarded during the 1980s. As a result, the practice of Western capitalism does not offer a stable model, with clearly agreed rules. Rather, it is a moving target, caught between the pull of complex and often opposing forces, whose longer-term direction is difficult to define. (de Jonquieres 1990, 2)

I believe this struggle can be analyzed not merely in terms of competing solutions to the crisis of contemporary capitalism (monetarist, fordist, global fordist, neofordist, postfordist, etc.; see Grossberg 1992), but also as a struggle over the spatial distribution of both capital and the different forms and practices of capitalism itself (i.e., of the different ways capitalism produces and extracts surplus value). Obviously such a struggle involves remaking the map of global capitalism and restructuring the nature of and the relations between the local and the global.

And in this restructuring, we cannot assume the continued hegemony of the United States in global capitalism. At least we have to recognize and begin to locate the conflict between the interests of the United States (recognizing that U.S. economic and political interests are not always the same) and the interests of global capitalism. It is this struggle and this conflict that I think has to be related to the project of the new conservative hegemony. In these terms, we might begin to consider the possibility that the moral agenda of the New Right may itself be appropriated and rearticulated by the entirely different interests and strategies of specific capitalist fractions.

Let me describe one such interest in the very simplest of terms, because I think it is crucial to understanding the depoliticization of American society. In a certain sense, the United States has to be depoliticized and moved to the right in particular ways so that capitalism can dismantle America's claim to retain its global hegemony, since the United States often acts as if such hegemony were its natural possession and right. At the very least, capitalism has to move the United States from the center stage of its own political life so that capitalism itself can have the space to construct a new economic map of the world and determine the United States' place within it. (It is not unlike giving a child something to play with while you go off to clean house or even restructure the household.) Of course, the United States, in the forms of the state and specific economic interests, does not always go along with this. It is only when we begin to map out these complex fields of forces and interests that we can begin to understand the agencies involved in the contemporary struggle for hegemony.

STRATEGIES FOR POLITICAL OPPOSITION

Rather than continue this line of argument, a line that will require a great deal of work not only on "economics" but also (at least for British and American cultural studies) on how to place economics within cultural studies, I want to conclude with some observations about the implications for political strategy of my analysis of the struggle for hegemony in the United States. I want to speculate about why the Left has been so ineffective in responding to this very real and visible challenge, while emphasizing that I am speaking of a particular context and a particular struggle. I do not think that strategies can simply be appropriated from one context or struggle to another, any more than can the form and practice of cultural studies. Strategic politics have to be built on an analysis of the political struggle to be waged. In a sense, I am speaking here to an imaginary audience, located in the United States. Whether these observations have any relevance elsewhere is beyond my ability to say. I also want to apologize ahead of time for what I'm sure will be the overpious tone of my assertions.[7]

First, we cannot reduce all of politics to the politics of everyday life, nor all cultural struggles to the struggle over symbols and representations. For example, in the United States today, many struggles over particular forms of racism seem more concerned with whether particular symbols (e.g., team mascots) are inherently racist than with the actual material conditions of the subordinate population and the possible relations between particular institutions (sports franchises, universities) and those conditions. If nothing else, such strategies reduce all political questions to the same level and urgency, and are likely to produce endless arguments over the meanings of the symbols.

This argument has important implications for much of the contemporary discourse about hegemony, where there is a tendency to reduce Gramsci's distinction between the state and civil society, first, to an opposition between the people and the power bloc (in Stuart Hall 1987) and finally, to an opposition between oppression and authority (in Laclau and Mouffe 1985).[8] There are at least two significant problems with the reductions performed by this particular line of theorizing. On the one hand there is no way to generate political opposition except from within the experience of the oppressed, since oppression and antagonism are mutually constitutive. In fact, the entire question of domination, where "subordination [is] judged illegitimate from outside" and which depends on a judgment of the political and economic system itself, is erased. Instead oppression exists wherever a subordinate relationship (in which one is subjected to the decisions of another) becomes the site of an antagonism. There is no discussion of the legitimacy of some authority or of the requirements of competence in some instances. All subordination is equally bad as soon as it generates its own antagonism.

On the other hand the vision that is supposed to unite all such antagonisms, the vision of a radical and plural democracy, assumes that the validity
of each struggle, of each identity or antagonism, can only be located within
itself and hence cannot be judged. The only possible principle is then the
maximum autonomization of the different spheres or struggles. But this egalitarianism has to be modified by a principle of equivalence that guarantees
that each struggle will be modified by its need to respect the equality of the
others. Their equality then is balanced by their common demand for democracy or liberty. But are all demands subsumable under the general principle of
"democratic demands"? And what happens when two demands conflict?

Of course, Laclau and Mouffe (1985) recognize that this democratic commitment cannot be defined, for that would surely eliminate some struggles
from its space. It can only be a moment of tension and openness; it cannot
define, in Laclau and Mouffe's terms, "a logic of the positivity of the social":
"No hegemonic project can be based exclusively on a democratic logic, but
must also consist of a set of proposals for the positive organization of the
social" (188–89). But where do these proposals come from? And what values
do they seek to inscribe on the social? In fact, in too much contemporary
discourse, democracy remains undefined or taken for granted: Who are "the
people" and what forms of power are they invested with and how? Where do
questions of rights, freedom, and so forth fit? Along these lines, we need to
rethink the conflation of politics and culture in which democracy is seen as
"a way of life, an on-going contest within every aspect of daily life" (Lefort
1986, 267). Such discourses end up defining democracy on the model of self-
management and cultural equality, and once again erase the political (state)
specificity of democracy and its relations to rights.

Second, we cannot conflate politics with moral purity. Politics is the art of
the possible. Our moral positions have to be tempered by the realities of the
world and the possibilities of change. Sometimes we need to be efficient and
effective, and that may require organization and even bureaucracy. Democracy isn't always the best local political strategy. Sometimes we need to make
compromises. Although we may be opposed in principle to capitalism, we
are unlikely to overthrow capitalism or even convince the majority of people
that we should overthrow it. That doesn't mean we can't criticize it, or struggle to rearticulate it, to change the ways it operates and its systems of values
and priorities. Capitalism is, after all, not a fixed system.

This also means that we should probably spend less time judging our allies and more time fighting our enemies. The debate over "political correctness," while perhaps unique to the United States insofar as it is deployed as a strategy by the Right, points to a significant failure of the Left: to bond together for a common struggle, the importance of which outweighs individual differences or even failures. The Left has to begin to criticize itself, not for its moral failures but for establishing its own system by which people's behavior, speech, and even thoughts are policed and measured against some constantly undefinable standard of moral purity.

Third, at the same time we as intellectuals need to find ways to reclaim our intellectual authority, to speak to and, when necessary, even for others. The fact that authority is socially constructed, that all knowledge is historically implicated with systems of power, does not mean that all authority can or should be rejected, or that all systems of power are equally condemnable. Too often, left intellectuals seem to think that their only responsibility is to give over their speaking position to others less capable of manipulating the codes of public discourse and perhaps less knowledgeable about certain matters. I am not trying to suggest that nonintellectuals are dopes or not worth listening to. On the contrary, I am suggesting that intellectual labor produces its own value which we must be able and willing to use.

Fourth, and perhaps most controversially, we need, for the purposes of this struggle, to escape the dead end of social movements organized around identities, even when such identities are formed in struggle. I do not mean to reject the importance of questions of identity, or their centrality in other real and crucial struggles, just their viability as an organizing principle for this hegemonic politics. It is the attempt to define identity politics into all strategic spaces, its occupation of the domain of politics per se, that I am opposing. After all, such identities are always exclusive and initiate struggles over who controls them. Moreover they proliferate endlessly, creating a constant need to fulfill the demands of new, previously unacknowledged identities. Even more importantly, they do not seem capable of defining or controlling people's political commitments, even as they have enabled the Right to construct such social movements as merely "special interests."

I do not think it matters whether identities are defined here in essentialist or anti-essentialist terms. The same problems arise. In fact, I am rather suspicious of the current celebrations of fragmented, hybrid subjects. I do not disagree with them; they do describe what or where we are, but not where we need to be. We need to ask where these fractured and hybrid identities come from, and the answer has to be, in part, from capitalism and capitalist culture. As Mort and Green observe, "there are some uncanny resemblances between lifestyle market segmentation and the individualities thrown up by the new political movements of the 80s" (1988, 32). But while they take this as support for a politics of postmodern identity, I take it as good grounds for suspicion.

Instead I want to turn to the advice of the African American feminist writer June Jordan: "People have to begin to understand that just because somebody is a woman or somebody is black does not mean that he or she and I should have the same politics. We should try to measure each other on the basis of what we do for each other rather than on the basis of who we are" (cited in Parmar 1989, 63). This may seem rather obvious, since it is entirely consistent with the emphasis in cultural studies on articulation and the lack of any necessary guarantees in history. And yet its implications for a radically different form of politics have been largely ignored. I would call this a politics of practice, in which people are organized around common opposition to certain practices and structures (e.g., antipoverty, antiracism, antisexism, a concern about those infected with AIDS) and around common support (e.g., the right of people to enjoy whatever sexual relations they want, including same-sex relations, without discrimination, punishment, or even an identity) that can be articulated together.

Fifth, we need to get beyond the opposition between the local and the global. This means giving up such slogans as "Think globally, act locally," since in some sense every action is both local and global. Instead we need to think and act strategically. This means that we need to identify the points of articulation, the points where the global becomes local and the local opens onto the global.

Finally, we need to strategically enter the struggle over people's affective lives by whatever means necessary. On the one hand this means that we need to speak to people in the languages they understand, starting from where they are. I am not talking here about how technical or difficult our language is (although I do think we need to develop better nonacademic writing skills and more effective nonacademic ways of communicating). But to assume that people are simply incapable of reading or understanding difficult arguments seems to me simply the worse form of elitism. The problem is not that people can't understand what we say; it is rather that people often don't care about what we write, and so they find no reason to make the effort. We need to connect to people's affective lives in order to organize our own politics, not to tell them what their politics should be, and we need to use the forms of culture that speak to them. Again, we need to give up the self-righteousness that characterizes so much of the alternative populist media in order to produce something else, something that operates within the popular culture but uses those popular languages and logics in new and different ways, to new and different ends. This would be a popular "minor" culture, in Deleuze and Guattari's terms (1987).

On the other hand, struggles over people's affective lives probably require a good dose of utopianism, but again it cannot come entirely from above. I believe that most people, if you could get past their pessimism and ironic cynicism, have what Dick Hebdige describes as "a shared responsible yearning . . . out toward something more and something better than this place and this now" (1985, 38). We have to remind them that Marx did not want everyone to be equally poor, he wanted everyone to be equally rich. But of course, such a project violates too many of our theoretical regulations.

A counterhegemonic struggle will require the creation of structures of affective commonality that do not deny differences, based on principles of justice, freedom, equality, and democracy in economic, political, and cultural terms. Is it naïvely optimistic to believe that such structures are possible? Probably, but as Gramsci (1971) suggests, politics requires "pessimism of the intellect, optimism of the will." And if we are unwilling to embrace optimism, or, better, to construct the grounds for a new optimism in the present context, then we have become part of the organization of pessimism. Let me close, then, with a different vision of optimism, in the words of the Chinese writer Lu Xin: "Hope cannot be said to exist, nor can it be said not to exist. It is like roads across the earth. For actually, the earth had no roads to begin with, but when many people pass one way, a road is made" (1921, cited in Gottschalk 1990, 26).

Conclusion: From Media to Popular Culture

to Everyday Life

As the focus for this essay I want to use a statement in the Victoria (Australia) curriculum: "The student's natural enthusiasm and interest in the media should be sustained in the more formal classroom structure. Even so, teachers must achieve a balance between developing a sound approach to media education and fostering the student's feel and excitement for it." I want to talk about this "balance" or, more accurately, why this balance is so hard to achieve. In a sense, I see this desired balance as the dilemma of teaching media rather than its chief difficulty.

The statement presupposes an interesting if somewhat predictable distribution of relations to the media: on the one side, students with their "natural enthusiasm," "interest," "feel and excitement"; on the other side, teachers with "a sound approach." This division seems to embody a desire to have it both ways, as it were. We have to see our students as lacking any sophistication, which is not quite the same as assuming that they are passively manipulated cultural dopes, for they are, after all, granted a very active affective or passional relation to the media. To some extent, this is necessary if we are to maintain our authority as teachers without condemning ourselves to guaranteed failure, since, if they are "dopes," we could never teach them anything. But if there is no problem, if they are not in some ways, at some times, duped by their relationship to the media, there is probably no reason for us to teach them anything about the media. Thus I do not want to dismiss outright the elitism inherent in the call for "a sound approach" as long as we take it as a demand that as teachers we constantly construct positions for ourselves *as* having a certain authority. Nor do I want to dismiss the goal of balancing our elitism against the affective strength of our students' investments in the media culture. But I do want to reject the particular sociological distribution of cultural capital implied, between emotion and passion on the students' side and intellect and reason on ours. I prefer as my starting point Frank O'Hara's lines:

> I am ashamed of my century
> For being so entertaining
> But I have to smile.

What defines a "sound approach" to media education? What do we mean when we say we want our students to be "critical" or, at least, "critical consumers"? Do we intend to wean them away from bad or dangerous programming, to inoculate them against the media's worst effects? Are we responding to some psychological crisis that the media produce in and for individuals? or perhaps to some crisis or disease that has suddenly appeared in the social body? Or do we intend to educate their palate, to teach them to discriminate quality (even if we recognize that such distinctions are always closely tied to economic and social relations of power)? Do we intend to give them the analytic tools necessary to interpret the media's messages, to ferret out the "hidden" or not so hidden meanings of the media texts they consume or, in many cases, the ones we choose to show them? Or, as I would advocate, do we intend to elaborate *with them* a theoretical and historical framework that would enable us to make sense of the complex social and political consequences of our different yet collective relations to the media?

I want to approach the question—of why it is so difficult to achieve the balance called for in the Victoria curriculum—from the perspective of my own commitment to theory. I want to think about teaching from the perspective of a cultural theorist (as opposed to, e.g., that of a critic, a practitioner, a policy advisor, or advocate), but I also hope to think about theory from the perspective of a teacher. All of this reflects the fact that these remarks are partly the product of my effort to rethink my years of teaching rock and popular culture. In that effort, I have tried to elaborate a framework that is both academic and pedagogical, a framework that belongs both to me and my students (because it has always been derived in part from the interactions between us). But these remarks are also partly defined by the fact that I teach and research rock music (rather than, e.g., television), a topic that is often noticeably absent from conferences on the media. I believe that if you begin with popular music you are likely to end up with a very different perspective on media and popular culture, as well as on problems of media pedagogy. But speaking as both a theorist and an American, to an Australian audience composed largely of teachers, places me in a rather awkward and perhaps paradoxical position: in order not to be purely academic, in order to cut into the pedagogical question, I have to talk at a fairly general or abstract level.

I think that the reason it is so difficult to actually achieve a balance between enthusiasm and "a sound approach" has a lot to do with the peculiarities of the dominant approach to media studies and media education, an approach that locates the practices of the media within a certain structure and a certain set of assumptions. That structure and those assumptions are signaled by the term "communication." Communication presupposes the existence of a difference or gap between two (or three) discrete and independently existing entities (although some contemporary theories try to avoid assuming their absolute independence): producers, texts, and audiences (senders, messages, receivers). It makes no difference how complicated each term is or if, as in some poststructuralist theories, it is the difference itself that is constantly being produced. The very essence of communication is defined by the attempt to mediate or transcend the difference, to create some moment or structure of unity, identity, or commonality, some moment of shared existence.

This model of communication has taken over our theories of culture, so that we increasingly take it for granted that culture—the space of experience and the "meaningfulness of human reality"—is reduced to the realm of communicative action. The "meaningfulness" of culture is reduced to the interpretation of meaning in its simplest and narrowest sense, to that which is easiest to talk about within the codes of Western academic theories: semantic content, cognitive significance, narrative meaning, and representation. Thus culture becomes transformed, before our very eyes, into ideology; and it makes little difference whether it is treated as content or structure. Once culture is reduced to meaning, meaning always reproduces the gap it is intended to overcome, for culture must now exist apart from reality. The result is a finite number of strategies by which this secondary difference can be transcended: reduce reality to culture (as if everything were meaning); locate the cause of culture in a reality outside of culture itself; or treat culture as a structural copy of reality (disregarding any question of causality).

Nowhere is this reduction of culture and meaning more obvious than in the arts framework curriculum, which talks incessantly of "creating and communicating meaning" and of "expressing ideas." In fact, in its list of eleven theoretical concepts to be brought to bear upon the media, five are concerned with this narrow conception of meaning, and one cannot help but get the impression that this is the only form of cultural effect that matters: "narrative"; "selection, construction and representation . . . translating reality into a representation"; "language of the media . . . create and communicate meaning"; "media influence . . . impact on our day to day lives . . . Our values, attitudes and assumptions about the world may be confirmed or questioned"; "meaning and interpretation . . . appreciating the variety of meanings of a media text."

I am aware that locating the media within an arts or cultural framework—with its emphasis on meaning—is often intended as a way of escaping the worst features of a scientific effects model. Yet it often merely reproduces them. We should not forget, after all, that the two perspectives actually may have related origins. Wilbur Schramm, often considered the founder of the effects model, was trained in literary studies and established the Iowa Writers' Workshop, the most famous and successful school of creative writing in the United States. His move into the Office of War Information enabled him to bring his training to bear upon questions of media, meaning, and information.

The fact of the matter is that whether one uses the traditional scientific effects model or the currently hip interpretive model of the mass media, the perspectives and questions available are severely constrained, depending on which of the three terms—producers (technology, economics, policy), texts, or audiences—is given priority and assumed to be the locus of power. For in every theory one term is seen to be ultimately determining so that, despite gestures to the other two, they remain at best tangential and at worst irrelevant (if not passive). Of course one might object that communication is an interactive, hermeneutic, or even systemic process. But contemporary efforts to "put the pieces together" do little more than acknowledge the problem and act as if naming the resolution magically provided the solution.

Within a cultural or interpretive approach there are basically two perspectives available: (1) media messages are the active agents that produce effects (meanings) for a largely passive audience (however constrained this process may be by other secondary processes); (2) media audiences are the active agents who determine the uses to which passively manipulated media messages are placed. The problems with both of these can be summed up rather simply: Effects have uses and uses have effects. Obviously the first describes a traditional literary-critical perspective; it makes little difference how complex the text is made (an "intertext," a genre, a media, etc.) or how complex the meanings it produces (it may open a space full of gaps, contradictions, and absences). It is the text that is the locus of power operating on an essentially passive (interpellated, subjected) audience. The second describes the more recent ethnographic or audience-centered perspective, which places the burden on an active audience and its power to bend an essentially passive text to its purposes and pleasures. Such approaches have a marked propensity to assume that such inflections embody active struggles within which audiences are constantly empowered. But perhaps more importantly, such ethnographic approaches reduce the audience to another textual production since, at best, what they can discover is another text (that of the audience's response), which is itself in need of the researcher's interpretation. When you are talking to an audience, all you can do is produce further texts, much like the critic who is caught in the constant spinning out of interpretations of interpretations.

What is wrong with such textual (communication) models of culture can be summed up in the following question: What do you know when you know . . . "the meaning of a text" or "the audience's statement of its interpretation"? In fact, you don't know what you know (in terms of its actual effects) when you have an interpretation (always the critic's) of a text, or when you have the text of the audience's statement of what they think the text means. What is it that one now understands? What claims can actually be made? Further what weight can be given to such interpretations in the face of the contemporary kaleidoscope of media practices and audiences? No one consumes a single media text, or even some neatly packaged set of media texts. And I doubt that any two people have exactly the same media taste or exposure.

Here I note—perhaps with a certain discomfort—that I agree with Trevor Barr's argument in his keynote address at the Oz Media 88 Conference (and subsequently published in *Metro* 82, Autumn 1990) about the continued domination of textual analysis, the continued appeal of textual evidence, and the potential disservice of such an emphasis (whether on the media text or the audience's statements). The discomfort I feel stems from Barr's description of such an emphasis as based in the 1960s and 1970s. While this may have been offered as a simple historical fact, I fear it is too easily inflected to a political conservatism (even a conservatism of the Left), too easily articulated to an antitheoretical position. Moreover, unlike Barr, I do not think it is sufficient to supplement such studies with other areas such as technology and policy (adding the producer into the gap, as it were).

But I do agree with Barr that the increasing power of such textual or, in my terms, communication models of culture has real consequences, especially with regard to questions about the politics of culture and the media. It has led to the view that what is at stake in politics is the struggle to construct a consensus, to construct and imbue the entire population with a shared interpretation of reality. Do we all agree with the dominant view of, for instance, what the family means and what it should be? If we don't, then presumably the function of culture is somehow to incorporate us into the consensus. And if we are not or cannot be incorporated, then we must be expelled. Yet from a different angle, if we are neither incorporated nor expelled, then we must be resisting the dominant consensus. Thus the model of communication allows only two political positions: domination or subordination, incorporation or resistance. This has seriously constrained the possibilities for defining critical media work: (1) you always find domination just where you expected it (e.g., the capitalist media produce sexist, racist, homophobic, Eurocentric, etc., messages), and there is little you can do except stand outside such messages and rail against them; (2) you always find resistance just where you expected it; the only response is to turn the means of cultural production over to the dominated (e.g., as if it were guaranteed that the form and content of cultural productions from the margins would embody a different and correct politics since, presumably, marginal populations are always resisting); (3) such questions of power are irrelevant in the end because people will always find ways of empowering themselves and producing moments of pleasure.

This last view is often based on the assumption of a logical difference between social power (hierarchical) and everyday life (anarchic) so that everyday life intrinsically resists cultural power. Such a view fails to see that while people might always get pleasure from their activities (which I actually doubt), not all pleasures are equally good and not all pleasures have the same political consequences. It fails to see the complex relations between strategies of control (including pleasure), resistance, empowerment, struggle, and opposition. It fails to examine the articulations between the forms of pleasure and survival with which people maintain some control over the construction of their own differences, their own lives, and their own possibilities and the structures and forces of the social formation.

The problem with a communication model of the media and culture is, to put it simply, that we know it is wrong, both as a description of people's relation to the media and as an analysis of the power of the media in contemporary society. We know that our students (and some of us) don't have the same relation to all media texts and that this is not merely a matter of "taste." We know that the media produce not only meanings and pleasure, but also displeasure, anxiety, boredom, drudgery, fragility, insecurity, empowerment, and even disempowerment. We know that the media are related not only to how we interpret the world, but to our emotional lives, our political lives, our social lives, our economic lives, and our material lives (e.g., the organization of time and space). We know that the media cannot be understood merely as a leisure activity independent of their relation to labor, education, and the other demands on and activities of people's lives. Moreover people's lives are never simply and singly determined; people's identities are always constructed at the intersection of their numerous social roles, differences, experiences, and activities. Consequently their place within relations of social power—the way they live their domination and subordination—is always active and complex. Understanding people's relation to the media and popular culture requires us to look at how both people and media practices are inserted into and function within the networks of everyday life, power, and history.

At this point we might well ask, Where did we go wrong? I believe that, at least at one level, the answer is obvious: We too quickly assumed that the mass media could be treated as a reasonably consistent and coherent set of practices or processes. Thus we assumed that there is no significant difference in the ways the media operate as a news or informational system, as a ritual system for the production of communal identity and shared meaning, and as a system for the distribution of popular culture. (I believe that the model of communication, albeit inflected differently, works reasonably well as a theoretical account of the first two functions.) We have failed to recognize that the different functions of the media may also point to radically different systems of relationships and modes of operation. In particular we too quickly identified the forms of popular culture with the mass media or the processes of mass communication. We confused a historically contingent relationship (in which the mass media became the primary means for the distribution of popular culture) with a theoretical identity. Consequently we forgot to explore the effects of this linkage and to consider the significance of the very *popularity* of popular culture.

Let me now return to my original question: Why is it so difficult to find the balance between students' enthusiasms and our effort to formulate "a sound approach" to the media? I believe that the answer lies largely in the ways we have gone about constructing what it means to have a sound approach. It is not then a question of simply substituting one theory, presumably a better one, for another, but of reconsidering the relation between our theories and the historical context in which we are living and teaching. It is a problem of having failed to respond to the historical context with the theoretical tools that are appropriate to it. Rather than responding to the historical context theoretically, we have attempted to make it fit our theoretical models even if this means abandoning everything we already know we know (e.g., we know the media have effects). Alternatively, "a sound approach" to media education has to be derived and understood contextually (the key word!) and strategically. That is, in some way it must already take into account and respond to the nature of our students' (and our own) enthusiasms in the context of their everyday lives at the present moment. And in that sense, what it means to be critical or critically educated has to be understood in the context of what they are to be critical of and why (i.e., what are the stakes in our educational projects). Consequently the theoretical, historical, and political underpinnings of media education are in fact inseparable in the attempt to forge a pedagogical practice. We need to define a perspective—a theory—that is able to fight against its own immodesty, a theory that always starts with its own context and that articulates itself in the project of analysis (not unlike Marx's notion of theory as the production of the concrete).

Let me then begin to suggest a different model, both theoretical and pedagogical, a model in which we as well as our students are constantly implicated (assuming of course that we as teachers also care about at least some popular culture). For it is a model not of the media and popular culture per se (although it certainly sees cultural practices in a very different light), but of theorizing the media and popular culture. I would offer two premises for this model: The first is a principle of articulation that says that no relations in history or social life are guaranteed in advance. To understand a practice then involves the task of constructing its context (the web of nonnecessary relations in which it is implicated) even as that context is being constructed. But quite obviously, cultural practices construct and are constructed within many different contexts (e.g., bars may have different videos and musics playing simultaneously, which changes the effects of both in ways that are specific to the context of social and cultural relations). In different contexts they are enacted in different ways, at different tempos. We have to begin by acknowledging, then, that cultural practices are the sites of many different activities and effects, that they are not taken up, lived, practiced, effective in just the same way and to the same degree in every context. The questions we must address have consequently changed: we must inquire into how specific practices work, through what modes of functioning, to produce what concrete effects. We must ask how cultural practices rearticulate or reshape the contexts of our lives.

The second assumption is that critical and pedagogical practices must be appropriate to the rhythms, forces, and densities of the lived contexts of everyday and historical life (which is not to say that they must be the same). Rather than beginning by separating culture from something else (called "the real") or reducing everything to culture, we must begin by recognizing the specificity of our relations to popular culture and to its enormous power. I would claim for example that, at least for significant fractions of the population of the contemporary United States, we *live in* popular culture. This is one of the signs of our (post)modernity: that popular culture cannot be treated as a domain separated from reality nor as somehow eclipsing reality. We live in popular culture as much as we live in the ideological maps of daily life and the relations of the economic structures. It is not just a matter of popular culture's having become the dominant forum for ideological struggles or the predominant source for the iconography of our daily lives. I mean the claim to be taken more literally: Popular culture is the material milieu within which we live, within which we navigate our narrative and emotional existence. Consider Billy Joel's "We Didn't Start the Fire": the song weaves history, economics, and pop culture into a seamless representation of the rhythm of our lives, as if there were no differences among these domains insofar as they function as contexts for living.

One result of living inside of or within popular culture is that, in a very real sense, the critical distance that for centuries has been a constitutive element of Western cultural practice and relations is actively negated in our contemporary relation to popular culture. The fact that there is an active opposition to critical distance makes it imperative that we find a different theoretical practice for analysis, criticism, and pedagogy. I want to offer a model of such a practice here, a practice by which we attempt, with our students, to construct a map of the effects of popular culture. More accurately, it involves a series of four intersecting maps, operating at different levels of description and abstraction, moving from popular culture to the political context, describing the struggles and effects organized by and around popular culture.

The first map involves describing popular culture itself, for we can no longer take for granted the boundaries that define the object of discussion and analysis. We cannot define some isolatable segment of popular culture—whether it is *Star Trek,* or the western, or rock music. We need to construct, with our students, the "formations" of popular culture in which they live (or to which they relate). I have, for example, described rock music in terms of "apparatuses." No one who is a fan of rock music is actually a fan of rock music in its entirety or in isolation. As a fan, you are located in specific apparatuses that include a particular selection of rock music (e.g., a lot of hard rock, perhaps some punk, but no heavy metal; perhaps this Midnight Oil album but not that one; perhaps this song by Men at Work but no other), but also a selection of other media texts, of styles of dress, of dancing, of movement, of ways of talking and relating to other people, of ways of crossing categories of social difference (whether gender or race or age), of relations to school and family. Once you begin to assemble a particular apparatus, the pieces often seem to fall into place, sometimes even predictably. Dick Hebdige (1988) described something similar as a "cartography of taste," but this still sounds too subjective. For such structured distributions of cultural practices are socially constructed, and they often define sites of struggle and power within everyday life.

Practices are always distributed unequally and that inequality is not random (e.g., increasingly in the United States, children cannot listen to certain music or wear certain clothing; blacks have access to different musics than whites). These are often the result of economic and political relations and struggles over the distribution of specific forms of practices. There are many ways in which this unequal distribution is carried out; some of them are obvious and common. Other techniques operate only by indirection and may be specific to particular contexts or moments. For example, in the United States there is an extraordinary response to the explosion of information and commodities: namely, the marketing of more information (e.g., a magazine like *Entertainment*) predicated on the assumption that you don't want to—or, even, can't afford to—make the wrong choices about popular culture. While in a certain sense critics have always provided information to guide consumer choices, such guidance has usually been presented as a way of defining "correct taste" rather than as a response to the fear of making an error.

After all, popular culture was—traditionally—one of the places where it presumably did not matter if you made a mistake.

A second context-specific way in which this distribution is accomplished involves a specific discipline of behavior or, more accurately, a notion that transcendence can only be accomplished through discipline. According to this discipline, the requirements of the healthy body (both the individual and the social body) dictate that the only legitimate form of pleasure is unpleasure: you have to work to be able to have fun (an apparent contradiction for rock culture at least). This has important links to other political projects for it legitimates the regulation of structures of pleasure and fun, for example, attacks on drugs and addictions and the regulation of women's bodies (defined increasingly by their responsibility to the foetus). Finally, there is a struggle over who has the right to speak for popular culture. There are numerous legal and economic struggles (e.g., struggles over labeling, trials over obscenity, liability for the behavior of fans), which all involve the claim of external—familial and state—authority over the structures of popular legitimation and the legitimation of the popular. The result of such techniques is that society produces and distributes, unequally across the population, clusters of cross-media popular taste; but we must remember that such formations transcend even popular culture, including structures of behavior and attitude.

The second map attempts to describe the effects that these different formations have upon us (and the struggles to determine those effects). I call this level, following Pierre Bourdieu (1984), the sensibility of the formation. That is, we simply cannot take for granted what the important effects are of any formation of popular culture. We often assume that the effects are always defined by structures of meaning, narrative, representation, ideology, and desire. My sense, especially in the context of teaching rock and pop music, is that this is rarely the case. Rock (and much of popular culture) works through very different forms of effects; it has very different effects on one's lives. For example, Adrian Martin's important work on teen movies (1994) emphasizes the power of "the spectacular" as opposed to the narrative. But it is always an intimate spectacle, a spectacle that depends upon the fact that the image already matters to its audience. Such intimate spectacles are clearly visible in that moment when someone lip-synchs a song with all of the passion (but always with some irony) that fans feel for their favorite songs. Such events seem to elicit and organize precisely that sense of passion for, that investment in, the popular iconography of the fan's daily life. It is a powerful affective statement of the importance of what actually matters. Often popular culture works less to define the meanings of what goes on in our lives than to define what matters to us. And what matters to us is not just the specific texts (musics) but also the things that are located on the mattering maps that the formations of popular culture produce for us, the maps that identify what matters: what forms of social relationships, what forms of practices. And the maps themselves matter: they are what give popular culture its enormous power and what define our commitment to the popular formations in which we live. We have hardly begun to explore the structures and possibilities of such mattering maps and the relationships they enable.

In that sense, I use the term "empowerment" to describe the specific relationship that is established between the sensibility of a formation and those who live within its spaces. The second map then describes the ways in which people use popular culture to empower themselves or, in some cases, the ways in which popular culture can disempower people. I assume that people are neither stupid nor self-destructive and that, for the most part, they always get something out of the popular culture they consume. That is why they consume it, because it gives them something. But that "something," the forms and structures of empowerment, is not in and of itself political. It is not necessarily also a form of resistance. For example, consider the way in which a particular song empowers Tom Cruise in *Top Gun:* certainly he is empowered, but he is empowered to successfully fly military missions. Hardly an act of political resistance! Empowerment refers to the kinds of energy or strength that people are constantly getting out of popular culture.

The notion of a sensibility refers as well to the array of attitudes that structure our cultural and everyday environment. For example, in the United States, one of the dominant sensibilities put into place by popular culture is what I have called a "postmodern logic" of "authentic inauthenticity." It legitimates and even privileges an ironic cynicism: You know you are faking it and you don't care. Everything is an image and so you put on an image. The cynicism dictates that nothing matters; and yet, even within the cynicism, something has to matter if only to avoid allowing your cynicism to matter too much. (As the Human League put it in the hit song "Love Action," "I believe in the truth though I lie a lot.") *The Simpsons,* for example, is an extraordinarily cynical vision of daily life. But it is not the narrative or even the ideology of the family that makes the show successful but its cynicism, a cynicism that in the last instance, doesn't matter, since those who watch it are just as likely to get married, just as likely to end up with a marriage more closely resembling the Simpsons' than the Huxtables' and just as likely to end up getting divorced. Given the high rate of divorce predicted for those who get married in the 1990s, one can only marvel at the steadily rising rate of marriage.

But this second map of sensibility or empowerment leaves too many questions unanswered: how the specific formations of cultural practices, which may produce a variety of effects—pleasures, meanings, subject-positions, formations that may empower or disempower their audiences in a variety of ways—are struggled over and connected to larger political and economic structures. The third map begins to address such questions by examining how these effects and sensibilities literally provide maps for living. It attempts to draw the lines that connect popular culture to everyday life, looking at the ways in which the mattering maps of popular culture provide a sense of the places and spaces in which we live. Music may be the most powerful agent in such relations. Music, almost independently of our intentions, seems to produce and orchestrate our moods, both qualitatively and quantitatively. (Consider the functioning of background and soundtrack musics.) Music as an environment constructs and maps the rhythms, tempos, and intensities of our activities. In a sense, it determines where we stop and make an investment in the world; where we stop and say "This matters, this place is important, this kind of activity is important. I am going to stop here and this will become part of my identity. This is where I will expend my energy—this place will become a marker of my itinerary, of the structure of my everyday life." The French theorists Deleuze and Guattari, in an atypically moving passage, capture this process, and for the sake of brevity, I will quote it here:

> A child in the dark, gripped with fear, comforts himself by singing under his breath. He walks and halts to his song. Lost, he takes shelter, or orients himself with his little song as best he can. The song is like a rough sketch of a calming and stabilizing, calm and stable, center in the heart of chaos . . . Now we are at home. But home does not preexist: it was necessary to draw a circle around the uncertain and fragile center, to organize a limited space. Many, very diverse, components have a part in this, landmarks and marks of all kinds . . . Sonorous or vocal components

are very important: a wall of sound, or at least a wall with some sonic bricks in it. A child hums to summon the strength for the schoolwork she has to hand in. A housewife sings to herself, or listens to the radio, as she marshals the antichaos forces of her work. Radios and television sets are like sound walls around every household and mark territories (the neighbor complains when it gets too loud). For sublime deeds like the foundation of a city or the fabrication of a golem, one draws a circle, or better yet walks in a circle as in a children's dance, combining rhythmic vowels and consonants . . . A mistake in speed, rhythm, or harmony would be catastrophic because it would bring back the forces of chaos, destroying both creator and creation. (1987, 311)

To use their term, culture literally "territorializes" our lives. If everyday life can be conceptualized as a kind of traveling, as an interplay of mobility and stability, this third map contradicts our normal assumptions about the nature of that interplay. We often think of travel as following a series of predefined trajectories traversing the unformed space between already existing places. But to speak of popular culture as having a territorializing power is to suggest a radically different image,[1] one in which the places of stability are constructed along the paths of mobility. Where you stop is defined as you are moving, by the rhythms of your movements. Just as the trajectories and rhythms of your movements are defined as you stop, by the rhythms of your investments or places. It is a matter of what matters and the possibilities of transformation and elaboration. In a sense, today it is popular culture that says, "Here is a place of stability, a place we can stop. And from this place, here is how and where we can move on; in that direction we will construct another place for ourselves, another place that will matter to us in our lives."

But even the level of everyday life is not sufficient to construct an understanding of how popular culture affects our lives and, ultimately, history. Finally we have to look at the relationships between all of these maps and the various explicitly organized economic and political struggles that are taking place in the world today. We need to consider how in fact the struggles organized to restructure contemporary society themselves operate with and through popular culture. We need to ask how popular culture itself can become a strategic weapon in the service of particular economic and political struggles and how, at the same time, popular culture can become the ground on which all such struggles are increasingly waged. This is the fourth and final map; it is here, at this level, that our critical and pedagogical practice is inevitably transformed from the production of a reflective distance to the production of an engaged intervention. And it is here, of course, that we will always encounter the limits of our claims to authority.

Admittedly the model I have offered here is exceedingly abstract. I believe that it can only be made more concrete by using it, by bringing it to bear upon a particular context: how I teach rock music in Illinois in 1990 must be different than how I taught it ten years ago and, I assume, than how one would teach it in contemporary Australia. The model will only work if teachers and students agree to use it contextually to address a series of questions. It is only in the strategic project of asking what it means to be critical in a specific context that the model can be fleshed out and its possibilities evaluated. Locating it within such a context we can begin to consider the appropriate level of abstraction and generality. We can begin to identify the subjects, agents, and agencies of contemporary history and, with our students, to consider what role we (as teachers, students, and individuals) have to play in the contemporary struggles of history. I think it is only by this circuitous route that we can understand the power of popular culture and that we can entice our students to think about that power as well. And I think it is only by this circuitous route that we can begin to seriously explore the possibilities of criticism and even resistance that might be articulated out of popular culture. Finally, such a project cannot be undertaken independently of the more depressing task of looking at how the dominant structures of power are being put into place and the grounds on which they can or should be challenged. It is this very specific and local and, I hope, modest model of teaching and understanding popular culture that I want to offer you. I would like to think it is the model that has implicitly defined my teaching in the past; I am going to try to make it the explicit basis of my future efforts. It may or may not work; it may or may not be useful to you. I merely invite you to consider its possibilities.

Notes

INTRODUCTION

1   For example, I began teaching courses in cultural studies in the early 1970s, gave my first public lecture on it in 1976, and published my first article on cultural studies in 1977. Of course other scholars in the United States, most especially James Carey, were talking about cultural studies even earlier. Obviously courses in popular culture have a much longer history, but even when combined with cultural studies, even implicitly, their history goes back into the 1960s. Again, I began teaching courses in popular culture in the early 1970s; my first public presentation on popular music was in 1981 (although I began teaching classes on popular music in 1977), and my first publication was in 1983.

2   Hopefully without overromanticizing the possibilities of cultural studies as a revolutionary agent. In other words, one has to recognize the political limits of intellectual work even while believing that it has an important contribution to make.

3   Some of my work addressing the first two of these concerns is collected in *Bringing It All Back Home: Essays on Cultural Studies* (Durham: Duke University Press, 1997).

4   Habermas is the clearest example, although I would also describe the particular appropriation of poststructuralism and postmodernism that became dominant in the United States in these terms.

5   Meaghan Morris has been arguing for some time now that one should replace the focus on culture with a concern for everyday life.

6   I have used "everyday life" in a very specific sense. It is not merely daily life but an organization of routinized structures under capitalism. That is, everyday life is already a product of power rather than an escape from it. Thus I do not think that everyday life can be equated with Foucault's description of micropolitics and discipline. My own view is taken from Lefebvre (1984) but would not have been possible without the help of Meaghan Morris. In fact, I think I should have more carefully followed Lefebvre in distinguishing everyday life and the everyday.

7   I do not mean to make either Hall or Morris responsible for my work, but to acknowledge my personal debt to and my admiration for both of them. Both of them have rather dispersed bodies of work, but good starting points are Morley and Chen (1996) and Morris (forthcoming). Additionally, I would point to Bennett (1990) as having made a significant contribution to my own perspective.

8   I am not claiming that my work has described all of the ways the new conservatism deploys popular operating logics. For example, there is clearly a logic of conspiracy involved in the success of this hegemonic struggle. Such a logic of conspiracy can be embodied in a variety of forms and sites of conspiracy theories, from the individual intentionality of control narratives, as in the work of Tom Clancy, to the collective intentionalities of the system in many popular conspiracies (e.g., Nowhere Man or the Illuminati). I am grateful to Jim Hevia for raising this with me.

ANOTHER BORING DAY IN PARADISE

I wish to thank the following people for their help: Van Cagle, Iain Chambers, Jon Crane, Simon Frith, Jon Ginoli, Sally Green, Dick Hebdige, Charles Laufersweiler, Dave Marsh, Cary Nelson, and Larry Shore. Please note that I use the term "rock and roll" to include all postwar, technologically dependent youth music. The attempt to distinguish "rock and roll," "rock 'n' roll," and "rock" would only confuse the argument I am trying to make.

1   "Cathexis" is a psychoanalytical term, based on an economic metaphor, that refers to "the fact that a certain amount of psychic energy is attached to an idea or to a group of ideas, to a part of the body, to an object, etc." (Laplanche and Pontalis 1973, 62).

2   There was a particular moment when this foregrounding of the postmodern structure of youth's experience was widely visible, in the mid-seventies. Consider the enormous popularity of Pink Floyd's *The Wall*, as well as such songs as "Love Stinks" by the J. Geils Band.

3   It would perhaps be helpful if I gave at least musical examples of these five apparatuses: hardcore (Dead Kennedys, Circle Jerks, Black Flag), oi (Exploited, Cockney Rejects), new wave (Human League, Echo and the Bunnymen, Stray Cats, Elvis Costello, Joe Jackson), postpunk (Gang of Four, Talking Heads, Joy Division, Public Image Ltd.), new music (Glenn Branca, Brian Eno, Laurie Anderson, Lounge Lizards).

4   For a critique of both the "folk culture" and "art" views of rock and roll, see Frith 1981.

5   For example, as soon as there was an age split within the rock and roll audience, the older fans often described "teenage rock" as co-opted, despite the fact that they had grown up on (within) similar affective alliances. In the seventies, both heavy metal and disco were rejected by significant portions of the rock and roll audience as "co-opted," despite the fact that many of those who dismissed such music either listened to comparable music at an earlier point in their lives or were now listening to what was essentially the same music (but in a different alliance).

"I'D RATHER FEEL BAD THAN NOT FEEL ANYTHING AT ALL"

This paper was first delivered at the Conference on Mass Culture sponsored by the Center for Twentieth Century Studies of the University of Wisconsin, Milwaukee, April 1984. I am grateful to all the participants as well as the audience for many hours of helpful discussions. The title is taken from a song by Warren Zevon.

1   Thus any reading of rock and roll must be contextual, treating it as an overdetermined and overdetermining local event. There is no analytic system that can write the history/ herstory of rock and roll from outside the relations of its multiple apparatuses.

2   One can see a number of contemporary theories as attempts to come to terms with this affective level of existence. For example, Lefebvre's notion of the "everyday," Benjamin's description of "shock effects," and Foucault's theory of "eventalization" all seem to offer interpretations of changes in contemporary life at a level other than ideologically constituted (or consciously experienced) existence. Further, the Freudian notions of a libidinal economy and cathexis, especially as these have been reshaped in Deleuze and Guattari's theory of desire and in Lyotard's theory of intensity and pulsions, are the most powerful tools we have for describing the energy we invest in the world and in our ideological representations.

3   I would like to thank Sally Green, Jane Gallop, and Judith Williamson for their help in unraveling some of the complexities of this issue, and for their support as women rock and roll fans.

ROCK, TERRITORIALIZATION, AND POWER

This paper draws on material from Grossberg 1992.

IS ANYBODY LISTENING? DOES ANYBODY CARE?
ON "THE STATE OF ROCK"

1   Actually, it may be less a matter of how "new" such rhetorical figures are in discourses about rock—certainly fragmentation has been around since the 1970s—than of their increasingly central and dominant role in the discourses of the death of rock.

2   It would be interesting to consider here the question of the relative ease with which certain forms of practices travel, for example, food travels more easily than music, which travels more easily still than language. Of course, we would then have to go on to acknowledge significant, determined variations within each of these forms. Moreover, ultimately it may not be a question of how culture travels, but how travel produces culture. (See Clifford 1988.)

3   For examples of this discussion, see Coupland 1991; Linklater 1992; Howe and Strauss 1993.

4   Andrew Ross (in personal correspondence) has pointed out that this distinction has been used to distinguish between "the masses" (who operate from ignorance) and "the intellectuals" (who operate from knowledge). Yet in this "traditional" reading, knowledge was supposed to lead to or call for changed behavior. In its postmodern articulation, no such change of behavior is involved, because irony has replaced the understanding supposedly constructed through knowledge.

5   For a discussion of the relation between rhythm, existence, and power, see Deleuze and Guattari 1987.

THE INDIFFERENCE OF TELEVISION, OR, MAPPING
TV'S POPULAR (AFFECTIVE) ECONOMY

I would like to thank Jon Crane for his valuable comments.

1   It is interesting to note that what counts as acceptable behavior in cinemas is changing, presumably in response not only to the normalization of films on television, but also to the in-

corporation of televisual practices, for example, the inclusion of advertising before the feature and, most recently, the practice of leaving the lights on until the feature itself begins.

2   There are three different versions of this: Williams's flow (1974), J. Ellis's rereading (1982), which emphasizes the segmentality of the flow, or Foster's polarization of TV practices (1985) into fragmentation/fetishization and flow/consumption.

3   The question of levels of abstraction significantly redefines the commitment to context, since each local analysis is defined by its appropriate level of abstraction. That is, local or conjunctural analysis is not locatable on an axis of big/small. In fact, one of the errors of much of the writing on postmodernism is the failure to reflexively acknowledge the level on which they are operating, for example, Jameson's (1984) incorporation of multinational capitalism into his descriptions of the texture of everyday life.

4   It is quite common to find the emergence of postmodernity linked directly to the development of mass media. One can distinguish between those who see the media in epistemological terms, as a new mode of rationality (e.g., the Frankfurt school) and those who see it in ontological terms, as a new mode of Being (e.g., Baudrillard).

5   The question of affective economies is not equivalent to discourses of pleasure that function as the alibi for the deployment of sexuality. They articulate affective struggles into a limited set of structures: as a victim to be momentarily liberated because already repressed (it is always threatening because it is anarchic, without organization); as an excess never entirely recuperable; and as a dangerous distraction—the ultimate imaginary because it is so immediately real.

6   This is not to deny that one needs to distinguish different forms of televisual irony.

7   Thus it is easy to see how a movie star could become a politician/ideologue. But a TV star? And it is easy to see why an ideologue could (and even has to) become a TV star. But a movie star?

POSTMODERNITY AND AFFECT

I owe a great debt to my graduate students for the many hours of fruitful exchange that have contributed to whatever strengths this paper may have. I wish to especially thank Jon Crane, Charles Acland, and Anne Balsamo for their valuable comments on an earlier draft. This paper is offered as a tentative move into the terrain of postmodern culture and contemporary politics.

1   Only if we recognize this diversity can we understand the changes and movements within the terrain of popular culture. Thus, for example, Springsteen's success has always depended on a certain neonostalgia, but his more recent "superstardom" has depended upon a shift in the form of his songs from mythic-fantasy to pop neorealism.

2   "Authentic inauthenticity" refers to a communicative logic in which the only truth is that there is no truth (and that is in fact true). In social terms, it refers to not faking the fact that one is faking it. It might be thought of as a set of codes of simulation that does not function in the name of either the real or the hyperreal. See Grossberg 1993a.

3   The question of contemporary popular heroes provides a good example of the need for recognizing historical complexity and the diversity of communicative economies if we are to note both the similarities and differences between various cultural and historical

formations. For example, I would challenge Beniger's (n.d.) identification of the popularity of Kate Smith in the famous war bond campaign (as reported by Merton [1946]) with more contemporary forms. Merton's explanation depends upon the audience's "acute need to believe" and their response to Smith's "perceived sincerity." He further points to their perception that they "could've been like Kate." Beniger equates this to a *USA Today* poll (3 December 1986, 8C) of "the most believable sports figures endorsing products" that suggests that their believability depends upon their ordinariness, upon how much they are like us. But he fails to see that these two identifications depend upon significantly different economies: the relation to Smith has "a social basis . . . [she belongs] to the ingroup. She is kinfolk." The relation to "stars" like John Madden or Bob Uecker takes for granted that their ordinariness, like their sincerity, is obviously inauthentic. It is for just this reason that a fan of Madden's is unlikely to make a statement like the following, by a "devotee" of Smith: "I trust *her*. If *she* were a fake, I'd feel terrible." We, on the other hand, expect our heroes to be fakes, not only as images (Rambo) but as realities (Reagan). We know that sincerity is just another pose, but so what? Beniger is unable to recognize the difference, partly because he fails to place the forms of heroes into larger cultural formations and historical contexts. But more importantly he attempts to understand the communicative economy within which such popular heroes operate in terms of a redrawn line between interpersonal and mass communication—the result being that the question becomes one of the audience's interpretation of the size of the intended audience—instead of in terms of the historically articulated relations between different communicative economies and planes of effects.

4   See "It's a Sin," in this volume, for an elaboration of the forms of empowering nihilism.

POSTMODERNIST ELITISMS AND POSTMODERN STRUGGLES

1   The critique of Foucault that follows is not meant as a rejection of his larger theoretical position. I do, however, want to challenge his appropriation of the collapse of difference into a theoretical strategy that commits him to a politics of negativity.

2   In fact, it might be more advisable to avoid describing this popular sensibility as "postmodern." I choose to use the term because it has already been used, and my argument is that we must win this sensibility back to a more progressive and optimistic articulation.

3   A politics of need cannot be reduced to the question of production and consumption. We in fact need to develop a theory that accounts for the generation of real needs that cannot be ideologically represented or empowered without inflecting them into apparently predetermined political positions. Within such a theory, the politics of the popular might be represented as "from each according to his or her abilities, to each according to his or her desires" (rather than needs). In such terms, celebration cannot be equated with liberation, and the positivity of the popular cannot be defined in traditional terms, for example, as freedom or rights.

4   Despite Tania Modleski's efforts (1986, ix–xix) to construct such notions of empowerment as noncontradictory celebrations of the popular, recent work in cultural studies, including my own, is clearly intended to argue that critics must avoid reducing the politics of popular cultural practices to any single dimension. Empowerment need not

deny the possibility of disempowerment, or of forms of empowerment that are oppressive. It does, however, register the fact that people must find something positive in the forms of popular culture that they celebrate. A brilliant example of such an analysis is offered in Winship:

> it is time that as feminists we thought carefully about the political implications of . . . an image [that] too easily produces a knee-jerk response in feminists . . . although superficially the image may resemble classic porno pics, the representation of gender is being actively tampered with. What we also need to bear in mind is that for the 1980s New Young Women (middle-class, educated young women) that image simply does not and cannot mean the same thing as similar images did five to ten years ago for us "older" feminists . . . it is partly because, however indirectly, feminism has given these young women a knowledge and a strength to act in the world which also allows them to laugh at and enjoy those images in a way many of us could not, and cannot. The question now is, are we strong enough to acknowledge that our politics have to shift in order to take account of these changes? (1985, 45–46)

"IT'S A SIN"

This paper was first delivered as the 1988 Power Foundation Lecture at the University of Sydney, Australia.

1   By "systemic politics," I mean to refer not only to the institutionalized politics of the state apparatuses, but also the unequal distribution of economic, cultural, libidinal, civil, and political values. Thus it refers to changing political and economic relations as well as to the changing structures of racism, sexism, and so on, and the ways these impact on people's lives.

2   I realize that using "America" to refer to the context of the United States is particularly imperialistic. Unfortunately there is no rhetorically acceptable alternative, and besides it is useful precisely for capturing much of the spirit of contemporary "American" attitudes.

3   It is worth noting that the current use of "negotiated" reading is not the same as Hall's original use in "Encoding/Decoding" (1973).

4   There are many parallels between the early formations of British cultural studies and the work of the Chicago School of Social Thought under the tutelage of John Dewey.

5   For an elaboration of these arguments, see "The Indifference of Television" in this volume and Grossberg 1988.

6   The following discussion is indebted to both the published work of and my conversations with Stuart Hall and John Clarke.

7   This section owes a great deal to Meaghan Morris (1988b) and Janice Radway (1988).

8   For an extended discussion of these issues, see Grossberg 1992.

ROCKIN' IN CONSERVATIVE TIMES

I want to thank Meaghan Morris for her generous help and the model of cultural studies that her work has given me. This paper was first delivered at the Trajectories Conference, Taiwan, July 1992.

1   I use the term "America" uncomfortably (and without any intention of insulting my Latin American and Canadian colleagues), but no other term is available.

2   An example of the regional myopia of many Americans, including left intellectuals, is the following: A colleague of mine told me not too long ago that if I wanted to be a serious political intellectual, I could not remain in the Midwest but would have to move to one of the two coasts. Hence we need a politics to "End bicoastal arrogance!"

3   Too often the Left seems to be concerned only with high art as a site of struggle. When it turns to popular culture, it seems to immediately ignore the Right's attacks and to leap into questions of, for example, American imperialism. But it is rarely concerned with the continuing European imperialism of intellectual life. I assume that too many people assume that we intellectuals can deal with it by appropriating it into our own contexts, but that the rest of the population cannot.

4   I want to thank Harris Breslow for this observation.

5   I do not want to actually claim that the Right's strategy is an appropriation (whether conscious or not) of the logic of the rock formation. Actually, I am trying to draw a line connecting these two normally distant points because I think that by articulating it in this way we can arrive at a better understanding of the Right.

6   I want to thank David Picker for reminding me of this point. Again I want to emphasize that I am not rejecting the notion of a politics of everyday life, nor am I denying that there are important struggles to be waged there.

7   My imaginary audience is difficult to define, existing somewhere in the overlap between the activist Left and cultural critics/intellectuals. Perhaps it might be described as the "cultural Left."

8   This discourse has apparently moved with great ease from its original context in Thatcher's Britain around the world, which is particularly surprising since, in some ways, as a political strategy, one would think that there is some reason to judge it a failure in its original context. For an excellent critique of Laclau and Mouffe, see Frow 1995.

CONCLUSION: FROM MEDIA TO POPULAR CULTURE TO EVERYDAY LIFE

A version of this paper was delivered at the Australian Teachers of Media Conference, Melbourne, October 1990. I am extremely grateful to the conference organizers for the opportunity and for all of their kindness and generosity. I am also indebted to the many participants for their expressions of interest. I have chosen to keep the lecture format even though the paper is not a transcript of my remarks there.

1   I am grateful to Meaghan Morris for this point and for her many contributions to the ideas presented here.

References

Adorno, T. W. 1976. *Introduction to the sociology of music.* Trans. E. B. Ashton. New York: Seabury.

Althusser, Louis. 1971. Ideology and ideological state apparatuses. In *Lenin and philosophy and other essays.* Trans. Ben Brewster. New York: Monthly Review Press.

——. 1979. *For Marx.* Trans. Ben Brewster. New York: Vintage.

Attali, Jacques. 1985. *Noise: The political economy of music.* Trans. Brian Massumi. Minneapolis: University of Minnesota Press.

Aufderheide, Pat. 1986a. Blue Velvet's uneasy moral twilight zone. *In These Times* 10 (October 29–November 4): 21.

——. 1986b. Sid and Nancy: Just say no. *In These Times* 11 (November 19–25): 14.

Bakhtin, Mikhail. 1981. *The dialogic imagination.* Trans. C. Emerson and M. Holquist. Austin: University of Texas Press.

Ballard, J. G. 1985. *The atrocity exhibition.* London: Triad/Panther.

Barr, Trevor. 1990. Keynote address. *Metro* 82.

Barthes, Roland. 1975. *The pleasure of the text.* Trans. Richard Miller. New York: Hill and Wang.

Baudrillard, Jean. 1983a. *In the shadow of the silent majorities.* Trans. Paul Foss, Paul Patton, and John Johnston. New York: Semiotexte.

——. 1983b. The ecstacy of communication. In *The anti-aesthetic.* Ed. Hal Foster. Port Townsend: Bay Press: 126–34.

——. 1984. On nihilism. *On the Beach* 6: 39.

——. 1985. The child in the bubble. *Impulse* 11: 12–13.

——. 1986. Interview. *FlashArt* 130 (October/November): 39.

Beniger, James R. n.d. Personalisation of mass media and the growth of pseudo-community. Unpublished paper.

Benjamin, Walter. 1968. The work of art in the age of mechanical reproduction. In *Illuminations.* Ed. Hannah Arendt. New York: Harcourt, Brace and World.

——. 1973. *Understanding Brecht.* Trans. Anna Bostock. London: New Left Books.

Benn, T. n.d. Sexual spaces/public places. *Z/G* 6.

Bennett, Tony. 1986. The politics of the "popular" and popular culture. In *Popular culture and social relations.* Ed. Tony Bennett, Colin Mercer and Janet Woollacott. Milton Keynes: Open University Press.

———. 1990. *Outside literature.* London: Routledge.

Berger, John. 1980. In opposition to history, in defiance of time. *Village Voice* (October 8–14): 89–90.

Bloom, Allan. 1987. *The closing of the American mind.* New York: Simon and Schuster.

Bourdieu, Pierre. 1980. The aristocracy of culture. *Media, Culture, Society* 2: 225–54.

———. 1984. *Distinction: A social critique of the judgement of taste.* Trans. R. Nice. Cambridge: Harvard University Press.

———. 1990. *In other words: Essays towards a reflexive sociology.* Trans. M. Adamson. Stanford: Stanford University Press.

Brooks, Rosetta. n.d. Between the street and the screen. *Z/G* 6.

Brunsdon, Charlotte, and David Morley. 1978. *Everyday television: "Nationwide."* London: British Film Institute.

Carson, Tom. 1980. Martha and the Muffins get disengaged. *Village Voice* (August 13–19): 59.

———. 1981. The David Johansen story. *Village Voice* (July 8–15): 49.

Centre for Contemporary Cultural Studies. 1969–71. *Report.* Birmingham, England.

Certeau, Michel de. 1984. *The practice of everyday life.* Trans. Steven R. Rendall. Berkeley: University of California Press.

Chambers, Iain. 1985. *Urban rhythms: Pop music and popular culture.* New York: St. Martin's Press.

———. 1988. Contamination, coincidence and collusion: Popular culture, urban culture and the avant-garde. In *Marxism and the interpretation of culture.* Ed. Cary Nelson and Lawrence Grossberg. Urbana: University of Illinois Press: 607–11.

Christgau, Robert. 1992. His hit parade. *Village Voice* (March 31): 87.

Clarke, John. 1991. *New times and old enemies.* London: Routledge.

Clifford, James. 1988. *The predicament of culture: Twentieth-century ethnography, literature and art.* Cambridge: Harvard University Press.

Considine, J. D. 1981. REO + MOR = heavy metal pop. *Village Voice* (July 8–15): 57.

Coupland, Douglas. 1991. *Generation X: Tales for an accelerated culture.* New York: St. Martins.

Coward, Rosalind. 1977. Class, "culture," and the social formation. *Screen* 18: 75–105.

Cox, Meg. 1992. Rock is slowly fading as tastes in music go off in many directions. *Wall Street Journal* (August 26): 1 and 4.

Crane, Jonathan. 1988. Terror and everyday life. *Communication* 10: 367–82.

De Jonquieres, G. 1990. The West's moving target. *The Financial Times Industrial Review* (January 8): 2.

Deleuze, Gilles. 1977. Active and reactive. In *The new Nietzsche: Contemporary styles of interpretation.* Ed. David B. Allison. New York: Delta: 80–106.

Deleuze, Gilles, and Felix Guattari. 1977. *Anti-Oedipus: Capitalism and schizophrenia.* Trans. Robert Hurley et al. New York: Viking Press.

———. 1981. Rhizome. *I & C* 8: 49–71.

——. 1984. *On the line*. Trans. John Johnston. New York: Semiotexte.

——. 1987. *A thousand plateaus: Capitalism and schizophrenia*. Trans. Brian Massumi. Minneapolis: University of Minnesota Press.

Edwards, Lynda. 1992. The focusing of the president 1992. *Village Voice* (June 23): 25–29.

Ellis, Brett Easton. 1985. *Less than zero*. New York: Simon and Schuster.

Ellis, John. 1982. *Visible fictions*. London: Routledge.

Farren, Mick. 1982. Surface noise. *Trouser Press* (August).

Fiske, John. 1989. *Understanding popular culture*. Boston: Unwin Hyman.

Foster, Hal. 1982. Postmodernism: A preface. In *The anti-aesthetic: Essays on postmodern culture*. Ed. Hal Foster. Port Townsend: Bay Press.

——. 1985. TV in two parts. In *TV Guides*. Ed. Barbara Kruger. N.p.: Kuklapolitan Press.

Foucault, Michel. 1970. *The order of things: An archaeology of the human sciences*. New York: Pantheon.

——. 1977. *Discipline and punish: The birth of the prison*. Trans. Alan Sheridan. New York: Pantheon.

——. 1980. *Power/Knowledge: Selected interviews and other writings 1972–1977*. Ed. Colin Gordon. New York: Pantheon.

——. 1981. Questions of method: An interview. *I & C* 8: 3–14.

Frith, Simon. 1981. *Sound effects: Youth leisure and the politics of rock 'n' roll*. New York: Pantheon.

——. 1987. End of an ear. *Village Voice* (May 19).

——. 1990. Golden lite. *Village Voice* (April 24): 91.

——. 1991. He's the one. *Village Voice* (October 29): 88.

——. 1993. Youth/Music/Television. In *Sound and Vision*. Ed. Simon Frith, Andrew Goodwin, and Lawrence Grossberg. London: Routledge.

Frith, Simon, and Howard Horne. 1987. *Art into pop*. London: Methuen.

Frith, Simon, and Angela McRobbie. 1990. Rock and sexuality. In *On record: Rock, pop and the written word*. Ed. Simon Frith and Andrew Goodwin. London: Routledge.

Frow, John. 1995. *Cultural studies and cultural value*. Oxford: Oxford University Press.

Gottschalk, Mark. 1990. China's old dirty hands. *In These Times* (June 20–July 3).

Graham, Dan. 1983. New wave rock and the feminine. *Open Letter* 5–6: 79–105.

Gramsci, Antonio. 1971. *Selections from the prison notebooks*. Trans. Q. Hoare and G. Nowell-Smith. New York: International Publishers.

Greene, Bob. 1986. TV becomes more real than real life. *Chicago Tribune* (October 27): section 2, p.1.

Grossberg, Lawrence. 1982. Experience, signification, and reality: The boundaries of cultural semiotics. *Semiotica* 41: 73–106.

——. 1983–84. The politics of youth culture: Some observations on rock and roll in American culture. *Social Text* 8: 104–26.

——. 1984a. The social meaning of rock and roll. *One Two Three Four* 1: 13–21, 81–101.

——. 1984b. "I'd rather feel bad than not feel anything at all": Rock and roll, pleasure and power. *Enclitic* 8: 94–110.

——. 1985. If rock and roll communicates, then why is it so noisy? In *Popular Music Perspectives*. Ed. David Horne. 2: 451–63. Exeter: International Association for the Study of Popular Music.

——. 1986a. Teaching the popular. In *Theory in the Classroom*. Ed. Cary Nelson. Urbana: University of Illinois Press: 177–200.

——. 1986b. Is there rock after punk? *Critical Studies in Mass Communication* 3: 50–74.

——. 1986c. Response to critics. *Critical Studies in Mass Communication* 3: 86–95.

——. 1986d. History, politics and postmodernism. *Journal of Communication Inquiry* 10: 61–77.

——. 1987a. The politics of music and youth: Billboards along the North American landscape. *Canadian Journal of Political and Social Theory* 11: 144–51.

——. 1987b. The in-difference of television. *Screen* 28 (spring): 28–45.

——. 1988a. Putting the pop back into postmodernism. In *Universal abandon: The politics of postmodern*. Ed. Andrew Ross. Minneapolis: University of Minnesota Press.

——. 1988b. Wandering audiences, nomadic critics. *Cultural Studies* 2: 377–91.

——. 1988c. You still have to "fight for your right to party": Music television as billboards of postmodern difference. *Popular Music* 7: 315–32.

——. 1989. Music television: Swinging on the (postmodern) star. In *Cultural politics in contemporary America*. Ed. Ian Angus and Sut Jhally. New York: Routledge.

——. 1992. *We gotta get out of this place: Popular conservatism and postmodern culture*. New York: Routledge.

——. 1993a. The media economy of rock culture: Cinema, postmodernity and authenticity. In *Sound and Vision: The Music Video Decade*. Ed. Simon Frith, Andrew Goodwin, and Lawrence Grossberg. London: Routledge. 185–209.

——. 1993b. Popular music and the new conservatism. In *Rock music: Politics, policies, institutions*. Ed. Tony Bennett et al. London: Routledge.

——. 1993c. Cultural studies in/and new worlds. *Critical Studies in Mass Communication* 10: 1–22.

Guattari, Felix. 1984. *Molecular revolution: Psychiatry and politics*. New York: Penguin.

——. 1986. The postmodern dead end. *FlashArt* 128 (May):40–41.

Hall, Stuart. 1960. Editorial. *New Left Review* 1: 1.

——. 1973. Encoding/decoding in the television discourse. Occasional paper. Centre for Contemporary Cultural Studies. Birmingham, England.

——. 1981. Notes on deconstructing the popular. In *People's history and socialist theory*. Ed. Ralph Samuel. Boston: Routledge and Kegan Paul.

——. 1983. The problem of ideology: Marxism without guarantees. In *Marx 100 years on*. Ed. B. Matthews. London: Lawrence and Wishart.

——. 1985. Signification, representation, ideology: Althusser and the post-structuralist debates. *Critical Studies in Mass Communication* 2: 87–114.

——. 1986a. The problem of ideology—Marxism without guarantees. *Journal of Communication Inquiry* 10: 28–44.

——. 1986b. On postmodernism and articulation: An interview. *Journal of Communication Inquiry* 10: 45–60.

——. 1987. Gramsci and us. *Marxism Today* (June): 16–21.

——. 1988. *The hard road to renewal: Thatcherism and the crisis of the Left.* London: Verso.

Hall, Stuart, and Tony Jefferson, eds. 1976. *Resistance through rituals.* London: Hutchinson.

Haraway, Donna. 1987. Apes, aliens, cyborgs and women: Feminist theory, colonial discourse, and the contest for science. Lecture delivered at the University of Illinois, Urbana (April 22).

Harley, R., and P. Botsman. 1982. Between "no payola" and "the cocktail set": Rock 'n' roll journalism. In *Theoretical Strategies.* Ed. P. Botsman. Sydney: Local Consumption Publications.

Hebdige, Dick. 1979. *Subculture: The meaning of style.* London. Routledge.

——. 1982. Posing . . . threats, striking . . . poses: Youth surveillance and display. *SubStance* 37/38: 68–88.

——. 1985. Some sons and their fathers. *Ten-8* 17: 30–39.

——. 1987. Digging for Britain: An excavation in seven parts. In *The British Edge.* Boston: Institute of Contemporary Arts.

——. 1988. Towards a cartography of taste 1935–1962. In *Hiding in the light: On images and things.* London: Routledge, 45–76.

Hoggart, Richard. 1957. *The uses of literacy.* London: Essential Books.

Howe, Neil, and Bill Strauss. 1993. *13th gen: Abort, retry, ignore, rail?* New York: Vintage.

Hunter, James. 1981. Think to the beat. *Village Voice* (October 21–27).

Hutton, Paul Andrew. 1986. Davy Crockett, still king of the wild frontier. *Texas Monthly* (November).

Jameson, Fredric. 1983. Pleasure: A political issue. In *Formations of Pleasure.* London: Routledge: 1–13.

——. 1984. Postmodernism, or the cultural logic of late capitalism. *New Left Review* 146 (July/August):53–92.

Laclau, Ernesto, and Chantal Mouffe. 1985. *Hegemony and socialist strategy: Towards a radical democratic politics.* London: Verso.

Laplanche, J., and J.-B. Pontalis. *The language of psycho-analysis.* Trans. D. Nicholson-Smith. New York: W. W. Norton.

Leavitt, David. 1985. The new lost generation. *Esquire* (May).

Lefebvre, Henri. 1984. *Everyday life in the modern world.* Trans. Sacha Rabinovitch. New Brunswick: Transaction.

Lefort, Claude. 1986. *The political forms of modern society.* Cambridge: MIT Press.

Linklater, Richard. 1992. *Slacker.* New York: St. Martin's.

Marcus, Greil. 1969. Who put the bomp in the bomp-de-bomp-de-bomp? In *Rock and Roll Will Stand.* Ed. G. Marcus. Boston: Beacon.

——. 1980a. Anarchy in the UK. In *The Rolling Stone illustrated history of rock and roll.* Ed. Jim Miller. New York: Rolling Stone: 451–63.

——. 1980b. Wake-up. *Rolling Stone* (June 24): 40–44.

——. 1981a. The shock of the old. *New West* (March): 113.

——. 1981b. Etched in tone. *New West* (September): 124.

——. 1981c. Lies about Elvis, lies about us. *Village Voice Literary Supplement* (December): 16–17.

——. 1992. Notes on the life and death and incandescent banality of rock 'n' roll. *Esquire* (August): 67–75.

Marsh, Dave. 1982. *Elvis.* New York: Warner Books.

Martin, Adrian. 1994. *Phantasms: The dreams and desires at the heart of our popular culture.* Victoria, Australia: Penguin.

Marx, Karl. 1973. *Grundrisse.* Trans. M. Nicolaus. New York: Vintage.

Matterlart, Armand. 1988. Communications in socialist France: The difficulty of matching technology with democracy. In *Marxism and the interpretation of culture.* Ed. Cary Nelson and Lawrence Grossberg. Urbana: University of Illinois Press.

Mattelart, Michele. 1982. Media and the cultural industries. *Media, Culture, Society* 4.

McRobbie, Angela. 1980. Setting accounts with subcultures: A feminist critique. *Screen Education* 34: 37–49.

Mercer, Colin. 1986. Complicit pleasures. In *Popular Culture and Social Relations.* Ed. T. Bennett et al. Milton Keynes: Open University Press: 50–68.

Mercer, Kobena. 1986. Post-modern man. *New Socialist* (October): 44.

Merton, Robert K. 1946. *Mass persuasion: The social psychology of a war bond drive.* New York: Harper.

Modleski, Tania. 1984. *Loving with a vengeance: Mass produced fantasies for women.* New York: Methuen.

——. 1986. Introduction. In *Studies in entertainment: Critical approaches to mass culture.* Ed. Tania Modleski. Bloomington: University of Indiana Press.

Morley, David. 1980. *The "Nationwide" audience.* London: British Film Institute.

Morley, David, and Kaun-Hsing Chen. 1996. *Stuart Hall: Critical dialogues in cultural studies.* London: Routledge.

Morris, Meaghan. 1988a. Banality in cultural studies. *Discourse* 10: 3–29.

——. 1988b. At Henry Parkes' motel. *Cultural Studies* 2: 1–47.

——. 1988c. *The pirate's fiancée: Feminism reading postmodernism.* London: Verso.

——. 1992. On the beach. In *Cultural Studies.* Ed. Lawrence Grossberg, Cary Nelson, and Paula Treichler. New York: Routledge, 453–72.

——. Forthcoming. *Upward mobility: Popular genres and cultural change.* Bloomington: Indiana University Press.

Mort, Frank, and N. Green. 1988. You've never had it so good—again! *Marxism Today* (May): 32–33.

Nelson, Cary. 1978. The psychology of criticism, or what can be said. In *Psychoanalysis and the question of the text.* Ed. G. Hartmann. Baltimore: Johns Hopkins University Press: 45–61.

Nelson, Cary, and Lawrence Grossberg, eds. 1988. *Marxism and the interpretation of culture.* Urbana: University of Illinois Press.

O'Brien, Glenn. 1987. What is hip? *Interview* 27 (July): 42–43.

Orestes, M. 1990. America's politics loses way as its vision changes world. *New York Times* (March 18): A16.

Parmar, Pratibha. 1989. Other kinds of dreams. *Feminist Review* 31: 50–65.

Parsons, Tony. 1993. Time to make music not headlines. *Daily Telegraph* (January 1): 14.

Penman, Ian. 1982. Review of Simple Minds' "Promised you a miracle." *New Musical Express* (April 3).

Pfeil, Fred. 1988. Postmodernism and a structure of feeling. In *Marxism and the interpretation of culture.* Ed. Cary Nelson and Lawrence Grossberg. Urbana: University of Illinois Press.

Piccarella, John. 1980. Fashion's future fusion conventions. *Village Voice* (January 14): 70.

———. 1982. Flipper's triumph of the therapeutic. *Village Voice* (15 June): 83.

Polonoff, David. 1988. Backward mobility. *Village Voice.*

Radway, Janice. 1988. Reception study: Ethnography and the problems of dispersed audiences and nomadic subjects. *Cultural Studies* 2: 359–76.

Reynolds, Simon. 1986. Ladybirds and start-rite kids. *Melody Maker* (September 26): 44–45.

———. 1991. Dazed and confused. *Village Voice* (January 1): 71.

Robbins, Ira. 1982. Lip service. *Trouser Press* (August): 46.

Rose, Jacqueline. 1984. *The case of Peter Pan or the impossibility of children's fiction.* London: Macmillan.

Safouan, M. 1983. *Pleasure and being.* London: Macmillan.

Schjeldjahl, Peter. 1981. Appraising passions. *Village Voice* (January 7–13): 67.

———. 1986. Irony and agony. *In These Times* 10 (August 20–September 2): 23.

Shiach, Morag. 1989. *Discourse on popular culture.* Stanford: Stanford University Press.

Spivak, Gayatri Chakravorty. 1988. Can the subaltern speak? In *Marxism and the interpretation of culture.* Ed. Cary Nelson and Lawrence Grossberg. Urbana: University of Illinois Press: 272–75.

Steedman, Carolyn. 1986. *Landscape for a good woman: A story of two lives.* London: Virago.

Straw, Will. 1987. Intersections and directions in cultural studies. Panel discussion at Carleton University, Centre for Communication, Culture and Society, Ottawa (March 4).

———. 1991. Systems of articulation, logics of change: Communities and scenes in popular music. *Cultural Studies* 5: 368–88.

Thompson, E. P. 1961. The long revolution. *New Left Review,* no. 9: 24–29 and 10: 34–39.

Toffler, Alvin. 1971. *Future Shock.* London: Pan Books.

Williams, Raymond. 1958. *Culture and society 1780/1950.* London: Chatto and Windus.

———. 1965. *The long revolution.* Middlesex: Penguin.

———. 1973. Base and superstructure in marxist theory. *New Left Review,* no. 82: 3–16.

———. 1974. *Television: Technology and cultural form.* London: Fontana.

———. 1981. *Culture.* London: Fontana.

Williamson, Judith. 1986. The problems of being popular. *New Socialist* (September): 14–16.

Winship, Janice. 1985. "A girl needs to get streetwise": Magazines for the 1980's. *Feminist Review* 21: 25–46.

Zion, S. 1981. Outlasting rock. *New York Times Magazine* (21 June): 16.

Žižek, Slavoj. 1987. The subject supposed to . . . (know, believe, enjoy, desire). Lecture delivered at the Symposium on "Wars of Persuasion: Gramsci, Intellectuals and Mass Culture." University of Massachusetts, Amherst (April 24).

Index

AC/DC, 45, 67
Adorno, T. W., 172
Althusser, Louis, 126, 153, 157, 200
Anderson, Jim, 237
Anderson, Laurie, 52 n.3
Attali, Jacques, 94–95, 97, 98–99
Atwater, Lee, 89, 259, 260
Aufderheide, Pat, 162, 169
Aztec Camera, 48

Bakhtin, Mikhail, 161
Ballard, J. G., 162
Bangs, Lester, 60
Barr, Trevor, 274–275
Barthes, Roland, 88, 155
Baudrillard, Jean, 77, 83, 137, 140,
    141–142, 150–151, 155, 156, 165,
    178–181
Beach Boys, 48, 215
Beatles, 40, 45, 48, 61, 66, 67
Beck, Julian, 139
Benatar, Pat, 70
Beniger, James R., 163 n.3
Benjamin, Walter, 75 n.2, 77, 88, 129,
    160, 171–172, 184, 193, 258
Benn, T., 83
Bennet, William, 214
Bennett, Tony, 10 n.7, 168–169
Berger, John, 34
Berry, Chuck, 48, 50
Black Flag, 52 n.3
Blondie, 48

Bloom, Allan, 89, 235
Boone, Pat, 89, 260
Botsman, P., 73
Bourdieu, Pierre, 12, 13, 65, 181–182,
    222, 247, 280
Bowie, David, 48
Branca, Glenn, 52 n.3, 54
Brando, Marlon, 34
Breslow, Harris, 257 n.4
Brooks, Garth, 107
Brooks, Rosetta, 85
Brunsdon, Charlotte, 201
Bush, George, 139, 257, 259

Carey, James, 1 n.1
Carson, Tom, 53, 58
Caulfield, Holden, 34
Certeau, Michel de, 121
Chambers, Iain, 86, 152, 155, 197
Chen, Kuan-Hsing, 10 n.7
Christgau, Robert, 106
Circle Jerks, 52 n.3
Clancy, Tom, 15 n.8
Clarke, John, 194, 207 n.6, 213, 254
Clash, 47, 48
Clifford, James, 107 n.2
Clinton, George, 67
Cockney Rejects, 52 n.3
Considine, J. D., 59
Cosby, Bill, 140, 237
Costello, Elvis, 52 n.3, 54
Cougar, John, 44

Lawrence Grossberg is Morris Davis Professor of Communication
Studies at the University of North Carolina at Chapel Hill. He is the
author of *We Gotta Get Out of This Place: Popular Conservatism and
Postmodern Culture*, and has coedited many volumes including
Cultural Studies (with Cary Nelson and Paula A. Treichler).

Library of Congress Cataloging-in-Publication Data
Grossberg, Lawrence.
    Dancing in spite of myself : essays on popular culture /
by Lawrence Grossberg.
    Includes bibliographical references and index.
ISBN 0-8223-1912-8 (cloth : alk. paper). —
ISBN 0-8223-1917-9 (paper : alk. paper)
    1. Popular culture—United States—History—20th century. 2. Rock
music—United States—History—20th century. 3. Rock music—United
States—History and criticism. 4. United States—Social life and
customs. I. Title.
E169.04.G756 1997   306.4'84—dc21   96-49940 CIP